# FINDING
## YOUR WAY

Marianne Johansen

**BALBOA.**
PRESS
A DIVISION OF HAY HOUSE

Balboa Press books may be ordered through booksellers or by contacting:

Balboa Press
A Division of Hay House
1663 Liberty Drive
Bloomington, IN 47403
www.balboapress.com
1 (877) 407-4847

Because of the dynamic nature of the Internet, any web addresses or links contained in this book may have changed since publication and may no longer be valid. The views expressed in this work are solely those of the author and do not necessarily reflect the views of the publisher, and the publisher hereby disclaims any responsibility for them.

The author of this book does not dispense medical advice or prescribe the use of any technique as a form of treatment for physical, emotional, or medical problems without the advice of a physician, either directly or indirectly. The intent of the author is only to offer information of a general nature to help you in your quest for emotional and spiritual well-being. In the event you use any of the information in this book for yourself, which is your constitutional right, the author and the publisher assume no responsibility for your actions.

Any people depicted in stock imagery provided by Getty Images are models, and such images are being used for illustrative purposes only.
Certain stock imagery © Getty Images.

Print information available on the last page.

ISBN: 978-1-9822-0125-8 (sc)
ISBN: 978-1-9822-0126-5 (hc)
ISBN: 978-1-9822-0161-6 (e)

Library of Congress Control Number: 2018903916

Balboa Press rev. date: 04/06/2018

# Contents

# Part 3: Body

# Part 4: Quick Tips

In loving memory of Jamil.

Throughout our lives, we have hundreds of experiences and
mirror ourselves in the souls and minds of others.
We weave in and out of each other's lives searching for
love, trust, support, and ways to improve our lives.
We sometimes forget that life is a journey to be
lived in tune with nature and ourselves.
Picture yourself at the last station thinking, *What made it all worth it?*
—Marianne Johansen

We, as souls, [need to] learn to carry the Light
with us through our personalities.
—*Testimony of Light—An Extraordinary Message of
Life After Death*, by Helen Greaves, 1969

# Preface

We will all have joyful moments and challenges in life. For many of us, finding lasting happiness seems to be a challenge of its own.

As materialism and unnecessary stress have spilled into most of our world, we have moved further from our spiritual nature and from Mother Nature.

With this book, I aim to infuse more awareness in your daily life. I wish to inspire you to reconnect with nature and your intuition to help you develop your common sense, gain more self-trust, and embrace your spirituality with one goal in mind: to reach your inner realm and source of calmness and happiness.

*Finding Your Way* raises questions you may or may not have considered. It suggests perhaps new ways to look at your situation and relation to the world, become more aware in general, weed out nonessential knowledge or information, discover yourself, and reconnect with your inner self to move forward and upward.

I hope the ideas and reflections in this book will help you connect with your physical, mental, emotional, and spiritual layers. Seeing yourself as a whole being could help you open up to your unique abilities to cope with your specific challenges.

I invite you to put your hands on the steering wheel and welcome the responsibility and accountability for the direction and contents of your life.

We can play and interact with the energies we are made up of and that surround us, so why not do that in ways everyone, including ourselves, can benefit?

Like most people, I have experienced joys, wonders, love, and miracles but also tragedies, the death of a loved one, external disputes, and internal struggles. Throughout these pages, I draw mainly on my observations, experiences, thoughts, and inspirations and share the roads I have traveled to learn and move forward.

I acknowledge that every person I have met and interacted with plays a part be it big or small in my life.

Finding *my* way through life is a challenge I have taken on. I feel it is time to share my thoughts, and I will be honored if I can help you find your way.

# Acknowledgments

I am forever grateful to the following people for their timely love, support, comfort, and inspiration.

My Jamil, our boys Raian and Daniel, Anubhaa and Pranay, Sarah and Hussain, Caroline B., Camila B., Dee and Walter, Paula, Dawn, Sharon G., Daisy and Jihad, Mary, Suma, Marianne and Dean, Naheel, Kalpana, Ditte and Richard, Sandrine and Patrick, Kim, Diana, Bjarke, Caroline, Julie and Roy, Christian, Susanne, Lidia and Martin, Dejana, Paulinne, Suzy, and Rien.

A very special thank-you to my close family in my home country. Loving prayers and thank-yous go out to my extended family.

Last, a warm thank-you to all the children in my life for being the greatest teachers!

# Part 1

...............................................................

# Mind

...............................................................

*Devote time and attention to yourself and your thoughts,*
*and walk through doors you never knew existed.*
-Marianne Johansen

# Chapter 1

························································

# Creating Awareness

························································

## 1. Thought Equals Creation

Different people in many ways and at many times have said we are what we think. But what does that mean?

Many more of us are just starting to realize how much truth that phrase holds because only now with increased awareness can we notice the manifestation of our thoughts more quickly than ever. We used to have to wait days or even months until something we thought about would actually manifest, but now, that may take only hours or minutes.

We get proof much sooner, and so it is easier for us to notice the effects of our thoughts since we can remember our most recent thoughts or actions. We can witness the power of our minds and how our thoughts create change.

Globally, it will take longer to change things because all our lives are interwoven and not everybody is on the same page. But with a concerted effort, whatever enough people want and think about will eventually manifest.

We can choose to live balanced and harmonious lives by choosing our thoughts and being aware of them continuously. But it all depends on our interest and trust in the matter.

## 2. Think of a Positive Life

- Would you prefer a positive, happy, fulfilling life or a sad, miserable one?
- Would you rather live in peace or in turmoil?
- Would you prefer a beautiful view from your home or an unsightly one?

- Would you prefer to have time to do things that make you feel full, rich, and alive or only to have time to do what others tell you?
- Would you rather be with kind people who care about you or with people who abuse you and trigger your feelings of low self-esteem?
- Would you prefer to be in an understanding and compassionate relationship or one in which you argue and bicker all the time?
- Would you rather feel self-confident or have no confidence?
- Would you rather have respect and voluntary cooperation from your employees or their fear and eventually defiance?
- Would you prefer to enjoy love and respect from your children or sadness and fear?

When we line things up in this way, I think it is safe to say that we all would rather choose the options that invoke positive rather than negative feelings in us. So why do so many of us live with the negative options?

Many may say, "These are just the cards I have been dealt," or "I've landed involuntarily in this situation," or "This is where life (or circumstance) has taken me so far."

Yes, what happened in the past put you where you are now, but every moment of your life is influenced by every choice you make. From where you are now, you can make a conscious choice to start changing things to the way you like.

We human beings are blessed with free will, consciousness, and memories so we can learn from our experiences and learn to steer our thoughts and actions and thus our lives in positive directions.

Our lives may not change overnight (though that can happen); it all depends on our continuous awareness of the thoughts we focus on. Once we start making even small changes, once we start doing things just a little differently, it is as if an unseen force starts to make new and different things happen around us. Call it the law of attraction or the universe responding to what we are sending out, or call it something else or nothing at all. The fact is that things will start to unfold and change around us to challenge us, make us rethink old habits, and help us understand ourselves and others better.

New doors will open, situations will suddenly present themselves, and we will suddenly have new choices to make and have to decide which road we want to take next.

Something new will happen—but we will have to take the first step. As we become more aware of the contents of our lives, we will notice them.

That first step depends on your situation and what you want to change—but if you do something consciously, new opportunities and choices will present themselves. Choose where you want to go and you will see that new doors open and new choices appear.

Think about what you want to do next, and feel what feels right to do next. Allow your heart and mind to agree on what your next steps should be. Then follows the responsibility of choice, which I will touch on later.

Depending on your situation and what you would like to change, your next step could for example be to

- make that call to someone who has been on your mind for a long time,
- finish that book you started reading,
- offer your help to someone who needs it,
- finish the work you have been postponing,
- apply for that job you think sounds great,
- declutter your home or room,
- clear up a misunderstanding between you and a friend, and
- accomplish other things that keep moving to the front of your mind.

Follow your inner voice, that quiet voice in your mind that tells you what you need to do.

As long as you constantly try to make decent, positive, and constructive choices according to your heart and keep faith in the positive, your life will take a turn for the better.

You will still come across challenges—they are as much a part of life as are the blissful moments—but how you react to the challenges in your life will make all the difference.

Things that can make us sad, angry, frustrated, or heartbroken will still happen to us because we are human beings with feelings and egos and lessons to learn. However, the more we let our egos be inspired by our hearts, our souls, the more we will ensure that our thoughts are positive and centered on the greater good. And the more we see that every challenge we meet is something to learn from, the more we will be able to draw something positive out of any challenging situation.

If you nurture your mind, body, and spirit, your time will expand. You will gain a new perspective that will allow you to accomplish much more.
—Brian Koslow

# Chapter 2

. . . . . . . . . . . . . . . . . . . . . . . . . . . . . . . . . . . . . . . . . . . . . . . . . . . . . . . . . . . . . . .

# You Are Not Alone

. . . . . . . . . . . . . . . . . . . . . . . . . . . . . . . . . . . . . . . . . . . . . . . . . . . . . . . . . . . . . . .

Sometimes and in certain situations, you may think you must be the only one in the world who has this or that thought or feeling. But after confiding in a friend, relative, counselor, or stranger or even reading something, you usually find that at least one other person (and usually more than one) can relate to your internal turmoil.

Since we all have different living circumstances, backgrounds, and challenges, we find it easy to think we are different inside. But no matter what our circumstances, backgrounds, and challenges are, we are still very much alike on the inside. The expression of life around us is different depending on our mind-sets, actions, beliefs, purposes, and lessons.

We all experience the same concerns, considerations, challenges, letdowns, and successes. We all at some stage and on some level feel fear, worry, jealousy, competitiveness, greed, motivation, joy, relief, grief, and bliss. We all are really just longing for love, understanding, and support.

Dealing with our negative thoughts, feelings, and emotions can be a challenge. Some of us face them head-on, deal with them, and move through them, while others of us run away from them. Still others pretend they are just not there.

But we can rest assured that our negative feelings, emotions, and thoughts do not go away on their own. Once they are there, we must face them, accept them, and let them go. If we do not, they will only grow into fears and fester and even be brought to our attention in our dreams or manifest in physical imbalances until we deal with them.

Another major concept that unites us is our quest for improvement, our desire to make things better for ourselves and in many cases for others. No matter on what grounds we base our existence, we are here to grow toward positivity, which is sustainable energy. It benefits our natural environment and us the most if we look at it over the long term. Deep down, we all know that.

5

Most of us are interested in changing our lives and often others' lives too into something more positive. No matter what level we are on materially, spiritually, or socially, we are all looking for ways to sweeten and improve life one way or another.

We could be looking for freedom to choose our clothes or food, a decent employer, or a way to do what we love to do. We could be looking for ways to better educate our children. We could be looking for ways to advance spiritually. We might also be looking for more free time, a second car, or a vacation home.

Yet the general desire for improvement—rather, for a return to our natural, blissful, loving state—is deep in us all.

> Conscious beings are like fractals evolving to
> ever greater scales of magnitude.
> —R. C. L., www.fractalwisdom.com, "Meaning of the Universe"

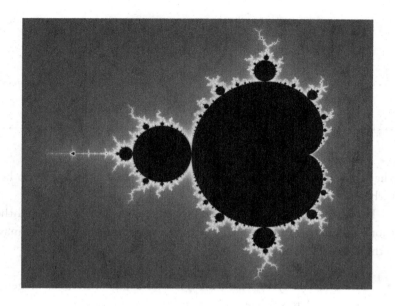

The Mandelbrot Fractal

To understand the small things, we sometimes have to zoom out. We then find the smaller picture is a downsized version of the bigger picture that if not identical is very similar.

Example: mothers are often the managers of their households. Others manage small companies, and others are the directors of governmental departments. Some manage towns, and others manage all the towns and cities in a country.

Though the number of people who have to be managed increases with each level, the mechanisms behind successful outcomes are alike on many levels.

Parallels to the fractal theory can be drawn in many if not all aspects of life and the universe.

(To read more about "A Fractal Theory of the Origin and Meaning of the Universe," see www.fractalwisdom.com.)

# Chapter 3

......................................................

# Life as We Know It

......................................................

So what is life really? Why are we here? What are we supposed to do here? And where do we go from here?

Hundreds of millions of people throughout history have asked these questions. Many theories have been put out there, and now there are maybe more than ever. Here are some.

- Life and reality on earth are parts of a big, universal, biogenetic experiment to study emotions and the laws of physics.
- The reality of our world is described in the movie *The Matrix*.
- Our world is a hologram.
- There is another side, and reincarnation is a fact.
- There is another side, but we all live only once on this earthly plane.
- We are eternal souls who are to bring heaven to earth ("As above, so below").
- Each of our cells carries all universal knowledge and experiences.
- We are eternal spirits having a human experience to learn about higher virtues such as love and service to others for the greater good of the universe, the source or organism we are all part of.
- Angels surround us; the spiritual world is part of our reality but in another dimension behind the veil of our limited consciousness and awareness. There are many levels of higher vibration beyond our heavy and murky vibrations here on earth.
- We have only one life, and our experience here is the only reality.
- We are energy. All around us is energy. We have the power to influence and attract the energies in and around us.
- Aliens and UFOs are among us and have been throughout the ages.
- There is an elite with a hidden agenda.
- We live in several dimensions at the same time.

- Time is an illusion and can be bent at will.
- Since the vibrations of earth are heavy and slow compared to vibrations in the spiritual realms, things manifest slower here on earth, and that teaches us about perseverance, trust, and patience.

Besides these theories of our existence, we find the established religions, which millions of people firmly believe in and live by. These religions state that a God or in some cases gods, goddesses, or other deities created everything and everyone. In the religions are rules and teachings the followers should live by.

Before established religions emerged, most belief systems were based on the natural world and people's intuitive abilities (paganism, shamanism, medicine men, etc.).

Nowadays, many people are also starting to believe in global mass consciousness; they believe that the sum of all our thoughts plays a part in creating our future. This ties in with the concept of self-fulfilling prophecies, which I will talk about later.

If we think we can change our lives by changing the ways we think and act, could we be jointly able to influence our planet and the way we live?

Even if we do not believe in a global mass consciousness, why not combat our fears and other negative thoughts, emotions, and feelings and turn them into trust, tolerance, and kindness? So much more is produced when people are fulfilled, respected, balanced, able to be creative, and able to be individuals who are part of something positive. Why not initiate a positive ripple effect by starting to make positive changes in ourselves?

Are the alternative theories, established religions, and hundreds of other cults, churches, and spiritual belief systems around the globe simply different ways of seeing the same thing?

Beliefs and actions that harm nobody and nothing are tolerated by all.

# Chapter 4

## Our World

Become Peace, for that is the Attractor of Peace to the World.
—The Essenes (200 BC—AD 100)

Earth, the blue planet, is our temporary home. It is our womb, our shelter from cold, dark outer space. It is our school where we take lessons in realigning ourselves with love.

On this planet, we have everything we need to sustain ourselves. Luckily, we do not rely on imported goods or raw materials from other planets.

We are our ecosystem, and everything and everybody on the planet is part of it. Every living cell and atom all over the globe, including us human beings, plays a part in this fragile, self-adjusting, and ever-changing ecosystem.

At any one time in history, numerous concurrent conditions have played themselves out and set the stage for the people living during that particular time whether those conditions have been natural such as meteorological or geological conditions or manufactured, man-made conditions.

Depending on where we stand, we paint different pictures of today's world. Some people may applaud the way things are going, while others would welcome a major cleansing and reshuffling. Some people struggle to find a way and a reason to go on living another day. Some rush along the paths carved out for them while others carve out their own paths.

## 1. Our Needs vs. Business

We all have to share our planet. Our survival depends on what resources are on earth and on how we administer them.

We need to eat and drink, and we need to rest in safe, peaceful places. To ensure our survival as a species, we have an innate desire to have children, and we want them to have their basic needs met in safe surroundings.

When our and our loved ones' basic needs have been met, we find ourselves with the urge to communicate at a higher level and to be stimulated mentally, emotionally, physically, aesthetically, and spiritually.

Over time, this concept of fulfilling all our needs starting with the basic ones has evolved into big business. Materialism and consumerism are filling our lives more than ever. We buy food, drink, and places to rest. We buy physical, mental, emotional, and spiritual stimulation and comfort in the form of books, education, TV, computers, furniture, movies, clothes, cars, phones, sports, seminars, and so on.

We often forget to think about what needs our purchases are actually fulfilling, and when we are not aware of that, it can lead to overindulgence, greed, and a satisfaction of our egos only. That does not mean that we need to forsake all material things to be spiritual. Positive stimulation and fulfillment through material comforts and joys can help spark imagination, creativity, and compassion.

Excessive buying on the other hand feeds only the ego, personal greed, and a wish to top others; it grants only temporary and superficial joy.

## 2. Are We Living in a Sim World?

Anyone familiar with the game Sim City would maybe find it interesting to compare it to how our world actually is. In Sim City, you have to construct and set up different conditions for people and see how they cope and what happens.

I am not sure if there is a country in the real world that has beautiful scenery, abundant food, a comfortable climate, and a rich lifestyle in which people live in harmony. People face some sort of hardship in every country. In some countries, just staying alive is a struggle due to lack of food, water, and hygienic facilities.

In other countries, those things are not an issue, but the people have to endure extreme weather conditions that can threaten to destroy their homes and livelihoods.

People in other countries seem to be luckier at least in terms of food quality, health facilities, and education, but maybe the unemployment rate is high and many people wander around wondering what their life purpose is. In some of these countries, taxes may be very high making it difficult for people to be financially secure. In yet other countries, people suffer from lack of food, hygiene, clean water, unemployment, proper education and have to live with potential natural disasters as well.

Then there are of course countries with extreme laws that deeply affect how people live their lives. Usually, a single person or a few people have passed the rules and laws in these countries.

One thing is sure—every country has its share of challenging and convenient living conditions for its inhabitants albeit at different levels. Some have challenges on the physical level while others face challenges on the more intellectual, aesthetic, or spiritual levels.

Every country has its rugged landscape and its beautiful and tranquil places. Every country has happy and unhappy people. Every country has people who contribute to the whole in positive ways just as every country has its share of people who affect the lives of others in negative ways.

In ancient times when humans were hunters and gatherers, climate and geography were the main causes of variations in living conditions. Nowadays, many people do not necessarily stay in their native country all their lives, and a different scenario has emerged.

Topics such as integration, culture, and traditions are on the mind of many people as we all try to live together. This seems to pose a challenge to many, but in every country and for millions of people, the cultural, social, and religious mix is no problem. They are in fact capable of accepting other cultures, traditions, and religions, and they live in mutual respect.

If you look at your own neighborhood, you may see people from different cultures and nationalities, and in many cases, you can live in peaceful understanding and acceptance.

So many factors play a role in disturbing this harmony, and often, it is because the acquisition of basic needs or personal freedoms has been disrupted one way or the other. Often, it is also because many let their egos run their lives and do not consult their hearts before taking action. Disharmony often erupts due to fear.

But deep down, everybody wants peace, harmony, and the ability to put smiles on other people's faces.

## Defining Utopia

Think about how people with abundant finances live. They buy beachfront houses or penthouses with gorgeous views to have a sense of space and beauty around them, or they buy houses surrounded by greenery. Some buy only organic food, macrobiotic food, pure spring water, and so on.

I think most of us would love to live like that, and I am sure most of us would upgrade our current conditions if we had the finances. (We can all have the lives we desire, and I touch on that throughout this book.)

In reality, if you look at every country, you will find ugly, uncomfortable apartment blocks or housing areas with little or no greenery around them, flats with less-than-perfect views, houses built very close to each other, buildings without proper sanitation and shelter from weather conditions, on and on.

Nobody with adequate finances and an informed outlook would buy or build a house in a dingy, unsanitary neighborhood with no greenery or facilities for children.

Given an informed choice and after other basic physical needs have been fulfilled, most of us would want aesthetically pleasing and beautiful homes that give us pleasure at all levels, not just the physical.

I believe we are in an environment that can teach us the lessons we are here to learn.

## 3. A World of Needs

So what is actually essential for living? Primarily, we need sufficient food, water, clothing, and shelter. After we have taken care of these things, we look at the world around us. We start looking for friendly and helpful people with whom we can interact in friendly and inspiring ways.

If we could fulfill all these basic needs, we would have created a very good foundation for our lives we could build on. After the basis of our existence is established and secure, we have the energy and desire to look at ways to evolve our minds, souls, and feelings in stimulating ways. Our aesthetic needs begin presenting themselves.

Think of how many things and concepts surround us today that do not actually fulfill any of the basic needs mentioned above. Which needs do many of these things actually fulfill? Have we acquired some of those needs through learning and influence from outside? Are some of the things we do and buy fulfilling only the needs of our ego and only in the short term?

You may be familiar with Abraham Maslow, who in 1943 proposed a psychological theory of a hierarchy of needs and called it "A Theory of Human Motivation."

He described five layers of needs, each one building on the previous layer. Once we fulfill the needs of one layer, we go on the quest to fulfill the needs of the next layer and the next. We may temporarily go back to lower needs but will not stay there once they are fulfilled. Once our basic needs are met, we may jump from layer to layer in our eternal quest for improving all layers. We are in constant flux as is all life.

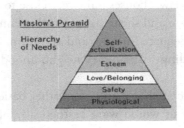

The hierarchy of needs is represented as a pyramid with the more primitive needs at the bottom.

> The first lower level is being associated with physiological needs, while the top levels are termed growth needs associated with psychological needs. Deficiency needs must be met first. Once these are met, seeking to satisfy growth needs drives personal growth …
>
> Physiological needs can control thoughts and behaviors, and can cause people to feel sickness, pain and discomfort [if not met]. (Wikipedia: "Abraham Maslow, Hierarchy of Needs")

He also pointed out our need to feel part of a group be it small or large and how when fulfilled, that can prevent anxiety and even clinical depression. In the layer of social needs, he thought that we basically just wanted to love and be loved in sexual and nonsexual ways alike. He recognized our need to work on our internal worlds—self-acceptance, self-love, and so on—and not rely entirely on our external circumstances.

## Some Criticisms of Maslow's Hierarchy of Needs

While Maslow's theory was regarded as an improvement over previous theories of personality and motivation, it had its detractors. For example, Wahba and Bridgewell found little evidence for the ranking of needs Maslow described or even for the existence of a definite hierarchy at all.

A 2002 study claimed, "The hierarchy of needs is nothing more than a fool's daydream; there is no possible way to classify ever-changing needs as society changes" (Wikipedia).

I do not believe that Maslow's hierarchy is a fool's daydream. I believe the headlines in the different layers would stay the same or at least be similar today despite societal changes as long as our human composition stays the same.

Over time, we may add ideas or concepts to Maslow's hierarchy that were not relevant, available, or in focus in the 1940s, but I think one would still be able to fit them into one of Maslow's levels.

Below is a suggestion for a perhaps incomplete and not finite list of needs, rights, and aspirations for everybody.

- abundant healthy food and clean drinking water
- comfortable, hygienic, and spacious housing
- healthy and clean environments
- access to unlimited natural environments
- access to medical care and alternative therapies
- clothing to suit weather conditions
- balanced, overt, unbiased, and noncommercial education including information on natural laws and human nature
- noncommercial information
- freedom to pursue positive activities, family structures, and careers
- opportunity to pursue individual senses of purpose
- opportunity to travel
- opportunity to enjoy nature's bounty
- freedom to select whom we want to be with
- opportunity and freedom to pursue positive dreams
- freedom to live by individual ideas of spirituality and beliefs

## What would be on your list?

Next, I will deal with some challenges we may be facing as we go through life and what happens when some or most of our needs are not met.

# Chapter 5

······································································

# Some Challenges in Life

······································································

## 1. What Happens When Our Needs Are Not Met?

Whether we agree with Maslow's hierarchy or use our own standards, we all know what it feels like when some of our needs are not met.

When that is the case, we may start feeling anxious, frustrated, angry, confused, lost, ashamed, and tense, and in the long term, we may begin to feel bitter and depressed.

We are however able to function even if only some of the basic needs are fulfilled. Imagine that you had enough food and water but no proper shelter. You could make it through another day but perhaps not comfortably depending on the weather or geological circumstances.

Similarly, if you knew for sure that a need was only temporarily not being met, you would in most cases be able to handle that.

Interestingly, predictability comes in and helps us. If we are very hungry but know we will have food shortly, we will handle our hunger and not get depressed over its temporary lack.

The more our basic needs are met, the more we can accept and handle that situation even if needs from the higher ranges of Maslow's hierarchy are not met at least short-term.

Imagine living in a decent home and having sufficient food and water. You have enough money to buy what you and your family need. You have access to medical care when you fall ill. You are happy with your children's school. You have access to information. Your family and friends are around, and you have a job.

But your home is not in a place you want to live. The weather may not permit you to spend as much time outside as you wish, the cultural scene may be lacking, and there may be only a few inspiring places for you to take your kids. Many of your basic needs are fulfilled, but you feel unfulfilled on some of your higher needs, for instance, confidence, achievement, and spiritual evolvement.

You will function and live happy and content, but from time to time, you will feel something is missing; you will feel the urge to fulfill your higher, more-aesthetic needs, and that urge becomes stronger over time. You might start feeling frustrated, irritable, and bitter if you don't do anything about it. In the long run, you cannot run away from your inner voice, your soul's calling, at least not without suffering.

## Your Internal Process

To change that around requires gratitude and wanting to be happy regardless of your external circumstances. So how do you get there? Finding things to be grateful for starting with the basic elements of your existence can help you feel happy. Focusing on your positive thoughts rather than your negative fears can also help you feel happy. This is mindfulness.

Consciously focus on appreciating whatever you can around you. Enjoy even the smallest moments. Cherish life and existence. Try to see opportunities and believe that there is a meaning behind it all and that you hold the key to your soul and heart. When you believe your core is peaceful, joyful, and filled with love, you will be grateful you have yourself.

We all have a strong desire that can be a catalyst to help us improve our situation. Sometimes, this desire is overshadowed by our doubts and fears, but underneath those is a desire for improving our lives, situations, and experiences.

When we focus on appreciating and feeling grateful for some of the things or circumstances we already have, we can start moving forward and upward. We can do that when we fuse our gratitude with our heartfelt desire for positive change.

## 2. Financial Challenges

We need money for most of the things we want and need—food, drink, housing, furniture, and experiences and events.

Before the concept of money was introduced, people bartered food, salt, goods, and commodity money such as beads, shells, and precious metals.

Life may have been simpler as everybody's basic needs were met then and there. However, you can imagine that it would take nothing more than a few greedy and powerful people to create imbalances in such barter deals. These rogues would give less and want more.

Greed still plays a major role in the global imbalance and availability of material things as well as in the imbalance of the distribution and production of food and water. But we can believe in the concept of abundance, that there is enough for everybody. We should acquire things only after following our hearts.

We see financial markets almost taking turns collapsing, sending shockwaves throughout the globe, and leaving thousands if not millions in financial distress. It seems that nothing is safe when it comes to economics be it national or global.

Two or three decades ago, IT stocks were the new thing right up until the market crashed and many people lost a lot of money. Some years after that, many people turned to real estate and made big profits. Real estate hit an all-time high, but that bubble also burst in many countries due to global financial crises.

We have seen oil prices go up and down, and we have seen the value of the dollar and other currencies fluctuate. Numerous banks required financial injections due to global financial crises. Food prices have soared in many countries.

These are just a few examples from the last decade, but they are repeats of what has happened historically due to circumstances that many do not even question.

Necessity is the mother of invention; that has applied to many people throughout the centuries, and it continues to do so.

## 3. When Structure Is a Challenge

Most people like structure in their lives. Some like fully structured, mapped-out working days while others like looser structures with wiggle room to determine their work. Yet others like to have the freedom and ability to be their own bosses.

Some like structure in their religions—fixed prayer times and established ceremonies, festivals, and rituals. Others lean toward nonreligious, self-established rituals or routines to make their days go smoothly.

It's only when structure feels like an inconvenience or we feel our lives are being held back because of societal, cultural, or traditional structures that it becomes a cause for concern. Then, we must find other ways to live more in accordance with our standards and routines. Sometimes, this could even mean moving to a place where we can live in our own way or by confronting the obstacles. Often easier said than done, but we all have the right to live according to our structures as long as we do not harm anyone.

It could also be that structure itself is a challenge for you, that you do not like structure and resist it even if you know it would bring some peace to you. I know of this challenge firsthand, and it has taken me lots of effort and self-exploration to find out what the blockages are and how to overcome them.

In some cases, these blockages can be lack of self-esteem, fear of success, rebellion against authority figures present early in life, and so on. Are you living under a type of structure that does not feel right to you?

## 4. Our Inner Landscape

Today, we are more and more influenced by things that seem to be controlled by others—soaring food prices, unstable housing markets, inflation, interest rates, crashing markets, poor or mediocre medical facilities, wars, and big-scale conflicts to mention just a few.

We seek to overcome these challenges so we can live balanced and simple but rich lives. Some of them can make it hard for us to believe we can make our lives more-positive experiences. These challenges can make it difficult for us to see how we can obtain inner peace and harmony, but we can overcome them! We sometimes forget we are also creators and cocreators of our own conditions. I am not saying we are creating these wars and atrocities; most people want to and can live under peaceful and respectful circumstances, and wars are created under completely different agendas.

We can realize we can spread positive ripples. Everything we do matters for ourselves and everyone around us. It will take some time to spread globally, but it is underway. Seen individually, it can take less time; in fact, we can make instant changes here and now. It all depends on our outlook, our inner harmony, and our ability to stay in the present, and it depends on our priorities.

Only when we are in a quiet, blissful, strong, and balanced state of mind can we tackle all challenges in a long-term positive way. Only when we learn to hold onto our positive thoughts and focus on positive deeds can we live in harmony with our inner selves and thus create those positive ripples in and around us.

Below are some examples of barricades in us that can prevent personal, internal harmony but that we can turn around with positive awareness and focus on positive outcomes.

- when we make choices based on outside influences rather than connections to our souls
- when we are consumed by fear or by a restless wish to impress others
- when we have little empathy or understanding of other people and their struggles
- when we are preoccupied with trying to digest the information we are bombarded with every day
- when we are too busy with our work, providing for our families, raising our children, keeping our marriages strong, nurturing our needs, and so on to stop and consider if we are living balanced and fulfilling lives
- when we focus on negative thoughts

Do you recognize any of the above? I think most of us have faced at least a few of these challenges. But when you become consciously aware of your internal mechanisms, you can stop feeling stuck or feeling inner turmoil.

Secure inner balance and strength step by step. Take it one challenge at a time.

## 5. The Challenge of Information Overload and Social Competitiveness

It is very easy for us to find things that occupy our minds. It is harder to become aware of what we actually allow our minds to be busy with. It is so easy to feel adrift and overwhelmed in today's information jungle.

We hear thousands of ways to lose weight, get fit, stop smoking, be successful, attract a dream partner, be popular, avoid getting fired, land a dream job, dress for success, be a good person, what to avoid, and other such advice most of which makes us compare ourselves to others or our surroundings, so competition may set in and pressure may build.

No wonder so many people are stressed and millions turn their attention inward to see who they really are, why they are here, what they are doing, and where they are going.

Many of us are trying to find spiritual answers to the bigger meaning of all this. We want to feel our efforts are not wasted. This spiritual awakening is happening all over the world. People are looking through the fogs of stress and consumerism for deeper things in themselves and in the world they know.

Many people are looking for practical ways to incorporate for instance spiritualism in their lives. Here are some questions they may have.

- How can I step outside the whirlwind of everyday life?
- How can I improve my life?
- Where should I start?
- How can I change things I am not happy with?
- How can I stay focused regardless of others' opinions?

I will address these questions and more later on. For now, back to the increasing information overload. We are constantly bombarded with information, technology, and materialistic temptations. We receive information via the news and TV, radio, the internet, and magazines. Millions are constantly connected to information links via laptops, mobile phones, and iPads.

We even look at big-screen TVs at some traffic lights with advertisements. A traffic light used to be a place where we could let our minds drift a bit while waiting.

Letting our minds wander is the best thing we can do for ourselves from time to time. It is in fact necessary for us if we want to maintain a healthy mental state. Nature is and always has been the best stress reliever.

What can we do to keep on top of the information load?

## Gain Perspective

Sometimes, we need to gain perspective to help us choose and prioritize the influences in our lives. For more on this, see the chapter "Perspective."

## Bring Calmness to Our Minds

Children often sit and stare into space, and if you call them, they will not react. They are in an instinctive meditative state and are letting their thoughts drift. That gives them a break; they can switch off from the outside world and reflect on and digest their impressions.

This is indeed a very useful habit, but we seem to push it to the back of our minds as we grow up. Nonetheless, we can recall this meditative, reflective state any time we want through meditation alone or in guided group sessions. A calm mind helps us see our paths more clearly.

## Focus on Positive Information

It would not be possible to keep up with everything going on around us even if we tried; we must make constructive and positive use of what is available. We should try to fill our minds with what is essential to us and creates free space that allows inspiration, vision, and creativity to enter.

The plethora of information available through the internet can be an incredibly valuable tool that enables us to

- search and gather information on almost any topic,
- increase our knowledge about what goes on in the world,
- become inspired and stimulated by others and their experiences, and
- evoke emotions and feelings.

In spite of all the negative news, the world holds lots of good news. You can start looking for positive stories and experiences all around you right now.

You can read books, magazines, and journals that empower, relieve, and support yourself. You can start noticing things that make you smile and give you good feelings.

You can notice strangers' smiles and see kids happily playing; you can enjoy a stunning landscape or cloud formation. You can listen to people laughing. Just think *healing*.

We can send healing thoughts and intentions out to every being on this planet including ourselves and Mother Earth. Every positive thought we send out echoes a positive deed just as every negative thought we have attaches to a negative deed and manifests negativity. It is so much more productive and healthy individually and globally to let the negative flow away and dissolve and then focus on what is positive and beneficial as a whole. People need people for dialogue, comfort, and progress.

## 6. The Challenge of Influence

Who is really influencing our opinions, beliefs, and values? Our families? Friends? Communities? Our broader society? Someone we do not even know?

How much time do we spend on movies, books, TV, newspapers and magazines? Below are some influences you may not even think twice about.

## High-Score Lists

We find high-score lists linked to different media and items such as movies, books, fashion, TV shows, consumer products, and others. The lists can reflect popularity, usefulness, durability, safety, effectiveness, and so on. The lists reflect the fulfillment of different needs in line with Maslow's hierarchy mentioned earlier.

However, if a book has made a bestseller list, does that mean it is universally good? If you think it is not good, is there something wrong with you? Absolutely not. It could just mean that the marketing for that book has been particularly effective with others, but it doesn't say anything about how helpful it has been or how deeply it has impacted those who have bought it.

We have free will to form our opinions, and we can choose to view these lists as merely guidelines or reflections of certain trends. But we should not view these lists as things that determine what is right or wrong. For that, we can use our values and common sense, which I will also talk about later.

## TV News

Bad things happen. We experience this in our lives and see it on the news every day or read about it on the internet if we so choose. Things that we perceive as negative happen. The way we digest and manage the information is up to us. How we let it influence us is very individual. We can change our perspective. We can monitor the effect it has on us, seek information that gives us a positive effect, and turn our attention to doing good for ourselves and others in whatever social circles we can.

## Movies

Different movies tell us many things about different national and global trends, social structures, and our knowledge of psychology, science, the universe, earth, and so on. The past three decades have sprouted themes from bloody horror movies portraying unsuspecting teenagers, alien invaders who connect with children and psychics, psychological thrillers that play with our minds and push the limits of what we perceive as normal, and we have seen the emergence of violent movies with subtle undertones that show little respect for certain people.

That said, there are also many thriller movies that give us a positive adrenaline rush. Many wonderful and positive movies out there portray the beauty and strength and immense powers in human beings. This all means we should choose mindfully and consciously who and what we want to influence our lives.

## The Internet

The flashing ads and links that constantly pop up on our computer screens can be a big distraction and may tempt younger users to explore a world of information that is not age appropriate as there is no filter that allows you to decide what types of ads you want to appear.

## Desensitization

The information jungle is influencing our children and our teenagers; it misleads them into believing that material abundance, war, terror, greed, and hatred are what our world and reason for being is all about.

They see negativity in so many places, and if they are not shown otherwise and do not learn to use common sense and trust their hearts and what they feel, they might think that life has no value unless they have many material things. They might think that fear is a natural part of everyday life, and they might not seek out, value, or be grateful for the positives our world and life have to offer. They become desensitized to negative things and are led to believe this is the norm.

We cannot allow this negative cycle; it spreads negativity, sadness, and in many cases trauma that need to be dealt with later on. Our children have to learn to express themselves as loving beings.

We like stable pictures of how our world is just as Maslow pointed out in his term *predictability*, which is important for adults as well as children. And we like positive things as reasons to go on. The more positive things we can find in our lives, the more they ignite our spark to go on.

However, our image of the world is shattered by frightening and negative news and information; we have to pick up the pieces and try to make sense of and stabilize our worlds personally and globally. To do this, we have mechanisms or tools to help us gain a sense of balance in the emotional, physical, mental, and spiritual senses.

How much we allow ourselves to be influenced by for instance TV shows can keep us from living in compliance with our inner selves. Depending on how things are presented, people can become desensitized to many things and move away from a positive approach to life.

If we see something on TV, we can find ourselves liking or disliking something because of the way it was portrayed whether it was a certain product, a way of doing things, psychotherapy, alternative therapies, UFOs, or ways to live spiritual lives.

It is useful to be aware of how TV characters can influence us and not let this interfere with our common sense or our courage to act in sustainable ways.

We should often stop, think, and become more discerning about the sources of information and ask ourselves, *What are actually their goals and values in bringing me this information?*

It is up to us as adults to show our children the beauty and value of life whenever we can. Here is an example of how we can extract information from the world around us. In a country where I used to live, many expats from poorer countries worked there as laborers, cooks, house cleaners, gardeners, and builders. Many of them had to ride bikes to work. Though traffic laws gave bikes the right of way, many drivers did not grant that; they forced bicyclists to wait until the cars have passed.

My native country in Europe is very different; bicyclists are considered "soft" road users; cars must give them the right of way. There are special bike lanes on every street, and there are traffic lights especially for bike riders.

People from all walks of life ride bikes; a vast majority of the people in my native country ride bikes; those who ride bikes are not sending signals that they are poor. This reflects the national notion that everybody is important.

This is just one example of how to zoom out and see the bigger picture and see patterns in society and the synthetic, man-made, societal layers around you. You can use the information to help you become aware of how many things surround us and signal that some are considered less important than others. And you can help change that notion by consciously taking actions that show the opposite.

## 7. Maintaining Personal Space and Boundaries

Many situations make us feel our personal space and boundaries have been disregarded. I am not talking about wars or violence, which are gross violations of other beings and life in general. I am talking about work or home situations that may make us feel disrespected or not heard.

When we are in such situations, we should remember that we have the right to choose what we want to allow in our personal spaces. But if our boundaries are disregarded too often, we may end up doubting our judgment and our belief that we have the right to choose. Our self-esteem may be low, we may question our psychological stability, and we may not know how to move forward. If we cannot find a way to do that on our own, we can look for help from elsewhere until we find stability within yet again.

Here are examples of things people may perceive as invasive.

- information we have not asked for (mainly business oriented)
- some events on TV reality shows
- some concepts of TV game shows—peer pressure by the media
- paparazzi following celebrities
- noise or other harassments and bullying from others

Countless TV shows push people's personal boundaries; they show us how much integrity, dignity, personal feelings, and privacy ordinary people will compromise to gain financially.

Often when we see something on TV and especially if it is done in an entertaining way, we find it hard to distinguish right from wrong. We often accept what we see as the norm, and we become afraid to feel and think otherwise.

Some people who watch personal boundaries being broken down in TV shows and elsewhere may believe it is okay not to respect other people's private spaces, but that could create a trend of disrespect.

One thing we can do about that is turn off our TVs and keep giving other people the respect we want to receive from them. This is how we can choose in these cases.

In the case of paparazzi and their relentless pursuit of celebrity photos, their usual defensive reply is, "It's what people want to see" and "It's a question of supply and demand." I see it more as a psychological trick for financial gain while feeding off readers' curiosity and their soft spot for comparing themselves or aspiring to something that in reality is not the way it is portrayed in these magazines.

Nevertheless, where is the limit? How personal do you think you have the right to be with others you do not know at a personal level?

The media frenzy and TV shows that have evolved over the past decades may influence many teenagers as well as young adults into erroneously thinking that disrespecting others' rights, privacy, and personal boundaries is okay.

I am sure that the paparazzi out there just "doing their jobs" will think back on these times and come up with a somewhat more profound answer than "It's what people want to see."

There are many other ways to get a kick out of life; is it right that people have to compromise their boundaries and values for the entertainment of others?

If you want to explore your personal boundaries and keep them intact, take the time to consciously define them.

## Healing Visualization

The next time you encounter a situation in which you feel your boundaries are invaded, picture yourself wrapped in a white protective light. Imagine that the light has roots in earth and has a cord connected to a source of love in the cosmos. The image of you wrapped in this white protective light can help you feel protected, and that can help you better deal with the situation.

The more you can visualize situations and evoke positive feelings, the more you will be able to hold onto positive thoughts and steer yourself in a direction that is more positive for you and your surroundings. Every time we focus within, we can find a point of balance and calm.

## 8. The Challenge of Staying Alive

Millions of people globally face starvation. It has been like that for as long as I can remember, and it goes back even further. It has always puzzled me how this could continue to be a problem.

Millions of people in Third World or developing countries are still malnourished because of drought, war, or inadequate supplies of food and clean drinking water. In addition, many do not even have proper shelter.

Starving to death has been the unfortunate fate of millions throughout the centuries. Weather-induced catastrophes such as hurricanes, floods, drought, and earthquakes have caused and regularly still cause shortages of food.

Now as then, diseases in domestic animals and plants have also caused food and water shortages as have regional, national, or world wars. Over time, as the population in developed countries increased, so did the demands on agriculture and cattle production.

When the feudal system (peasant vs. lord) as well as money and taxes were introduced, people gradually lost access to their supplies and needs. Nowadays, government subsidies and structural changes in trade agreements play a big part in the production and distribution of the global food supply.

With an ever-growing population and a planet going through significant changes at the moment and over the past few centuries, it is difficult to predict what the situation will be like for the generations to come. We can all see that the world is changing; the ecosystem—our planet and all that lives on it—will balance itself out eventually one way or another.

The challenge is how to deal with the life-threatening problems so many people face today. Hundreds of government and nongovernmental organizations help alleviate the situation, and thousands of workers and volunteers offer their help to people who are hanging onto their lives. Can more be done? With the enormous amount of food waste and pipelines everywhere, it should not be a problem to help all people in the world gain access to adequate food, water, and shelter.

It all comes down to priorities.

# 9. The Challenge of Tradition and Culture

Most of us live to some extent according to our traditions and cultures. Many people live fully according to old tradition.

Our food habits, social status, ability to choose life partners, the way we raise our children, our livelihoods, and the way we perform and celebrate certain festivals or ceremonies are all aspects of our lives that in many cases have been influenced by our traditions and cultures.

Often, actions and values based on tradition fulfill mainly our basic needs (physiological, safety, love, belonging) with a few exceptions of fulfilling the higher needs (perhaps only esteem; see more in chapter 4.3. on Maslow's theory of human motivation.)

Some members of a family may accept and live according to the rules of their traditions and cultures. We often see that tradition is intertwined with religion or other spiritual beliefs. Many people find great comfort in the fact that many aspects of their lives are laid out for them, and they may find it very helpful that certain rules apply to almost every step they take.

Others may feel that the rules and habits are stifling and very difficult to accept, and they may even find that these go against their wishes and values. They may experience a lot of pressure from their families and find it difficult not having the right to choose for themselves. They can face great challenges in that sense.

The experiences that make us go through various feelings differ, but the feelings each of us holds are the same.

## 10. Frustrations with Established Society

In every society in every part of the world throughout history, certain groups of people did not know how to fit in or did not want to fit in the established society. Some people are quite content with not fitting in; they find their own ways to create rich and meaningful lives for themselves outside the establishment.

Others who feel they do not fit in may unfortunately go in the opposite direction and spiral downward into a negative state of living; they feel different and not worthy and strange compared to others. Though they could benefit from a caring therapy, they are often not able to reach out and ask for help.

Many frustrated and angry young people in every country have lost faith in their systems and social norms. Their degree of frustration can vary from country to country depending on how invasive the regime or system is in their lives.

The causes of their frustration depend on what their expectations are, and those depend on many factors including the conditions in their countries compared to those in other countries.

Comparing our lives to those of others can be inspirational and aspirational, but it can also provoke envy. Taking responsibility for one's own life can be hard for many and can result in frustration with how things are.

Frustrations can also build up when a regime blatantly mistreats people or treats certain of its people unfairly. Many young people vent their frustrations in violent ways because they feel there are no channels for their voices. There could be many reasons for their violent behavior. Maybe they have no contact with others who live within the system, or maybe they never had anybody to teach them how to deal with their frustrations.

Maybe they feel they received nothing from their schooling. Maybe they had problematic or even traumatic childhoods due to abusive parents or peers. Maybe they feel misunderstood, misguided, misled, and abandoned. Maybe some are just looking for an outside source to blame for their circumstances.

They may be looking for a purpose, they may be looking for better things to fill their lives with, but they have a hard time finding that and thus find comfort, meaning, and companionship in others who are in the same boat as them.

The system—established society—does not know how to react to this group and tends to shun them because of their destructive behavior that influences their surroundings negatively. But shunning them can make their situations even worse because everybody needs the same comforts and feelings of security and purpose. The violence and destruction they cause is not a sustainable answer to their situation; it is probably the last resort.

As discussed earlier, if our needs are not fulfilled, we can end up frustrated and angry. Many may have gone through most of their lives with unfulfilled needs. If that were the case, they may have gotten used to having to put a lid on their needs to avoid feeling unfulfilled and disappointed.

Having trouble finding avenues to express themselves so they can feel heard, many teenagers and adolescents turn to drugs or alcohol for relief from their pain and to blur reality.

Abusing drugs and alcohol may make people think they are happy in their clouded reality. But we have all heard many stories of people coming out of substance abuse and saying they have come back up again and see the positive side of life. They label their times of abuse as low points in their lives—"I was down in the dumps and didn't see things clearly."

Drug and alcohol abuse does indeed make you see things not clearly. And when you see things clearly, staring into the reality of your hardship could be too much to cope with.

Many who come out of their abuse often report having found a broader perspective on life that includes the natural environment in one way or the other. Often, our disconnectedness with nature and our natural selves, our inner selves, is the cause of so much suffering and despair.

Many countries experience demonstrations (some of which end up as riots) because people are angry about the choices their governments are making. Many who take part in those demonstrations may be frustrated with certain aspects of the systems that personally affect them; they join demonstrations to make a statement. They may not actually have an alternative system in mind, which can cause further frustration. Or they may have an idea of what they want but find it difficult to start making changes when met by a wall of red tape and often force.

Another source of frustration that many people experience is due to the fact that we all have to live together in spite of our beliefs, values, interests, and actions. But millions all over the world live in peace with whatever neighbors they have.

It can be hard for people who are part of a minority to find their own places and find acceptance in societies that disagree with them in many ways.

Many of the conflicts today go back centuries, but one thing they have in common is that they rely on people's cultural and traditional sensitivities, feelings, and emotions, including fear. Many clashes are caused by this, and fear is a widely abused tool to cause those clashes.

Dividing people into groups, castes, or classes depending on financial levels, skin color, location, beliefs, and traditions can provoke jealousy and misunderstanding that create many of the negative situations we witness today.

If everybody started perceiving others in accordance with their actions and values rather than their religion, color, or wealth, the world would be a completely different place.

One can only begin to imagine how different.

*The Native people were ruthlessly destroyed because they were*
*an inassimilable element to the civilizations of the West.*
—A Basic Call to Consciousness, Iroquois People, 1977

# Chapter 6

........................................

# Preparing for Change

........................................

## 1. Taking Stock of Your Life

To make any changes in your life, you first need to stop and take stock of your situation. If you do not, you will feel you are not in control of your life. You may feel you are drifting with the winds and do not have a say in where life takes you. You may not even take time to think about how you feel. Day after day goes by until one day, you realize you feel stuck and dissatisfied with life.

So ask yourself, *Is there anything I want to change in my life?* You may have thought about this before, and you may have some vague ideas, but you may not have taken concrete actions to define what you want to change. Here are some questions you can ask yourself.

- Do I feel unhappy with many things in my life?
- Am I carrying an inexplicable unsettled or fearful feeling?
- Am I short-tempered?
- Do I rarely burst out laughing?
- Do I let the beautiful details of life go by without noticing and being grateful for them?
- Do I keep complaining about the same things?
- Do I repeatedly seem to encounter the same types of situations or confrontations with others?

If you answered yes to any of these questions, do not worry. You can start right now in a different direction; it is never too late to do that. Your awareness and willingness to initiate change will trigger change, and it will start the moment you focus on the positive.

You can focus on your positive thoughts and go in a more positive direction by answering the above questions and others you may have and think about the following more-specific topics that can give you an idea of the cause of your negative thoughts. You can write down whatever comes to your mind first.

- What do you imagine your life to be like?
- Are you in the geographical location you want to be?
- Do you enjoy your work or studies?
- How are you helping yourself and others?
- Who are the people in your life? Do you care for them and love them? Do you feel they care about you? Do you help each other enjoy life?
- Do you spend your time the way you want to?
- Do you fill your life with things that make you feel joyous and fulfilled?
- How do you feel when you have moments to yourself?
- When you are in bed ready to sleep, how do you feel?
- How do you feel and what do you think about when you wake up?

Your answers to these questions may give you clues about what you want in your life that you do not have and what you want your life to be from this day forward.

## Healing Visualization: Visualizing Your Ideal Day

Being a very visual person, I use images to help me define certain things. I thought of dividing my ideal day into a pie chart to see what actually mattered to me and what my ideal day would be like.

You can apply this pie chart to your workday, your spare time, or your whole life. Use it to become more aware of how you feel and what you think of throughout the day.

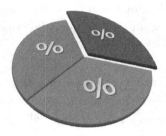

Fill it in with feelings and actions that could fill your day. You can make your own list and use it as a guide for your daily activities including how you work, interact with others, recharge yourself, and deal with situations.

Compare your pie chart to your current life. In what areas do you need to change things? It's easy to forget to pay attention to our thoughts and actions. We often operate on autopilot and do not always consider how we can make our lives more efficient and fun.

Maybe we could improve the way we play with our children. We could find new ways to rest and recharge. We could get better at time management. We could do more things together as a family. We could see the world through a child's eye. We could do more to help and be kind to others.

Once you start paying loving attention to yourself, the information you need to move on will suddenly find its way to you so you can improve yourself, your life, and your relationships with yourself and others.

How you begin each day can tell you about your life. As mentioned earlier, one way to get an indication of your current state is to notice how you feel and what you are thinking of when you wake up after a good night's sleep.

Every day is a new beginning for you. This is when your body has had a chance to recharge. Your dreams will have reshuffled any mind debris from the previous day, and you will be left with what is on your mind temporarily as well as long term.

If you spend just a few minutes every morning consciously noticing your state of well-being—what your predominant feeling is and what thoughts you are focusing on—that will give you a good idea of what level you are on and how you feel about your life or certain aspects of it.

Do you wake up with a good, calm, and secure feeling? Do you feel anxious, uncomfortable, and uncertain about your next steps? Are there certain things that dominate your thoughts, or do your thoughts flow in a stress-free manner and let you take action? Do you focus on the positive rather than the negative thoughts that fly by?

Things that keep entering your mind and leave you feeling restless, irritable, or upset are telling you they need to be addressed in a positive manner that works long term; you can do that step by step.

## 1.1 Dreams Can Tell You about Your Life

Your dreams can also tell you about what is on your mind if you are having trouble sorting through your conscious thoughts. Dreams of course tell you about what is going on in your subconscious as well.

Many online dream dictionaries, apps, and books can help you interpret your dreams, and can tell you what is going on in your inner world and what your subconscious is trying to tell you.

Your dreams are actually you, your soul, trying to communicate with you and trying to tell you about aspects of yourself you are not dealing with, are afraid of, are ashamed of, or not accepting.

Your dreams are friends, trusted parts of yourself that are trying to get important messages to you to help you evolve and sort through your thoughts, actions, and emotions. They will help you discard thoughts, actions, and emotions that do not serve your best interests.

## 1.2 Physical Signs of Your State of Being

To become more conscious of what goes on inside you, take a minute to notice your physical body.

- Notice your breath for a minute—air flowing in and out.
- Notice your train of thought.
- Notice how you feel. Do you get goose bumps when you think of certain things? Butterflies in your stomach? Dislike?
- Do you get headaches when you think about certain things?
- Do you clench your teeth or make a fist?
- Does your breath change from deep and relaxed to shallow, stressful, and quick when you think of certain things?
- Define what makes you feel uncomfortable physically, mentally, or emotionally and thus define what you would like to heal.
- Listen to your body when exercising.
- Listen to your inner voice. What is it telling you?
- Make conscious decisions on what you feel you should or should not put into your body as in food, drink, drugs, etc.

## 1.3 Use Your Body as a Barometer

Become aware of your body. Have a good look at it, and use it as a barometer of how balanced and harmonic you are in the moment.

## Healing Visualization: Healing Shower

The next time you are in the shower, tune in to your train of thoughts and feelings. The soothing trickle of water renders a great sense of calmness and openness to ideas if you let it.

Imagine the water washing away negative thoughts and experiences. Watch them flow down the drain and into the ground, where they will be purified by light, crystals, or energies of Mother Earth perhaps.

Create a vision of your own. Imagining yourself being purified can help you feel more purified and cleared of negativity. It can help you step out of the shower or the bath with a fresh perspective on your situation. All you have to do is let it. Be open to noticing signs and information from within or around you that prove more positivity is opening up for you.

If the shower isn't the place for you to relax and recharge body and mind, find other ways that can help you in this regard. Maybe dancing, walking, singing, swimming, or doing chores can help you get into that frame of mind. Doing things that do not require your full conscious attention are often the best ways to reach your inner self.

The beauty of it is that we all have ways to relax and recharge. Our relaxed but aware minds help us relax our bodies and tune in to the signals our bodies are sending us.

## 2. Create Space for Creativity and Healing to Enter Your Life

When you have given the above questions some thought, it is time to delve deeper into your treasure chest of wisdom and knowledge, and here is a tip that can help you get started on that.

You may want to start incorporating into your daily routine some time to help you calm your mind, clear your thoughts, and just be. Let the negative thoughts fly by. Start focusing on and holding onto your positive thoughts. That way, you will create space for creativity, vision, and healing to enter.

You may have your own ways of doing this. Maybe you enjoy music, meditation, yoga, riding a motorbike, walking in nature, watching a sunset, or enjoying the view from a mountain. You may have many other ways that can help you clear your mind and sort through your thoughts so you can discard the negatives.

You alone can best define your best times and find ways that help you feel calm, relaxed, and aware enough to notice what is going through your mind and how that leaves you feeling.

## 3. You Know Best

Learn to listen to your inner voice, which is your positive true self. It can help you choose what to do, how to be compassionate and sensible, how to know right from wrong, and how to relax and have fun. It is always positive.

Invite your inner voice, your soul, your higher self, your guardian angel, or whomever you want to invite into your life as your guide for the highest good. You will wonder how you ever lived without listening to it!

## 4. Countering Negative Thoughts

Through every situation we face, we have to deal with the accompanying thoughts we have. They are our inner conversations, our inner monologues.

Depending on our awareness of ourselves self and our level of mental, emotional, and spiritual understanding, our thoughts can be our best friends or our worst enemies.

One way to help yourself move forward and upward is imagining having a temporary inner parking lot for your negative thoughts. Whenever you hold a negative thought (fear, doubt, worry, anxiety, guilt, etc.) there will be in your mind some advice, a meaningful answer, or a wise observation you have obtained earlier ready to respond to or counter that negative thought temporarily.

I stress the word *temporarily* because although you may hold a piece of advice, an answer, or an observation that counters your negative thought, you may still experience that negative thought over and over until you believe a hundred percent the answer you are holding. The answer to your negative thought can become so integrated in your thinking and living that you will be able to dissolve that negative thought every time it shows its head.

When you can replace the negative thought with a positive counterpart, it will eventually become nullified. Your negative thought will no longer be able to create a negative experience. Its reason for existing will no longer be.

## 5. Focus on Balance in Your Life

We all want to create comfortable, safe, and nurturing homes for ourselves and our families. We all have to think about how to teach and prepare our children to create useful and meaningful lives for themselves.

We all think about how to balance work and time off. We often worry about bills. We constantly meet challenges just trying to make a living and creating decent, fulfilling, inspiring, meaningful, and fun-filled lives for our families and ourselves.

So naturally, since we are so caught up with the everyday challenges, our lives sometimes become unbalanced. We may not have the energy to think beyond our circles of family and friends, to take care of the environment, or to connect with nature and the subtle energies that surround us.

But when we are so busy and mainly concerned about the practical issues of life, that means something else in our multifaceted state of being is out of balance and that we have to make changes in our lives to regain equilibrium in our physical, mental, and spiritual aspects.

With that comes the need for us to consider what is essential to us and what are our priorities. The more we focus on feeling positive, the more we will actually feel positive.

Surround yourself with people you love and care for and who give you inspired boosts upward and forward. Do not spend your time with people who seek to bring you down.

# Chapter 7

········································································

# Perspective—How You See the World

········································································

You will enhance your life when you choose to focus on the positive instead of the negative.

## Six Ways to Gain Perspective on Your Life

Sometimes, we become so engrossed in the daily grind that our focus gets lopsided and we put greater emphasis on things that do not benefit our well-being or positive growth.

If you feel you need ideas on how to get a little balance and focus into your perspective of life, try the following examples.

## 1. Detach from the World Occasionally

If you are feeling overwhelmed, stressed, careless, or complacent about everything going on in the world, step back to create some space and look at an overview for yourself.

- Turn off the news
- Read only what really interests you.
- Take a mental break, meditate, light a candle.
- Turn down the volume when TV commercials come on.
- Take time out from seriousness.
- Engage in something funny and positive.
- Read a cartoon.
- Watch a funny or a warmhearted movie.

- Call a friend.
- Get grounded; turn to music or nature. Keep your ears open to nature's sounds.
- Allow your mind to be occupied with something positive, cleansing, and soothing that you deliberately choose.

We all need that positive, grounding feeling; it creates an unseen bond between us all. The world is as complex and unclear as it has probably ever been. Be critical and selective about any information you receive. You cannot absorb all the information around you, so do your best to be your own filter.

## 2. Think of a Disaster Movie You Have Seen

I mean one of these movies in which the world comes to a halt due to a weather catastrophe, an epidemic, an alien invasion, or a similar event.

If you have not seen such a movie, imagine a new ice age has come overnight. Snow covers everything. Cities and towns have been flattened. There is no electricity. Phones are not working. Cars cannot drive through the masses of snow. You are stuck where you are and cut off from the rest of the world except for maybe your nearest neighbors.

Then think about what would be most important to you in the next day, the next month. What would really matter to you? What would be your priorities?

After the first month, things start to slightly clear up. What would be most important to you the following month and year? Think of the plethora of things, information, and gadgets you normally have and decide which could help you in your new situation.

Is there anything you are spending your time and energy on now that is actually insignificant in the bigger scheme of things?

## 3. Find Comfort in the Fact That Negative People Will Probably Not Stay That Way

And even if they do stay that way, they will face more resistance from others over time and find it increasingly difficult to be at peace with themselves.

In time, we tend to become more patient and considerate. Maybe we begin to surrender more to the fact that nothing lasts forever, and maybe after many different life experiences, we start to see the bigger picture more clearly.

Healing ourselves so we can help others becomes a big priority for us. The people with negative behavior we are concerned about now will probably one day realize the same.

## 4. Fast-Forward to When You Are Seventy-Five

Imagine yourself being at the age when you will have passed through the longest part of your life. You have had many experiences, and you have time to reflect.

What actions and experiences would you look back on? What feelings would you like to have when you are older? Would you like to feel contentment and bliss and know you have had a positive impact on yourself and others? Define the feelings and memories you would like to have.

Bring that knowledge to the present. You can start going that direction now by making choices that make you feel good at whatever level is possible for you. You can feel good now and later in life.

This exercise does not mean that you have to live as if you were already seventy-five! It means that it might help give you some perspective on your goal however distant it may be, and it might help you with some of the choices you make starting now. It might also help you remember to have fun along the way!

## 5. Turn Down Your TV's Volume and Just Look at the Picture

Look at the pictures that flicker across your screen without sound, without biased comments, and think about how it makes you feel. You will suddenly see the absurdity of all the suffering and the desperate situations people across the globe face.

Turn down the volume when a commercial comes on; you'll be amazed to discover how you feel! Alternatively, close your eyes and just listen to your TV. This way of sorting out the visual noise works with movies and commercials too. You will feel much more capable of noticing what is important and what is just filler.

Once you are no longer absorbing the full visual and audio impact but concentrating on only one, you will find it easier to allow your mind to be the filter of what you are taking in.

## 6. Picture Yourself as a Small Universe

I imagine all the cells I am made of and how they are constantly changing, renewing themselves, and moving about. Then I think how much I would benefit if all my cells were healthy and positive. I imagine my cells drawing in positive energy that benefits them and me. I then expand my perspective to thinking about earth and all living beings on it including all humans as the cells.

Imagine how much we could benefit earth if we were all busy thinking positively and lightly. We would benefit, and the earth would benefit just as each cell in my body would benefit.

Take it one step further and think of the universe as a whole and how all the stars and the planets are now the cells.

# Chapter 8

## Our Children

*One Generation plants the trees; another gets the shade.*
—Chinese saying

*Parents are the first teachers of the children.*
—Burmese proverb

Our children are our biggest assets. They give us so much when they come into our lives; it is only fair to think about what positive experiences we can give them.

Treat children with respect. They are born helpless, vulnerable, and innocent. People who abuse children in any way ranging from unknowingly damaging their self-esteem to abusing them physically or otherwise psychologically would benefit from seeking help so they do not transfer their shortcomings to their children. We all have lessons to learn, so we should not feel ashamed, embarrassed, or guilty that we need healing one way or another.

Our children come into this world on their own path and with their own range of lessons they need to learn and issues they need to heal. If we clear some of our issues, we will at least project less negativity onto our children.

If we replace our dark feelings—guilt, jealousy, anger, fear, and others—with positive feelings, we will acquire a surplus of positivity that we can offer others and give our children a different experience than the one we had.

Think of the journey you and your child are taking, and focus on having a positive experience together.

## 1. Good Intentions

It is great to have good intentions for your children, but be patient and let them be their own judges of what they like as long as it does not harm anybody. Allow them to use their intuition. Be encouraging, supportive, and aware of their reactions to situations and suggestions you present them.

Whatever you want to teach your children—swimming, reading, playing football, fishing, being a good friend, etc.—remember that your child wants to have fun doing it. It is heartbreaking to see a parent forcing a child to learn something because the parent thinks it is important.

A nurturing nudge in a certain direction can be fine; children sometimes need a little encouragement and support to be okay with trying something, but if they keep resisting something, maybe it is time to let it go for now and turn their attention to something they enjoy. Pay attention to how your children react to anything they encounter, take it seriously, and make it a positive experience.

Even when we parents are having a bad day, we should look at our parenting as a positive thing and do our best to bring out the glow and smile in our children rather than tears of shame. That does not make our children stronger or build their character.

Children will learn to deal with different situations if they have a solid, warm, secure, and loving foundation and a support network behind them. That helps them develop a positive confidence.

## 2. Having Children

Once you have a child, you will be needed twenty-four hours a day every day. It is a big responsibility; how big and how demanding it is is hard to imagine until you become a parent.

It is not easy to predict the impact a child will have on your life. Once you get to hold your baby, you realize you will have to be there for him or her for a long time. Your child needs somebody, preferably you, to take care of him or her day and night and offer positivity.

Timing is of great importance when you have children. They will need you at any time whether you are busy with something else or not. You have to incorporate nap times and baby feeding times into your daily routine.

Finding time for yourself and your partner can become a challenge when you become a parent. As your children grow, you will need to squeeze in time to help them with schoolwork, when they are sick, and when they engage in outside activities; they will continue to need your support and know they have a special place in your life and heart. In return, your children will give you the best times of your life!

Everything with children comes in phases, and nothing ever stays the same. Sometimes, I felt trapped in recurring tasks—changing nappies, breastfeeding, cleaning bottles, getting up at night, thinking about safety in the home, and running after a two-year-old bundle of energy.

However, as time passed, I realized they would grow out of one phase and enter the next, and I would be thrilled noticing their look of pride and a bit more independence with each accomplishment.

Our job as parents is to be there for our children, guide them, love them, be patient with them, and work alongside them. We need to take time for that. If you feel you cannot do this, maybe having children is not the right choice for you at the moment, or maybe you could consider in what areas of your life you could compromise to offer a child a good existence.

Of course, we parents cannot give our children the best experiences a hundred percent of the time. We also get tired, we have our difficulties, our moods change, our energy levels go up and down, and we still have to go through challenges and frustrations. And we just don't know everything about raising children; we are also learning as we go. But if we are willing to accept that we are learning, we have come very far in our positive growth.

Thankfully, many great books on raising children are available. We can also speak with friends, parents, and professionals when we feel hopeless and that we are losing positive contact with our children or when we feel their behavior is going in the wrong direction. We parents are their constant guides, and we must share responsibility for the turns our children take as well as teaching them to take responsibility for their actions.

Children want to be loved, and they want to learn; they are naturally curious, innocent, and loving. We cannot wrap them in cotton to protect them from the negativities of the world; we have to let them drift and soar, but we should be there when they land.

## 3. Children Having Children

There are now more teenage moms than ever. These mothers are so young themselves. They have not had their own time to develop, grow, and explore themselves and life.

In some countries, they get government help and free housing; they often live alone with their children, the fathers not being around. Many of the young moms have not finished their education and have not fully matured intellectually, socially, emotionally, and spiritually.

They face the difficult task of bringing up their children and teaching them about the world, other people, positive values, and so on because they still have so much to learn themselves.

Instead of using their adolescent years for their own purposes, they have brought another person into the world. They have babies who need a lot of their attention, care, and time.

Another group of teenage mothers lives in countries where social norms and traditions direct them to go into hiding, give up the children for adoption, or just leave the children literally at the doorstep of another house.

Think of the devastation and trauma they must endure not only being very young with a child in a society that doesn't approve of that but also having to deal with the emotional trauma of unwillingly letting go of their children.

If you are a teenager heading down this path or thinking about heading down this path, think twice. Make sure you are fully aware that a new life, a new person will be there with you at all times, and he or she will need emotional, social, material and spiritual comfort to get a good start in life.

## 4. Breaking the Cycle of Bad Role Models

As an adult and a parent, how often do you encounter situations that bring back memories of your childhood? How often do you think about how your parents or guardians handled certain situations, what their mood was, and what they said about specific situations? I think that happens quite often.

Now that you are an adult or adolescent, you may have a clearer opinion and a more experienced view of where they went wrong and where they went right.

If you have a clear picture of negative behavior from your parents or guardians that happened to you in your childhood, actively steer away from that behavior so it does not affect your children.

That is of course easier said than done because sometimes, we do not know our reactions to certain events until they happen. Even then, we may not notice it. However, with increased awareness of our behavior, we can change it to constructive guidance instead of negative influence.

Think about your childhood. What situations made you feel comfortable and secure? Maybe you remember your dad fixing something in the house while your mom was in the kitchen making lunch. Maybe you remember hearing your mom's sewing machine buzzing and you knew your mother was mending your pants or making a new shirt for herself. Maybe the sound of the lawn mower told you your dad was in the garden and you felt secure knowing normal chores were being handled. Children take comfort in atmospheres that include activity and stability.

What would you like your children to think of you once they grow up? Think about how you were influenced by your parents and about how you are influencing your children and other children in your life as well.

## 5. How Are Our Children Influenced?

We parents or guardians of children are the biggest influence in their lives. Many of us spend a lot of time with our children at least when they are young. Children treat us with honesty, innocence, and unconditional love, and they expect us to treat them the same way.

In their innocence and honesty, they can easily see through us if we are not being honest with them. They are also very good at reading body language—our gestures and facial expressions. The best way to interact with children as well as all others is to be honest within age-appropriate boundaries of course and with the exception of little white lies as long as they harm no one.

Being honest saves us so much energy in sorting out uncomfortable situations, remembering what was said to whom, trying to hide hidden motives, and so on. And being honest teaches our children a very important spiritual virtue.

Where else do our children learn about self-esteem, ethics, and kind behavior? Do they learn them from TV cartoons and other TV shows, from toys or books?

Do you think about how your children are stimulated at the daycare or at school? Do you learn how they are doing, or do you trust the influence the caretakers or teachers have on your children? To become kind, empathetic, and loving individuals, they need good teachers and teaching materials including toys.

Thankfully, many dedicated teachers and assistants have the social, emotional, and educational welfare of the children in their care in the front of their minds and engraved on their hearts.

Think of how everything around you influenced you as a child and a teenager. Then fast forward to the present and think about what the teenagers and young adults are exposed to today. Which influences do you think teach them compassion, empathy, care, and respect?

When children start school, their sources of influence diversify. They become more aware of other people's ideas and often want to be like their friends. They also start becoming more aware of the contents of TV programs and books.

Have you thought about how older children ages ten to thirteen respond to the world around them? Do you know who their role models are? Do you know about their activities during and after school?

Do you feel you are in touch with your children when they are between fourteen and eighteen? Do they come to you for advice? Do you guide them without forcing anything on them? Do you give them liberties but also boundaries?

## Loving Boundaries

If you set up guidelines and boundaries for your teenagers, if you take an interest in their activities, if you help them with what to spend their money on and so on, you are letting them know, "I care about your well-being, and I care about what you do and how you handle things. I'm here for you if you need me no matter what situation you are in."

The importance of sending this simple yet powerful message to our children cannot be emphasized enough. (I will touch upon the pagan spiritual principles in Part 2).

## Television and Computer Games

TV and computer games are of course another big influence on children of all ages. Different TV programs are aimed at children in different age groups. It is up to us as parents to judge what we want to inspire and influence our children. There is an array of topics and concepts available.

- inspirational and positive programs or games with simple and friendly story lines
- educational programs that teach words, counting, colors, shapes, numerous concepts, and art

- TV programs in which the characters or puppets have what resemble spiritual experiences and worlds with voices that tell the puppets what to do
- alien landings, children, and adults with super powers and interplanetary war situations
- violence, bullying, and other disrespectful behavior in other programs and games
- TV shows that show children or young teens living luxurious and glamorous lives

Whereas many programs and games evolve around a positive sense of humor and many teach something constructive in a fun way, there are also programs, games, and TV shows that demonstrate a notable absence of parents or other adults providing realistic and useful guidance to various scenarios.

As parents, we can choose what we allow our children to watch and play. Before we make the choice, we should think about which message a certain plot is sending our children and think about how often we want our children to be exposed to it.

Another way that might help us choose what is appropriate for our children is simply to watch their reactions. We can see if their behavior changes after watching some programs or playing some games. If their behavior seems to reflect something negative they have seen, maybe it is time to change to another TV show or game.

## Role Models

If you look at the world as a whole through the eyes of the media, the picture you see is very negative. We all have negative experiences, but in between our trials and tribulations, we all have positive stories to tell as well.

When we share our positive as well as negative stories with friends and relatives, we often share ideas on how to become more positive in certain situations or how to handle certain challenges.

If we look back at family gatherings or other social events from our childhood, we may remember snippets of conversations between our parents and other adults. Even if we were not old enough to understand the topics, we would have at least witnessed how their interaction was and we would have noticed our parents' reactions then and afterward.

If we parents can show our children an interest in and a willingness to help others, we are sending them powerful messages.

## Your Standards

Many parents feel guilty if they cannot offer a constant flow of entertainment or activities for their children. However, I do not believe our children want or need to be busy all day. Today's children are the same as children thirty years ago and before that.

They cherish the same kinds of activities we did—a fun walk in the forest, swimming, hiking in the mountains, ice skating, fishing with friends, playing ball, and so on. Think about the activities you remember fondly, and incorporate those into your children's routines.

Children are curious and eager to learn, so take advantage of that in a positive way! Be critical as well as realistic about the influences your children receive.

## 6. Observe Your Children

Taking time to observe your children can be very rewarding. Looking at them quietly without them knowing when they play on their own or with friends can tell you a lot about how they are feeling and how balanced they are.

What are they doing? Are they playing happily? Are they singing, talking, chirping, engrossed in something positive? Are they playing rough? What do they say? Is it positive or negative?

Think how much you love them and feel grateful. Think of how you can make your children proud. How can you boost their confidence? How can you praise them? How can you reward them for good behavior? How can you show them you are interested in their world and what they are experiencing? How can you show them empathy? How can you help them become loving people? What do you need to work on and heal in yourself before you can give all this? Think about that.

We are not meant to be miserable and unhappy. We need to work on the negatives we feel, think, or experience and see them as opportunities to heal and let them melt away.

Nobody is completely balanced, in tune, and stable emotionally, mentally, and spiritually; we all need to work on something in us, but we have healed many aspects in us already; that helps us function well. The more healed we become, the more we can share and give to our children and help the next generation tremendously.

## 7. Children's Feelings

When your children are upset, let them know you love them no matter how they feel or no matter what they need to vent even when there is no immediate or obvious reasons for their emotional outbursts. That can be difficult to do at times depending on the circumstances and whether you are busy doing something else. But whenever your children are upset, they need your comfort and reassurance that all will be okay.

I cannot stress enough the importance of acknowledging your children's feelings; they are as real as yours. The issues and situations that trigger your children's feelings may be very different from the ones that trigger yours, but the feelings are real!

Your children consider you the best person to get them through their feelings because you give them love and support. It is so important for children of all ages, including teenagers, to feel safe, useful, and supported no matter what they are going through.

Do you take time to comfort your children? How do you react when you notice a frown on their faces or when you notice trembling lower lips? Do you take it seriously when your three-year-old shouts at you out of frustration? Do you get down to your children's level to find out why they are frustrated? Could they be just tired or sad? What do you do when your teenagers seem distant and grumpy? Do you even notice their moods and behavior?

Children and teenagers are very sensitive and receptive to what is going on around them. Many things can seem quite scary and daunting, so holding the hands literally and figuratively of trusted grown-ups is comforting and very often all they need.

As parents or peers, we are needed all the time, but whenever possible, we have to push our needs aside and give hugs and comforting words to children in distress no matter how small we may consider their problems to be. To them, they are huge.

Giving positive attention to children may be a challenge for many of us parents; our children discover how often they need our attention and time only when we are in their lives, and it can seem a daunting task.

But many parents are exhausted by perhaps paying too much attention to their children at times. The parents can pay so much attention and make sure they are fulfilled that the children end up just wanting more.

As with everything else in life, the key word is *balance*. We can give too much attention, and we can give too little. We learn as we go along, but if we pay attention to our children—to their moods and behavior patterns, we can find out how balanced and harmonious they are.

## 8. Traumatized Children

Millions of children around the world have mental and emotional scars caused by thoughtless grown-ups or other children who have had little positivity in their lives.

Think about all the children who live in war zones, who are given weapons, or who see family members being shot or taken away by soldiers. Think about the children who witness parents abusing drugs or alcohol. Think about those children who see their parents fighting every day verbally or maybe physically. Imagine the picture these children have of the world and human relationships.

## Putting Experiences into Boxes

When we are six or under—our formative years—we are like sponges. We absorb everything that is happening around us and store these experiences in little boxes in our minds.

Children who go through negative or even traumatizing experiences may not know how to digest these experiences on their own. Often, they are not offered any counseling or therapy, so they have to put a lid on a particular box in an attempt to avoid dealing with the pain of that experience.

Over time, children may add more unpleasant experiences to that box and end up as adults with boxes full of feelings such as fear, bereavement, sadness, shock, and others. They may have also securely locked the box.

However, things cannot be locked up forever. Emotions and feelings will find their way out eventually; we have to deal with whatever we put in our boxes.

One way to deal with severe issues is through therapy with professionals. Dealing with our issues is often less painful than living with them stuck inside us year after year.

Moreover, contrary to what we may believe or hope, stuck feelings, emotions, and even thoughts do not go away over time; instead, they tend to grow stronger and begin to affect us by creating fears and anxieties over seemingly unrelated matters.

Whatever is stuck will also begin to affect our behavior, dreams, and even our worldview. This new behavior and mind-set may bring about a negative cycle of experiences triggering yet more negative feelings.

With professional help, therapy, or healing, we can consciously work through negativity. Depending on how we work, we can choose a method that will help us start living in a positive and constructive way.

Another thing to contemplate is what is behind the behavior that has driven a person to inflict this kind of harm and trauma on their own or others' children?

Adults usually end up in situations like this because they themselves have experienced hard times they had no means or intellectual tools to handle in constructive and positive ways.

However, as mentioned before, pent up emotions and feelings are bound to surface one way or another, and one way of letting out anger, fear, and despair is to deliver it to somebody else's doorstep. That is done either consciously or subconsciously. Some people act viciously because they do not know how else to act. Others may not even realize the immense impact their negative ways have on children or their surroundings.

The key is to become conscious of your own behavior and break a cycle of trapped and new negative behaviors, thoughts, and emotions.

## 9. Learning from Our Children

Once you start seeing your children as equals and as intelligent human beings with their own reasons to be here and not as your property or as lesser than you are, you will find you can learn a lot from them.

With their innocence and sense of trust still intact, children's observations come from a much simpler worldview. If you pay attention to their remarks, they may help you put things in the right perspective.

My son taught me a useful lesson about shouting at somebody. Although it is an unkind way of communicating, shouting is often an instinctive way of getting somebody's attention if you are scared (if your child is doing something potentially dangerous), if you are tired, or if you feel you are at the end of your tether.

I found myself sometimes shouting at my son until one day, he said, "Mom, it's not nice. It makes me scared." So I asked him, "What do I do when I have told you something nicely five times and you don't listen? Then I don't know what to do." He replied, "Just tell me nicely, Mommy. And then once again tell me." A simple answer yet so difficult to pursue sometimes. I felt guilty.

I am aware of my reasons for resorting to shouting—feeling ignored, frustrated, losing control, or tired. However, becoming aware of my reaction prior to its eruption and reacting in a calmer way has been a challenge.

Learning to become aware of that a split second before you lose your temper and start shouting can be hard. Sometimes, a comment from your child may be enough to make you aware of it. It may also take a physical reaction—heart palpitations, your face turning red, your body tensing up—to help you become more aware of your behavior.

Some of our behavioral patterns will take longer to change than others. It depends on how deeply rooted our behavior is, what triggers it, and how regularly it is triggered. We often have to encounter the same situation repeatedly before we finally find the key that opens the door to a new way of handling certain situations.

## Back to Basics

When we were born, we all needed the same things—comfort, love, social interaction, security, warmth—besides the basic physical needs—oxygen, food, drink, and shelter. But we need and crave the same things throughout life. What could make us not need love, comfort, security, social interaction, and so on?

As we grow older, we add many layers to our psyches and our bodies through our experiences, and we learn different behavioral patterns and coping techniques. But the core we come into this world with still needs the same things throughout life.

Looking at children and noticing their innocent and trusting behavior can teach us a simpler way of life. They do not come into the world needing or wanting too many material things; these are things we bring into their lives.

They come here wanting to learn from us, how to live on this planet in a safe, comforting, loving, and secure way in harmony with others.

That is something worth remembering.

## 10. Sharing Experiences with Our Children

When we share experiences with others who find the same experiences positive, that gives us a heightened sense of comfort, fun, and trust, and we create a special bond with them.

Notice how excited most children become when they see or experience something positive and fascinating. They may call us over to watch their favorite TV show and share in their excitement; that can make the experience more fulfilling for them as well. Further, they use the sharing experience to mirror themselves in your enthusiasm, and it makes them feel they belong with you. Take time to give your children this emotional security.

On the other hand, they will also want you around for comfort if they experience something unpleasant or scary. As in any situation, children watch how you handle unpleasant or scary situations; they notice if you are calm and show confidence or if you show fear.

As parents, guardians, or friends of children, our ethics and philosophies become guidelines and inspiration, and children learn from us consciously and subconsciously. We should let that guide us. Our children and teenagers will be the adults of the future.

## 11. Food and Children

Millions of children around the globe are diagnosed with obesity due to unhealthy diets. Ironically, and regrettably, plenty of other children are malnourished and struggle daily just to stay alive.

Until children are old enough to live on their own and sustain themselves, their parents or guardians are responsible for teaching them healthy lifestyles.

But many adults and parents are unable to live healthy lives; the number of TV shows about losing weight is proof of that. Many obese people may know what they are doing wrong, but they need help in slowly introducing healthier routines into their lives.

Many people feel they are too busy to look at what they actually eat and drink; they will eat food that is fast and easy to prepare and consume. Many find the variety in the supermarkets too overwhelming, and yet others may not feel they need to think consciously about how to live healthy lives.

Other psychological reasons may be behind people not living healthily. However, parents' unhealthy lifestyles can be adopted consciously or unconsciously by their children. To help us with guidance and advice, we can turn to dieticians, naturopaths, fitness professionals, doctors, healers, and others.

We should find a way to get the topic of eating and drinking in healthy ways back on the popularity scale. We care about putting the right type of gas in our cars, and we buy the right food for our pets, so we should care about what we and our children eat.

I read an article entitled "Healthy food makes healthy children." It was apparently the result of a study. I find it strange that something so obvious needed to be researched. However, this ties in with the chapter "Common Sense" in which I look at how we can get back to using our common sense more.

## Showing Children the Way

Educational systems around the world could be used more to contribute profoundly to healthy eating. Sharing a few healthy recipes with children is one thing, but it is equally important to teach them about the value of basic organic foods and how to appropriately combine foods from the different groups—carbohydrates, protein, acids, sugars, and others.

Schools could teach children how to make basic, traditional, and healthy foods from their region or other places. That could be an integral part of learning about different cultures. And it would help children develop an interest in living healthy lives.

Children have an innate curiosity in virtually everything as long as it is presented in an inspiring and fun way, so it is so important that they learn the value of the basics—food and drink.

## 12. Archetypes in Relation to Our Children

The concept of archetypes was put forth by the famous Swiss psychologist Carl Jung around 1919. He suggested,

> Archetypes are innate, universal prototypes for ideas and may be used to interpret observations ... The existence of universal content-less forms that channel experiences and emotions, resulting in recognizable and typical patterns of behavior with certain probable outcomes. (Wikipedia: "archetype")

He defined archetypes as meta concepts that humans seem to relate to or respond to in the same way and connect with certain emotions or feelings.

According to Jung, many of the archetypes are exposed in our dreams. The meaning or symbolism of certain images and concepts seems to be shared by humans around the globe. For example, according to Jung, a house represents you, the dreamer. The basement of the house represents the subconscious. The windows of the house represent your eyes, your outlook at the world. You can find many clues as to how you feel in your wakened state by noticing what state your "house" is in.

Jung mentions other examples of archetypes including mountains, caves, horses, elephants, turtles, water, and celestial bodies to mention a few. They each seem to have a specific meaning and connotation universal to all humans.

Other recurring archetypal images in a presumably limitless catalogue are the wise old man, the trickster or fox, the great mother, the mentor, and the devil. Jung saw archetypes as psychological organs comparable to our physical organs in the sense that we developed both through evolution.

If you believe in such archetypes, it is easy to believe that we find the same things to be positive, delicious, or beautiful and find the same things to be negative, appalling, or ugly.

This knowledge is very useful for the advertising business to mention a more down-to-earth use of psychology. Many of us may have seen a fizzy drink in a cold glass with droplets of water running down the side in a commercial and suddenly became thirsty. We may have seen a waterfall, an erupting volcano, or a humpback whale jump out of the water and felt in awe of nature or an excited rush of adrenaline.

We may also have seen images of a baby in distress with tears running down his or her cheeks and felt a sting in our hearts and an urge to hold and pamper this baby and all other babies for that matter who were in the same situation.

Keeping in mind this universal nature of our feelings and emotions may sometimes help us understand our children better. Whatever we as adults feel is positive, they will feel as positive; whatever we perceive as negative, they perceive as negative.

This may help us become more aware of our behavior toward our children before we often unknowingly affect them in negative ways.

# 13. Preconceptions in Relation to Life and Our Children

Our preconceptions can sometimes make it difficult to accept things that happen to us as just part of life. Since my husband died, I have naturally had a difficult time in many ways, but it has also been difficult seeing myself as a widow.

In my mind, a widow is an older woman who had a long life with her husband until he passed. My preconception of a standard widow is not someone fairly young as I am. Naturally, I am aware that many other fairly young women lose their husbands and partners, but I think most women become widows later in life.

Most of us do not normally expect that fairly young people as my husband would suddenly die. At least in the Western world, I think most of us expect that people live until they are in their seventies or eighties, not dying in their forties.

We may make sense of what happens to us through our views on life and the world based on our preconceptions. Maybe if we realized life could mean anything and offer anything at any time—it could even knock us down—we would more easily find meaning in what happens on our journeys.

We have inner strength and wisdom to get through challenges such as a loss of a loved one. And we have the support of people around us to help us get up again.

Our intense experiences are bound to change us. They may change our outlook on life, the way we handle future situations, or our thresholds for things that bother us.

If you have a religious or spiritual outlook on life and the universe, you may be able to zoom out to look at the bigger picture amid your trauma and mitigate the emotional wounds it may have caused.

Some think that everything happens by chance or luck, sometimes bad luck. They believe that things happen to us for no special reason and that we can do nothing about it.

Often, the same people do not have a very spiritual view of the world but rather a more scientific view, as if they needed tangible proof before they subscribed to a particular idea. Thus, they also tend not to believe in the afterlife or reincarnation and related concepts that often have no physical proof.

However, when you have had many extraordinary, extrasensory, nontangible experiences, the notion of coincidence does not seem adequate to explain reality. The spiritual realm does not seem strange or unreal to me, so I will have an influence on my children different from the that of parents whose worldview is more scientific and proof based.

Someone (I do not remember whom) defined three categories of people in your life.

- those who come into your life for a specific purpose
- those who enter your life for a time and then leave perhaps due to death, or moving away, or simply breaking off communication
- those who are with you throughout (most of) your life

As I started to think about some of the people in my life, I found that categorization to be very applicable.

It provided me with a tool to take a snapshot of the people in my life and it made me think especially about those who were there for a specific purpose. Thinking about people being in your life for a specific purpose is comforting, but it also presents a challenge to define what those purposes could be. Looking at why certain people are in our lives may help us see how harmonious, incompatible, or conflicting those relationships are.

When you think of events and people in your life as lessons, you may suddenly feel a sense of gratitude.

Conveying this categorized view on the people in our lives to our children could help them as well. If we know our children and spend time with them, we will find ways to help them understand and learn from this idea.

Many things influence our views and understanding of life and other people. How exactly we are influenced clearly depends on how concepts or ideas are presented to us.

In the next chapter, I will look at the type of education our children are receiving.

# Chapter 9

## Education

It is the mark of an educated mind to be able to
entertain a thought without accepting it.
—Aristotle (384–322 BC)

## 1. All Knowledge Is in You

Have you thought about what your children are learning in school? Have you thought about the methods of teaching in their schools? What is the substance of the lessons? How do the teachers convey it? What kinds of materials are used? How do the teachers deal with individual students? What values do your children learn every day at school through teachers, classmates, and older students? How are their lives affected by going to school?

How are confrontations dealt with? How is social interaction taught to children? Do you find it important that students who affect others in negative ways should be guided toward being more positive? Do you communicate regularly with your children's teachers? Do you attend parent-teacher meetings?

Do your children learn about compassion and how to build self-confidence? How are world events conveyed to them? What aspects of life are they exposed to – is it fear or positivity?

What would be useful for your children to learn so they can help others? Do you value growth, compassion, and prosperity? Do your children learn about those values?

Do you think teachers' race or nationality is important? Aren't the quality of their personalities and ability to guide your children in a caring way the most important matters?

That is a number of questions! However, think about your answers to some of them.

## 2. Circumstances in School

One topic that teachers, parents, school councils, and educational ministries in many countries debate is class quotas—how many students per classroom so they learn in a valuable and socially positive way.

Some countries allow up to thirty-five students in college classrooms. Currently, many countries allow twenty or more students in primary and secondary school classrooms with only one teacher. In other countries, there are twenty-five or more students in classrooms with one teacher and one assistant.

With the class quotas going up in many places, parents and teachers fear many students will fall behind because teachers will have less time to attend to students individually. Students on all levels of skills and abilities will be forced to conform to the same standards. There will be little time to nurture different personalities or abilities to absorb and process information.

As I will touch on in a later chapter, Howard Gardner proposed in 1983 his theory that intelligence was multifaceted and that we have multiple intelligences and thus various strengths and weaknesses when it comes to our intelligence.

The eight types of intelligence according to Gardner were spatial, linguistic, logical-mathematical, kinesthetic, musical, interpersonal, intrapersonal, and naturalistic.

Gardner questioned the way intelligence was traditionally defined in psychometrics. He believed that a child who for example mastered multiplication was not necessarily more intelligent overall than a child who mastered a type of intelligence different from the logical-mathematical.

The second child may have a different, potentially highly intelligent approach to the multiplication process as opposed to memorizing the multiplication table, which could be the strength of the first child. Gardner's theory of multiple intelligences has both supporters and opponents (Wikipedia: "Howard Gardner's Multiple Intelligences").

## 3. Systems of Teaching

I believe in the theory of multiple intelligences and that people learn under different circumstances or systems of teaching.

If a student falls behind in one system of teaching, that does not mean he or she is not smart in general; he or she could show a high intelligence in many other ways and in a different system. Here are examples of systems of teaching as I see them.

- the learn-it-by-heart way
- the Montessori way, which acknowledges the diversity of personalities and characters in children; in it, children are guided toward exploring different topics rather than facts being dictated to them
- the conventional way in which teachers tell the students about topics with little or no discussion about the veracity of the facts and with little or no room for alternative ways of thinking or questioning things

Teachers and students relate to each other in a variety of ways. Some schools maintain strict hierarchies. Teachers are clearly above the students, and the tone is very disciplinary and often a bit cold.

In other schools, the structure is more flat—teachers and students have more of a dialogue, and students are free to question their teachers and the topics.

Other schools may be a mixture of the two; the teacher's authority can be questioned, and a friendly atmosphere allows room for the students' imagination and general speculations on what they are being taught.

There are more systems and relationships than just these three, but students should be in systems and relationships with teachers that allow them to perform as best they can and in a socially positive way. Quite a challenge, naturally.

Academic standards, support, and encouragement are equally important ingredients in a balanced educational system.

# 4. Teaching Perspective

We learn so many things in so many ways throughout life. Our education is important in terms of what knowledge we absorb and how we learn to grow up to be respectful, compassionate, and positive thinking people. We must learn to respect earth and to create a sustainable future for all. This knowledge and support can come from the educational system and from parents, guardians, other family members, and friends.

The more you know about your surroundings, the more comforting it can be. Think of how comforting it can be to know about the geography of not only your own country but also the whole world. Knowledge can motivate us to take positive action in terms of taking care of the environment.

Think also about how awareness of different ethnic backgrounds, the location of natural resources, land use, the quality of life in different countries, the importance of nature's balance, and so on can enhance mutual understanding.

Having knowledge about these basic things can give us a sense of belonging, care, and unity—we all live under one roof—and our concern with conditions in other parts of the world may help improve the difficult conditions many people live under.

Unfortunately, these topics seem to have a low priority in many schools. Unless the children have an inherent interest in the subject or are already in an international environment, the lack of education in these subjects may deprive many children, teenagers, and adolescents of establishing an interest in the world.

## 5. Presentation of Topics

The ability to absorb knowledge and develop interest in a topic depends largely on how the topic is presented. In line with the theory of multiple intelligences, I believe some people prefer visual symbolism while others need help visualizing the solution to a problem and coming up with real-world sentences to know better how to solve that problem.

Due to the many personalities, levels of intelligence, and abilities of students, school systems find it hard to cater to everybody's needs. All educational systems need to pay adequate attention to the basic needs of children growing up in a positive way in a positive environment. It should be the foundation of any education system.

## 6. Is Compassion Taught in School?

How do we teach our children to become humane human beings? We all have shortcomings, misconceptions, and emotional obstacles, but we can be good examples for them.

Bullying and teasing occurs in schools and at workplaces. At times, the bullying can be astoundingly cruel and severe. What causes children and adults to act like this? What and who teaches our children to have little respect for or acceptance of people's diversity? Parents? Extended families? TV programs? Movies? Violent PC games or other types of games? Peer pressure or pressure from home?

The answer is probably yes to all of the above. Let us think about what our children are exposed to. As young children, they are so innocent and pure. But as they grow up, their values, visions, and virtues get more colored and blurred by what they see and hear. It becomes a challenge to hold onto the innocence and trust in the good we are all born with.

## 7. Your Book of Knowledge

You can add your observations about your and other people's experiences of any kind to your personal book of knowledge, and you can teach your children to do the same.

Every day, we can learn from others' positive actions and senses of humor, their ability to stay afloat when things fall apart, and their mistakes.

Sometimes however, our egos may get in the way of our interest in learning from others. We may be too proud to admit we could be better at something. We may believe that our ways are the best ways. We may feel insulted or embarrassed if somebody suggests we need to improve something about ourselves.

In addition, some people do not compare results or notice how other ways may make something easier, and some people do not think about the consequences of their actions and thus may not know they can do things differently.

If you feel you have found a great and maybe safer way to do something, you may feel the urge to share your idea with others so they can benefit from that. Hard hats and construction boots are better ways to dress at construction sites for obvious reasons.

We can all do some things better, and since we are all in the same boat, there is no need to feel embarrassed, insulted, or ashamed if somebody points out something to us. These feelings are triggered inside us because of something that has happened to us earlier, but we can learn to deal with it in a positive and even humorous way and let any negative feelings go.

It is an art to accept that others may have different ways of thinking. It is also an art to accept that people learn at different speeds and under different circumstances.

# Chapter 10

## Your Thoughts and Feelings

Visualizations are powerless unless we breathe life into
them through the power of emotion and feeling as if
those visualizations had already come to pass.
—Gregg Braden, *The Lost Mode of Prayer*, 1999

If you are not getting what you want, it is because
you are still getting what you need.
—Unknown

When we are in balance and happy, we tend not to think about our thoughts and feelings too much. We just enjoy the moment and spread our positivity to those around us without thinking consciously about it. Our natural state of being is just beaming out of us and infusing others with joy.

But when we face difficulties, challenges, and problems, we often feel we are on shaky ground. We may react in ways we wish later we had not. We might also be surprised by our reactions to certain circumstances or triggers.

To solve any of life's problems and act and react positively, we must start by observing our thoughts and feelings. We can face issues that affect our behavior in the same way we face any physical challenges; it just takes practice.

If for instance your bed breaks, you become aware of the fact that it is broken, you look at it, define the problem, and think of a way to get it back to its original state.

Likewise, when you want to solve or heal a negative emotional or mental pattern or issue, you must first become aware of it, observe it, define what the issue is, and find a way to readjust and rebalance yourself to get back to your original state of peace and love.

Getting through these four steps does not have to take long depending on the complexity of the issue, but it also depends on how open we are to admitting there is a problem, wanting to conquer it, and moving away from it.

Our negative thoughts and feelings will not go away by our avoiding or ignoring them. Remember the metaphor of the ostrich hiding its head in the sand because it thinks its enemies cannot see it when it does.

We also cannot hide from our negative thoughts and feelings by ignoring them and thinking they are no longer there. They will keep on knocking on our doors until we acknowledge them, deal with them, let them go, and learn to move on feeling enriched by the experience.

Accept that your negative thoughts and feelings are as much a part of you as everything else is. Acknowledge them, deal with them, and focus on positive thoughts.

We all have things we need to face and work on. Those around us remind us of our issues. The world around us is our mirror that reflects our inner world. Often, we do not want to face our issues, but if we face our not-so-fine qualities and work with them instead of hiding from them, that will help us find a way out of negative cycles. They help us grow in positive ways and return to our state of inner peace and happiness.

To move in a positive direction, we need to clear away our emotional and mental clutter. Once we have decided to face our negative aspects and move past them, we need to gain clarity of mind—we need to find silent space in us so we will have room and time to work on our issues. Throughout this book, you will find several ways to obtain that, including natural healing therapies.

You can actively break a cycle of negative thoughts!

# 1. Creating Positive Thoughts and Feelings

## 1.1 Finding Your Uniqueness

We all have skills and abilities that can benefit others as well as ourselves. We have unique ways of doing certain things, and we have specific areas of expertise. You can choose which ones you want to bring out:

Explore your thoughts and feelings; feel what gives you positive thoughts, goose bumps, and butterflies in your stomach and leaves you feeling good in a selfless way. If your thoughts are not harmful to you or others, head in that direction because your unique potential will lead you to your purpose in life! Your purpose always involves others.

Try not to compare yourself in an envious way with others who are successful, and try not to doubt your chances of success. You are unique, and you are already a success. You just have to bring it forward through your body and actions.

Many young people compare themselves and their lives to celebrities or characters on TV or in movies. It can be very inspirational to have role models, but it can also be easy to become carried away with wanting to be or look like them or having the same lavish lifestyle as them.

We see only a portion of those celebrities. We may think we know them from what we read about them in the tabloids, but we see only snapshots of their lives. We do not know how they think, what they really like and dislike, how they really behave among friends and relatives, and so on. Based on that, how can we wish to be like them? We have to look for our snapshot moments and create moments in harmony with our uniqueness and our paths.

In your search for your unique skills, you might meet others who are doing what you would like to do or who are how you would like to be, but whatever it is, you can do and be that too. You have a unique approach and methodology that will make your way special. Trust and believe in that.

To get to that place where you feel fulfilled, happy, and comfortable with your thoughts and feelings, you will need to focus on what you can do to get there. Maybe you can start by carrying out your ideas that give you positive feelings when you share them with others and imagine the positive impact your ideas will have on yourself and your surroundings. Those ideas originate in your soul and will lead you to new ideas, situations, and experiences that will take you to the next level.

Pursue those ideas that give you positive feelings and seem to draw you to them. If you keep encountering things on the same topic, go for it. And if you encounter obstacles that make your plans fall apart, do not despair; that happens for a reason too. Maybe you are not ready for your idea yet, or maybe other circumstances need to fall in place first. Maybe it is the universal law of forward movement creating resistance.

If you make choices according to your inner guidance and intuition, you will end up standing in front of doors to possibilities that are the right ones for you. All you need to do is take one step forward.

Never doubt that you have skills, abilities, and characteristics; we all do. Don't compare your skills to others. Yours are unique to you.

# 1.2 Acknowledging Your Intelligence

You are an intelligent being in many ways. Howard Gardner's theory of multiple intelligences, proposed in 1983, involved "explor[ing] and articulat[ing] various forms or expressions of intelligence available to cognition" (Wikipedia).

Gardner, whose theory found supporters and opponents, identified spatial, linguistic, logical-mathematical, kinesthetic, musical, interpersonal, intrapersonal, and naturalistic intelligences.

I support his theory and believe we can still be intelligent even if we do not score high on an IQ test based on logical-mathematical knowledge alone for instance. A test based only on those aspects does not necessarily depict our uniqueness or our abilities in other skill areas, exactly those skills we were meant to use to spread positivity around and within us. Those are the skills we are here to use and shine to the world. We must believe in our skills and accept praise from ourselves, families, and friends.

We should start doing what we feel or know is right because that is when we will excel.

# 1.3 Realize You Are Not Alone

We may sometimes fear we are the only ones in the world with certain strange thoughts, feelings, or ideas that pop into our minds. But at some point, we realize others have the same thoughts, feelings, or ideas to our great relief.

Everyone wants love, understanding, and compassion because these experiences make us feel good, loved, and full of life. Love is the foundation of our lives; it gives life meaning. When we think about what makes us feel loved, understood, and cared for, we should realize that those things make others feel the same way.

If we all have the same positive needs and feelings, we all probably have the same negative feelings. Whatever makes us feel disliked, mistreated, misunderstood, abandoned, insecure, betrayed, and confused probably makes everybody else feel the same way.

With seven billion people on the planet and not two of them exactly the same, it takes different events to cause the same feelings in us. Nevertheless, we all have the same pool of feelings and emotions. Remembering that we may be in different seats but still in the same boat may make us feel better.

No matter what personal image someone might show the world—tough, ruthless, snobbish, in control, aloof, and so on—that person will have the same feelings and needs the rest of us do. He or she just does not show it or know how to show it for whatever reason. Rest assured; the feelings and needs are still there underneath a shield.

We all need healing of our outer layers in some form or another, and we all came here with the opportunity to shed them or at least some of them. No one is in perfect harmony or free from negative thoughts, deeds, feelings, and emotions. The more layers we can release and heal, the more of our core we will be able to show. I believe our core is love, light, and sustainable balance. Imagine a world in which everyone was in a state of bliss, harmony, and balance and feeling at peace with everything. As unreal as that thought is in our current global situation, that is the utopian ideal I use to assess where I am and where we as a whole are today.

I see life as a step-by-step approach toward fully expressing something positive; we take the steps as they come and as we become aware of them. I find that a comforting notion, don't you?

## 1.4 Taking Charge of Your Inner Dialogue

Once you decide to turn your life around and head in a more positive direction, you can use one of the strongest indicators you have that can tell you where you need to focus; that indicator is your inner dialogue.

You can learn a lot about yourself by paying attention to your inner dialogue. This is a bit like connecting with your higher self during meditation. It is that place in you where you know, feel, or see what is right for you.

We may get insight into our states of mind and general conditions of being when we are in the shower, exercising, hiking, looking at people rushing by—everywhere and at any time.

Once we start paying attention to our inner conversations, we can learn to play ping-pong with them. We can counter all our worries, fears, doubts, and uncertainties by thinking positively, extracting the lessons to be learned, and focusing on positive thoughts.

It is a lot of work; it may be exhausting, and you may feel you are having the toughest negotiations of your life, but keep at it. You will soon realize that you have an answer to your next worry, fear, doubt, or uncertainty because you may have heard it before and you can neutralize it before it has a negative impact on your mind or body.

Your ego will want to keep the ping-pong game going; it will come up with new fears or put a new slant on an old fear in your mind, but keep the focus on the positive, the bigger picture. Remember that all fears are simply layers of old emotions, so keep the focus on you being the one spreading positive rings in the water. Focus on your fears melting away as you acknowledge their presence, and then ask them to be healed and cleared. Learn from the lesson, and move on.

We must endure our thoughts and feelings, so we need mechanisms to deal with them, to cope with life, and to believe we can do something positive for ourselves and others.

## 1.5 Challenges Are Lessons

When asked from which university they graduated from, many people proudly answer, "The university of life." I respect them for acknowledging that. Just being a living part of this world gives you the best schooling imaginable. My take on this stems from the fact that I believe our souls, our spirits go somewhere afterward, and I believe whatever we gain from the lessons we learn we get to take with us when we leave because we are a sum of our experiences.

We are not able to understand exactly what lesson we are supposed to learn until we have been through the experience. Often, it takes a good while to see what an experience or challenge has taught us—patience, love, forgiveness, humility, empathy, and others.

We are all here to learn many lessons in life and will meet the challenges we need. What seems like a huge challenge to one may seem like just a minor bump in the road to another. We all make mistakes, and we may all act unfairly in some situations.

We will read books, have conversations with others, and pick up guidelines here and there, but with all the information readily available, we can have a hard time trying to figure out how to live through what we encounter when emotions—usually based in fear—seem to get the better of us.

The first thing to accept is that good things and bad things will happen to us; we never know what is around the corner.

## 1.6 Creating an Overview to Process a Challenge

When I was a child and was afraid of something, I would ask my mother, "Can you die from this?" That is a natural question for children of a certain age to ask, but I feel it is also a way of establishing an overview of a situation, a way of finding out the extreme outcome—what would happen if I did this and where it could take me. This innate urge to predict the effect or outcome of a certain situation or event can help us decide our next step.

## 2. How Do You Process a Challenge?

Become aware of how you process negative input from a situation or people. Here are some examples of how you might tackle difficult situations.

1. You grit your teeth and wait until you are among friends to share your frustrations and feelings.
2. You feel personally attacked and let that fester in you.
3. You show no feelings and do not talk about the situation.
4. You react then and there and let people know how you feel.
5. You quickly look for a solution and end up solving the problem with no negative feelings attached.
6. You feel anger but do not let it out.
7. You feel intimidated, humiliated, or ashamed and do not know how to process the situation at the time.
8. You imagine a shield of protective light around you.
9. You have other ways of dealing with such situations.

Which number(s) illustrate your reaction?

## Healing Visualization I: Washing away the Layers

This is an efficient way to deal with negative emotions or feelings. See your challenge as something only you can deal with because whatever you are feeling is internal and personal.

A situation or a person has triggered a feeling in you; acknowledge the feeling and pinpoint where it sits in your body (e.g., your stomach), and place your hands there.

Imagine the feeling flowing through your body from its origin to your toes and through your legs to your stomach area and up through your arms and shoulders to your head and back to your stomach. Let the feeling flow through you until you feel it is losing its power and is melting.

Is there another negative feeling underneath it in your stomach? If so, repeat the procedure; let the feeling wash through your body until you feel that it loses power. Keep doing this until all negative feelings have been washed away and you feel peace, bliss, warmth, or light in that particular place in your body. This is a powerful and easy exercise you can do whenever you feel like it.

As we move through life, we pick up negative feelings and energies from our surroundings and other people often without our conscious knowledge. If left there unattended, layers of feelings will build up.

However, if we pay attention to our feelings in a physical sense, that is, by locating the feeling in our bodies, we can do the above exercise and reestablish feelings of peace and positivity by washing away our negative feelings.

Another way we can overcome negative emotions or feelings is to imagine a positive feeling instead to reprogram our outlook and way of thinking.

## Healing Visualization II: Imagine Positive Feelings

Imagine the feeling of fulfillment you will have when you are successful in that job you want.

Imagine the relief and happiness you will feel when that conflict between you and your partner is resolved.

Imagine the feeling of bliss and empowerment you will hold when you can react in a positive way to a conflict.

Imagine the feeling of comfort and contentment you will hold when you spread love and understanding to another person.

## 3. More Ways to Get through Challenges

The following pages contain examples of challenges and obstacles we might encounter through our thoughts and feelings. I offer insight and ideas about how to get through challenges, release them, and observe our lives unfolding in positive ways.

The ideas in each section may apply to more than one challenge because we often experience a mixture of feelings.

## 3.1 If You Are Not Listening to Your Heart

Many people have stopped listening to their souls, their hearts, their inner selves, and their bodies; they listen instead to their egos and minds. Everyday life is distracting enough to keep us from taking time to listen to what is going on inside us.

However, any action we take that is ruled by the ego and does not involve the heart creates an obstruction to living in full harmony in our minds, spirits, and bodies—our totality.

If your goal is to be balanced in mind, spirit, and body, you must take them all into consideration when you choose your actions.

## Ego vs. Heart

I am always tempted to put the concepts of heart, inner self, higher self, soul, spirit, and intuition under the same umbrella. With slight variations, they are all names for the same part of us.

Once you know how to make choices according to your heart or whatever you feel is the best name for it, you will see the difference in the choices you have made and are making that are based on your ego.

Your ego will fulfill some needs only temporarily. In the long run and on a bigger scale, following your heart leads you to fulfillment on all levels—mind, spirit, and body. Additionally, things will fall into place and start to work out in your favor. Often, you will also benefit others around you. How do you know if you are letting your ego rule your life?

If you make decisions with your heart, you will feel a long-term peace and joy and feel you are growing in a positive way. You will also see positivity emerge around you.

If you think and do things that satisfy your ego, you may attain peace, joy, and a sensation of growth in a materialistic, selfish way, but that growth will be only short term and in the long run will not benefit you or others.

Here are examples of feelings that satisfy the ego rather than the heart.

## Ego

1.  pride
2.  gloating
3.  control
4.  feeling better than others
5.  selfishness

## Heart

1.  humility
2.  happiness for others
3.  release and surrender
4.  knowing that everyone is reaching up from where they are
5.  service (your actions help you and others grow in positive directions)

It is all about learning to choose to listen to your heart. With practice, you will be able to define whether your motivation comes from your ego or your heart. With practice, you will be able to define whether your decision will create something that will help others positively.

## 3.2 If You Are Feeling Stressed

Millions of people feel stressed. Many are struggling to find jobs or keep their jobs. Many people work too many hours a day just to prove themselves. Many have too much work to handle.

Many parents feel stressed; often, mothers and fathers both have to work to provide for their families. Parents have to meet the needs of their children for help, guidance, love, and support and meet their own needs for loving relationships, individual time, and time with their parents, other family members, and friends. Imagine the constant pressure on their minds, bodies, and emotions as they try to keep up with everything.

When you listen to fast, upbeat music, you feel that you want to move your body. And when you listen to slow, calming music, you feel like putting your feet up and relaxing. When you are on the go and feel stressed, you may prefer upbeat music and find peaceful, slow music boring and end up feeling impatient.

But if you give slow, relaxing music a chance, if you give it thirty more seconds than you normally would, you will experience relaxation in your body and mind.

You need to take time to destress and recharge. If you do not listen to your body's signals and consciously take time to recharge, your subconscious will do it for you at some point by making you slow down for a physical reason.

When you make time for music, yoga, stretching, meditation, biking, and other such activities, think of the good it does your body and of the negative impact constant movement, stress, and trying to keep up with everything has on your body.

## 3.3 If You Are Creating Your Own Pressure

Sometimes, people create their own pressures. They have an urge to be at the top of the social ladder, to be number one, to fulfill their ambitions for themselves and their families. They feel a need to live up to certain people or keep up with certain traditions or rules even if they do not agree with them. Or maybe their routes toward their goals are filled with immense challenges.

Many people today, especially in the aftermath of the recent global crisis, find themselves in dire financial straits. Many have problems making ends meet each month. Others are looking at their needs and desires to determine if the desire for material things is putting pressure on them.

At times, people may not be able to pinpoint the source of their feelings of pressure; they may feel just inadequate, or unable to keep up with things, or not satisfied with their lives.

If you feel dissatisfied, get in touch with yourself and listen to your heart, your instinct, your gut feeling—whatever term you want to attach to it—and use that connection to find out what you actually want. It is time to start living the way all of you—mind, body, and heart or soul—wants to? Is it time to start taking actions that mean something to your true self?

When you listen to and follow that little voice or hunch inside, you will know you are living according to your true self.

So many people have lost the overview of their lives. They let quick judgments and decisions as well as other people rule their actions, and they end up living empty and sometimes very materialistic lives. They buy what they think they cannot live without and what they think will impress others.

If materialism rules your life, you are not in control of your life and something will keep irritating your thoughts and feelings.

## 3.4 If You Feel You Are Forgetting to Think Positively

As mentioned earlier, we should sometimes stop and think about whether we have become desensitized or even numb to negativity. Crime, violence, disrespectful behavior, and seeing people living in poor circumstances or being cheated of pay or free time are all negatives we face. We also hear about war, catastrophes, accidents, and such on the news.

If we watch or hear about anything many times, it eventually becomes the norm for us; we stop asking why it is so and say, "That's just the way things are and will stay that way."

Someone said, "The world responds to chauvinism, nationalism, racism, exploitation of personal integrity and other negative concepts," but I believe people respond to those things out of fear, boredom, or even emotional numbness induced by all these things around us that influence our lives and shape our understanding of the world.

We can learn to direct our energy toward positive things. We can learn to focus on what makes us feel hopeful rather than fearful. We can learn to filter out the dark noise. We can choose to focus on where to find and give trust, support, love, and care. That is far more sustainable.

Focusing on the positive does not mean ignoring the negative, the counterpart of positivity; we cannot have one without the other. Nature is a duality. If everything were positive, we would not classify it as positive; it would just be normal. In that sense, the negative shows us the way to the positive.

The negative is in our minds, feelings, and bodies. Ignoring it will not make it go away. Focusing on it will only increase it.

When we learn to acknowledge and accept the negative and then heal the feelings it has caused us and the situations we might have created out of fear, the negative will no longer stay with us because the circumstances will have healed.

Challenges and obstacles help us find the resolve and drive to get through the negative. Even anger can be used in a positive way by helping us create forward momentum!

## 3.5 If You Feel Fearful

Most people harbor fear to varying degrees; it is another obstruction to living balanced, harmonious lives. Fear is circulating in many minds and bodies; people are afraid of many things.

Except for life-threatening or dangerous situations, much of the fear we feel is created by our thoughts. Getting through a challenge is the way to let it go. Trying to jump over it, crawl under it, or run away from it will not make it go away.

But fear can be conquered.

To many people, faith in a religion or a spiritual belief is the cure for many fears and deep-seated worries. For others, actively focusing on positive thoughts is the answer. Others conquer fear by talking to others—friends, professional counselors, or others.

Whichever way you find works for you—any of the above or something else—dealing with your fears and seeing them off is better than leaving them inside.

*You will encounter only that, which you are able to handle.*
—Unknown

## 3.6 If You Feel Down

If you feel down for a long time, you will tend to let things drift. You may not care about how your home looks or how you look. You will not fix things that break; you will not pay attention to details around you anymore and feel less motivated at work.

You can become negligent in many areas of your life. Nothing stimulates you, nothing seems to please you, and you rarely have a good laugh.

That is a downward spiral you should remedy as soon as possible. If you are experiencing many of the points mentioned above, maybe you should seek professional counsel. You will have to take the first step and those that follow, but if you have somebody to help you along the way, the steps will seem less frightening and daunting. You can get help to take things one step at a time. Rome was not built in a day.

If you are feeling down, start taking simple steps that may not require too much effort.

- Take time to make yourself look better. Do your hair, put on nice clothes, pamper your feet, buy a shirt or some shoes. This may seem shallow to some, but beauty is part of our higher aesthetic needs, and doing yourself up can help motivate you to do something about your basic needs and sort out other things in your life. Often, it helps to switch things around consciously.
- Tidy your home or clothes; declutter and throw away things you do not need.
- Take a refreshing shower, a dip in a pool, or a swim in the ocean.
- Cook a nice meal for yourself or your family.
- Listen to cheerful music.
- Read something that inspires you.
- Ride your bike, take a drive, or go for a brisk walk.
- Watch a funny movie; laughter is still the best medicine!
- Talk to someone dear to you.
- Every day, do something for someone that makes you feel good.
- Spend time alone in nature. Connecting with nature is the best remedy for almost anything as it connects you with your inner world.
- Do something new you have wanted to do for a while.

Once you start feeling better because you are doing things you enjoy, you may soon be ready to face the world again and find out what caused you to feel down.

Maybe you are ready to have a talk with the person who triggered your feelings. Maybe you have found a new approach to solving a situation that made you feel down. Maybe you will be inspired to seek advice from a friend, colleague, or relative.

You can also visualize yourself in a new, improved state; your imagination is a powerful tool. Focus on your visualization and imagine how you would feel there. Let ideas on how to get there come to you.

It is always okay to seek professional help; opening up and letting things out will give you a sense of relief. You can talk to a life coach, psychologist, psychotherapist, cleric, or whoever makes you feel comfortable.

Nobody can or should go through life alone. We are all here to help each other the best we can.

If you lack the very basic needs—proper housing, nutrition, clothing, and education—focus on ways to fulfilling those needs. That is often easier said than done, but maintaining a focus on fulfilling those needs will help you fill them.

We must define our desires, listen to our intuition, and follow up with action. Our souls, minds, and bodies work best in unison.

No matter what level we are on, we yearn to improve our situations. We all have a drive to achieve the next level. We can do that by being determined and following our inner guidance.

## 3.7 If You Feel Life Has Been Treating You Unfairly

Most of us are familiar with this feeling. It is very easy to feel a victim of circumstances or that life is not fair. However, we can move away from those feelings and develop a new way of looking at life and why we came to feel that way.

At times, we face very upsetting situations that cause us to wonder why they are happening to us. We might feel ashamed to be in those situations. It could be the loss of a loved one, a missed potentially life-changing opportunity, the loss of a job we deeply loved doing, or the ill-fated circumstances of a close relative.

Sometimes, we may be mistreated by someone with no concern for the feelings they inflict on others. At times, we realize we have to define our boundaries more clearly to others so they will know what we find acceptable and unacceptable.

When you feel you have been treated unfairly, you may feel ashamed, guilty, and ridiculed and think you are the only one who is experiencing that situation.

The situation may be unique to you, but many others will have experienced the same feelings. Often, feeling the odd one out overshadows other feelings, but everyone at one time or another has had the same depressing feelings.

Spiritually speaking, nothing in life happens just to make us feel ashamed, mistreated, guilty, or awkward, and nothing in life happens just to rob us of our self-confidence. The situations we encounter may trigger these feelings in us, but it is up to us to move through them, learn from them, and release them and the people involved.

We can try to accept the feelings or heal them through meditation, hypnosis, or another method, but we should remember we are not the only people having those feelings. We can talk to someone about them or learn how others got through them.

As soon as we start doing something about our negative situations, we will be much closer to healing. It then becomes a question of finding out which way suits us best.

## 3.8 If You Are Not Comfortable in Your Own Skin

At times, we just do not feel comfortable with ourselves. Many things can make us feel that way. When we find it difficult to determine why we are feeling uncomfortable in our own skin, we can try out some positive ideas to help us get the ball rolling again.

If we start to improve one thing, that can easily start a positive chain reaction and reveal the parts of us that really need healing. We should continually do what pleases our bodies, minds, and hearts.

The ideas listed below may also assist you in getting out of feeling down.

## Ground Yourself

Do something that makes you physically feel better even if it means indulging your taste for foods you consider less than healthy; it is okay to indulge yourself once in a while.

Get a foot rub or massage, take a soothing shower, do some gardening or your favorite exercise, visit a beach or a mountain and just look at the sky.

## Stimulate Your Mind

Do something that makes you feel better mentally. Read a book or article on a topic that interests or challenges you. Talk to a good friend or relative. Call a professional life coach. Watch some TV programs that stimulate you in a positive way. Help your child with some homework.

## Get Comforted

Do something that makes you emotionally feel better. Visit someone who will support you and make you feel good by giving you hugs, supportive remarks, and pats on the shoulder. You could also meditate, pray, do yoga, dance, or listen to music. Just do something that makes you smile and that does no harm.

Maslow's hierarchy of needs illustrates how we need to fulfill our underlying needs before we can move upward and get out of our uncomfortable feelings. This is true no matter what level we are on in that pyramid of needs and motivations.

## 3.9 If You Feel You Need a Tough Image

You may show the world a tough exterior. You may feel a need to show off in front of your friends. You may bully others and brush off others' acts of love, kindness, and generosity. You may act as if you never get hurt. You might start joking about others when you are feeling insecure. You may think showing your emotions and sharing your true thoughts is a sign of weakness. You may be distrustful of others.

But what do you think about when you have a moment to yourself? If you are feeling lonely, scared, hurt, confused, lost, unsupported, or unloved, do not worry. Those are human feelings, and everybody has them to various degrees and at various times.

You can overcome the negative feelings! You can pull out all positive feelings from inside. Never think you are alone with your issues or problems! Look for help, guidance, love, and support that make you feel warm inside and give you positive glimpses into your situation.

When you feel you have found a confidant or some other way to get those glimpses, feel grateful for that because these glimpses are guaranteed to make you feel better and stronger, and they will guide you toward shedding your negative layers. Learn to seek help and guidance.

## 3.10 If You Are a Worrier

If you spend a lot of energy worrying about anything and anyone, there are ways to learn how to think positively and guide your thoughts rather than letting them guide you.

Be aware of your thoughts. As soon as you sense a worry coming up, imagine a positive outcome and believe that you and others involved will be just fine.

Believe everything is okay no matter how bleak things seem. Tell yourself this many times until you feel calm. Believing in the universal law that everything happens for a reason may also help you become calm.

Maybe you can ask God, an angel, or a loved one who has already passed for protection and achieve a sense of calm. With practice and with consistency, you will instantaneously trust the calmness and reassurance you receive. You will also feel you are freeing up a lot of energy and time you can then spend on positive things and actions.

The time and energy you spend on worrying about things, situations, or people will not fill you up; it will merely drain you. If you worry about something you cannot control, let it go; let things happen as they will.

If you are able to prevent a disaster or other negative, by all means do something! With life comes responsibility, care, and sensibility, but do not spend a lot of time and energy worrying about things that may or may not happen.

We all have worries and thoughts, but they are grounded in fear, and we often realize there was nothing to worry about or things happened anyway and did not turn out as badly as we had worried they would. Sometimes, things turn out badly, but in the end, it is all about trusting that no matter what happens, it was meant to be and is part of a natural development we may not yet know the end result of.

## 3.11 If You Are Stuck in a Situation

If you find yourself stuck in a situation, ask yourself how you got into it. What choice did you make that made you end up in that situation? How can you get out of it in a positive, constructive way? How can you prevent it from happening again?

Think about what areas of your life you want to change. You can always start by changing the way you think. Do you feel you are a victim? Do you feel bitter and unable to move on? Do you blame others for your situation? How can you separate yourself from them? How do you interact with others? How do you treat others? Do you forget to put up boundaries for what you let others do to you? What is preventing you from getting out of the situation?

It is all about empowering yourself to take control of the situation in positive ways that help propel you and others upward. Imagine the outcome of the choices you are considering now. How will they affect you and others?

Some things take longer to learn than others, and we will keep bumping into the same hurdles especially if we are unable or unwilling to see our negative aspects.

## 3.12 If You're Just Having a Bad Day

We sometimes find that things go wrong and we get frustrated with the smallest things. Our energy is depleted, everything we want to accomplish somehow gets blocked or does not go the way we want it to, and we say things that may hurt somebody else. We lose our temper, our self-confidence plummets, and we wonder, *What am I doing here* or *What am I doing wrong?*

Everybody has days like those. If you find yourself having a day like that and you cannot pinpoint what is bothering you, try to accept that you have that feeling. It is already there, so denying it will not make it go away. But what can you do to get through it?

- You can choose to get on with your day and will eventually find out what was bothering you or a solution to your problem.
- You can listen to your thoughts; those that come up repeatedly are the ones that need attention. When you deal with whatever issue they represent, they will go away.
- You can talk to a friend.
- You can meditate and feel grateful for other things in your life.
- You can make a to-do list for that day and attack the urgent things first. You will soon feel less stressed because you are doing something.
- You can spend time doing what you love to do to raise your mood and energy levels.
- You can also just cocoon for a while to recharge.

Our minds, bodies, and souls need solitude and time to reflect and digest. Some people need this respite more often than others to digest the world and their lives.

Withdrawing temporarily to refuel is a very important process for all living things. Take a look at nature again; plants and animals hibernate during some months to recharge and then grow when the time is right.

We also need to rest and recharge to have balanced minds, bodies, and souls. We need to rest our minds to make room for our hearts. We need to rest perhaps more frequently than other living beings depending on our activities and stress levels.

When we clear our minds of excess thoughts, information, and feelings, more space is created to let creativity, spontaneity, and positivity enter.

There is somebody out there with positive intentions who can help you if you only ask. You can talk to a psychologist, psychotherapist, or counselor. You can also talk to a friend who is willing to listen to your trials and tribulations. Getting things out in the open can offer you relief. In addition, hearing yourself talking about your thoughts can give you perspectives on your issues that could help solve them.

The occasional moan about this and that is okay, but if we turn that into a hobby, it will keep us focusing on the negative instead of the positive and prevent us from finding long-term solutions to our problems.

Sometimes, we look for others' approval of many of our actions and thoughts. We can attain internal peace if we learn to trust our feeling of what is good and positive for us.

## 3.13 Negative Relationships and Ending Relationships

There can be many reasons for being in a negative relationship. What may be difficult to accept is that we are responsible for staying in negative, even abusive relationships. Our choices have taken us to where we are. We are surrounded by those we let surround us.

All relationships are unique, but the feelings that negative relationship foster are common. If we feel a relationship is detrimental to our development, if we feel it opposes our true desires and selves, maybe we should break off that relationship.

A breakup may be the best solution though it can be a major upheaval especially if children, finances, and family expectations play roles in that.

Talk to others about your situation; get views from friends and family. And when you are on your own with your thoughts, picture yourself in other scenarios and notice how they make you feel. Deep down, you will know the solution that is best for you.

After a relationship ends, you will feel a loss and a void; you will miss the person even if he or she was abusing you. Take time to settle into your feelings and thoughts so you can gain a calm and collected overview of your new life.

In many cases, you will not need much time to realize you made the right decision. In other cases, you may return to the relationship, and it may or may not last. The future is hard to predict.

But we have to listen to our deeper selves and learn to live with our choices' consequences. We will make wrong decisions, but so be it. We will also make right decisions.

## 4. Accepting Your Past Behavior and Actions—Living without Regret

Very few can honestly say they have never regretted anything they have done or said. Most of us have at one point or another thought, *Oooh! Had I only said something else* or *I wish I had [or had not] done that.*

We can regret minor incidents such as failing to give someone a goodbye hug or saying something hurtful to someone without thinking. We can also regret major mistakes we have made such as deliberately hurting someone by certain actions or by failing to seize a special opportunity.

No matter what we may have done or said or not done or said, we should not let regret linger. We can think about what could have been or what should not have been, but what does that help? Things are how they are now; we cannot turn back the clock. But we can mend or heal the effects on others of what we said or did by apologizing to them or helping them with something. That can also heal our feelings.

We can learn from our experiences that our actions produce consequences, and we can do our best not to do certain things again or do them better next time. Sometimes, we may need to dig deep to find out why we behaved in hurtful ways; we hold the answer within.

We should never be afraid to admit things to ourselves. We all have negative thoughts, feelings, and actions in our baggage, but we can all do something about them. We can change our focus. Talking to a professional or a friend can help us let it out and lighten our burdens.

(Please note I am not talking about major criminal offenses or other major events; those circumstances demand more-elaborate explanation, attention, and healing).

# 5. Intention and Focus—Keeping It Positive

I have learned the immense power of good intentions and keeping faith in positive thoughts and feelings. You will not avoid heartache in life, but holding onto positive thoughts can make a difference in your life.

If we believe that certain things were meant to be and that we will experience something new and good even after a challenge, our perception of life will become very different.

Look at whatever happens in your life from a broader perspective, and notice other opportunities presenting themselves. Keeping faith and focus will help you choose your next steps in a wiser way, one that will work for your greater good.

Those who believe in the spirit realms will say that thoughts on the other side manifest almost instantly whereas here on earth it takes longer because of slower vibrations. What you focus on will happen. You are attracting it with your thoughts, feelings, and behavior. But because vibrations are slower on earth, we may not realize that what is happening to us now is based on thoughts we had yesterday or a week, a month, or a year ago. We may not even remember what our thoughts were back then!

The speed at which we manifest what we think is increasing, and it may even become close to instantaneous someday. We see the effects of our thoughts almost immediately in the spiritual realm; that makes it easier to believe we are the products of our thoughts.

It felt completely natural to me when I was young to think of wanting something or being with someone and then being able to have it or be with that someone as soon as I focused on it fully. I was always confused when that didn't happen. I feel that this proves the notion that we as children do remember a lot from our spiritual reality. That is, until we learn not to. I hope future generations will be encouraged to honor their spiritual sides as natural elements of their being.

But because we cannot always consciously remember our spiritual side, we have to rely on and trust in our other senses including intuition—a knowing, a feeling, a sensation we get—or a vision we receive; these are messages from our souls.

· This is a challenge for many of us, but when we have overcome that challenge or are on the way to overcoming it, we will no longer question the veracity of the spiritual realm. It will gradually blend in with our lives.

I have worked with energies for the past twenty years. Earlier on, after I reached the master level of Usui Reiki, I realized more and more how important it was to keep our intentions and focus positive especially when we work with clients. With positive intentions and focus, I feel and sense when positive energy flows through me, and I feel, sense, see, and know the positive and releasing effect it has on my clients.

"The Secret—The Portrait of the Key to Life" produced by Rhonda Byrne is also very much about positive intentions, thoughts, and focus. Listening to the positive observations and statements from a variety of inspiring people was then to me like hearing pieces of a puzzle clicking into their right places.

It is easy to fall into a state of feeling down and complain about things, people, and places; I have done that many times. It takes a lot of conscious effort to change our ways of thinking to realize we create our surroundings and circumstances and to turn complaints into positive, grateful statements.

If you think about and focus on something negative, something negative will manifest. If you think about and focus on something positive, something positive will manifest. If there is something you do not like, do not focus on it. Do not give it your attention. Starve it. Do not give it a chance to feed off your negative thoughts.

Instead, feed the positive things you want to have around you. Think, believe, and feel that all is positive, good, and the way it is supposed to be. Be conscious about that. Even after something bad has happened to you and you have recovered from the first shocking impact and are again able to hold onto positive thoughts, make sure you focus on the positive and hold onto that. That way, more positive things will be attracted to it.

A dear friend of mine does not believe in positive reprogramming of old habits and thoughts. She believes she would be cheating and not be living in compliance with her true self. She wants to feel better before she acts differently in certain situations. That way, she knows she is living her true self.

Ironically, she has been stuck in the same type of negative situations for many years! She handles the same situations in the same way over and over, but she feels she is simply a victim of circumstances. (See the previous chapter.)

I can see where she is coming from, but I can also see that she has her perception of the universal law upside down. Even if you feel you are only kidding yourself while you are trying to instill positive thoughts in your thought patterns, just give it a chance. Point your actions and thoughts in a positive direction and wait for the outcome.

Whatever you think of comes from within, so there is no reason to feel you are acting out of character or that it does not feel like you. Your new action plan will start to feel natural to you. The positive and intuitive way of living is in you. Your core is positive. You can bring it out via conscious positive actions.

Once you start thinking and equally important acting differently, you will get new ideas, impulses, and experiences that will lead to something else.

You will become consciously aware of your actions and behavior and focus on trying to change them. The process will give you new insights about yourself and the world in which you live.

> *Destiny is what you run into when you run out of willpower.*
> —Jonathan Cainer, astrologer, author

## What Drives You?

What makes you feel excited and energetic and makes you accomplish things you feel good about afterward? What drives you to do what you do? Are you driven by

- heartfelt passion?
- a need for money?
- wanting to ensure your children's futures?
- self-fulfillment?
- a desire to please others and get recognition?
- other reasons?

Go with what gives you positive feelings and could be positive for others too. Go with what your mind and heart agree on. Then you will be certain you are driven by spiritual, heart-based virtues rather than ego-based virtues.

## 6. Other Challenges and Alternative Healing

I would like to mention other challenges some people face, namely mental disorders such as psychosis, depression, obsession, schizophrenia, and neurosis to mention a few.

I am in no academic position to explain or document these types of imbalances scientifically or professionally, but I do have a holistic opinion about them.

Later on, I refer to the excellent book on Reiki by Bodo Baginski and Shalila Sharamon in which they explain the underlying reasons for mental disorders seen from a spiritual perspective and in connection with Reiki, the universal life force. Through my awareness and intuitive knowingness, I have come to agree with their views on various mental, physical, and emotional imbalances.

Baginski and Sharamon realized how all our mental and physical imbalances stem from imbalances in our conscious and subconscious minds. Our perception of ourselves and the world can sometimes be so skewed that the imbalances manifest and affect us physically. Often, we are not aware this is happening.

There are of course many degrees of mental and behavioral disorders. Baginski and Sharamon believe that mental illness most probably is a manifestation of a withdrawal from a reality some people see as unmanageable or unattractive. They open their consciousness toward areas that until then have been accessible only to the subconscious mind.

My sister, a highly trained and skilled manager in social work, has for many years worked with people with mental disorders and addictions. I have often wondered how her clients would react to Reiki treatments or other energy treatments I do, such as resetting their energy field and so on. I have yet to research the topic in depth, but with the positive feedback I am getting from my clients, who have a variety of other imbalances (not mental disorders per se), I would like to find out what the reactions of clients with mental disorders or addictions would be.

I am intrigued because I feel an urge to help people with any imbalance and help even out their imbalances so they become whole again spiritually, mentally, and physically. I am certain Reiki and other forms of energy healing would also show its overall benefits and healing properties here.

It is commonly accepted that yoga and meditation are beneficial therapies. These exercises are very popular because we are actually taking part in the therapy ourselves.

With Reiki and other types of energy healing, we are also taking part as we have to allow healing to take place, but the participation is initially usually happening at a deeper level (or higher level if you will). However, for many who are not in tune with their intuition, this seems not tangible enough for them to believe in the effect.

Those who feel they need something more tangible may go for acupuncture, homeopathy, kinesiology, massage, NLP, hypnosis, or other types of therapy.

It is up to us to choose which therapy we are most attracted to, and it should be our right to choose. It is all about finding ways that speak to who we are and to where we are consciously and spiritually.

Yoga and meditation can also open up new psychological and spiritual doors in us and give us something to work with just as Reiki and other forms of energy healing do.

When new doors open, when new aspects present themselves, we often need help integrating these new aspects into the puzzle that is us so we can feel and become whole.

Some years ago, I read about a yoga experiment that had been conducted in a prison. The inmates attended some yoga sessions to release their pent-up anger, fear, or other feelings. However, the outcome was disastrous as there was no follow-up and there was no outlet for those involved to work with their newly emerged feelings and tempers. A healing process had been started but not followed up and completed.

When you start opening up doors, you need to have someone or something ready to greet whatever presents itself. The main point is to not fear whatever feelings or thoughts emerge. Whatever happens is all part of you, and it presents itself so that you have a chance to balance it with its counterpart and give it a quiet place in you.

When we accept the duality of life—dark and light, fear and acceptance, anger and peace, control and humility, and so on—we can look at our lives and what we encounter and get an idea of what in us needs to be balanced.

A crime-prevention experiment was conducted in England to help teenage boys in poor areas de-stress and stay away from drugs, drinking, and crime. The Positive Futures program conducted more than 120 projects in the most deprived neighborhoods in England. The boys tried Indian head massage, cooking lessons, golf, foot spas, and Reiki to mention a few therapies. The reaction was overwhelmingly positive. The boys felt more alert and focused due to the different natural ways of detox and healing (www. guardian.co.uk/uk/2007/mar/19/schools.children).

What a wonderfully positive experience. Just imagine how encouraging it would be to young people everywhere if similar projects were carried out and followed up in all countries. As in many other cases, it is often only a question of priorities.

We learn throughout our entire lives; we learn different lessons at different times. There is no right or wrong place you should be spiritually speaking at any one age. Any age is an appropriate time to open up to new channels, ideas, and views.

# Chapter 11

. . . . . . . . . . . . . . . . . . . . . . . . . . . . . . . . . . . . . . . . . . . . . . . . . . . . . . . . . . . . . . . . . . . . . . . . . . . . . . . .

# Thoughts and Feelings
# after Experiencing Loss

. . . . . . . . . . . . . . . . . . . . . . . . . . . . . . . . . . . . . . . . . . . . . . . . . . . . . . . . . . . . . . . . . . . . . . . . . . . . . . . .

I lost my husband when he was forty-three. He suffered a heart attack after exercising. We had no warning; his health seemed fine. The shock everyone felt was numbing, indescribable. For a long time, it felt overwhelming and painful. Our two small boys will now grow up without their father, and my husband and I will not grow old together. We had so many plans.

The night he died, I received a call from his coach; she told me that he had fallen and was not breathing. I was putting our children to bed, when I got the call, and our oldest son had just fallen asleep. When I got to the fitness center I ran inside and saw my husband on the floor, lifeless. He was gone.

If you too have had a traumatic experience recently or long ago, something inside you will want to reassemble the pieces and get back up on your feet. You may not be able to feel that force inside you in the beginning when you are in shock. Nevertheless, it is there inside you, and it is important to allow it to come forward when it presents itself in glimpses. This force will keep you going even after life-altering, course-changing experiences.

You will be overwhelmed by emotions and thoughts and not know what to do. You may feel you have been hit by a stun gun. You may feel the world is closing in on you. Nevertheless, allow all these emotions and thoughts to come to you and pass through you. Allow yourself to react; it will not help to fight them. Have somebody be there with you to hold you, give you water, and comfort you as long as you need it. Do not try to be strong and think, *I don't need anybody's help.* You need others near you. Let in those who want to be with you.

## 1. Finding Strength

In the early stages of a trauma, we may search for strength. In the shock stage, just being physically present may suddenly seem hard and pointless. You want to be wherever your loved one is. It is important that someone is there to hold you and tell you to just breathe. Maybe the feeling of somebody rubbing your back gently may give you a sense of grounding, which you will need.

It is equally important that you take everything from then on gradually. You cannot rush anything in the present or in the coming days and months. The process you are going through will take as long as it takes; it is all individual, and it needs time.

Find someone who can guide you even if it is guiding you to simply breathe and walk. Find someone who can take you home or wherever you need to go, give you something to drink, tell you to lie down and relax, or just sit and hold you. Our needs are different, so try to have those around you who know you and who are not afraid to guide you gently and lovingly.

Maybe someone will suggest that you see a psychiatrist or psychologist who works with shock and bereavement. In the initial stages, let yourself be guided as much as you can. You are not able to make any major decisions in the initial stages, so trust those around you and go with what they suggest as long as you do not feel too opposed to it. They could know what is best for you.

Tell someone about what is going on inside you. You will cry and think you will never be able to feel complete again. It may seem that you have too many holes in your soul; you may feel your energy field will need mending, and you may have no idea how to start the process of repairing.

You may ask yourself, *How do I gather strength to even move on?* If you have children, you will think about how to handle them, how to be alone with them, and how to fulfill their present and future needs.

If friends or family offer to take your kids for a play date or the like, say yes; your kids will probably enjoy a break from the sadness and will enjoy the normality of visiting friends.

## 2. Basic Daily Rhythms

Do not think too much about the future; that can be painful early on. Take life minute by minute, hour by hour, day by day. Think about eating and drinking something. Think about the basics. Make sure your children are eating and getting to school. Cuddle them and talk to them.

Talk to someone, have someone hold you and bring you tissues, have someone help you shop for groceries, make you tea, and pick up your kids from school if need be. Have someone help you handle urgent legal and financial papers and such. Things may seem worthless and unreal, but normalcy in a new form will settle in your life again in time. And let it take time.

What struck me in the beginning was hearing the same thing from so many who had also experienced loss. Many of them said, "I survived, and my children survived. This is part of life. We have to move on." People said, "Life brings us smiles and tears," "In time it will heal," "Be strong and be strong for your children," "Take care of yourself," and "It will get better." They may just seem like words to you in the beginning, but if you take time to absorb these little proverbs, you will see that they hold truths. And they are said in love.

Love will take on a surreal, almost nonphysical shape. I found that I was able to discern deep love with my heightened senses in a way different from before. I saw that as a phoenix rising from my crumbling world.

## 3. Physical Reminders

The day after my husband died, I saw his shoes next to mine. I thought how strange it was that he would never wear those shoes again. I took them upstairs. I felt I was mentally burying him with that action but I also knew that if I left them there, they would become a constant trigger of sorrow.

I saw his belt on a hook in our bathroom. I had a strange feeling that every physical reminder of him was bizarrely foreign. I took it off the hook knowing he would never put it on there again.

I buried my face in his bathrobe and took in his scent. I started crying uncontrollably. I folded it and put it on a shelf. For months, I would breathe in his smell. It always made me cry, but it was as if I could feel him there with me.

I would place my foot in his footprints on the carpet (until the carpet was vacuumed), and I would feel this connection with him. I would sit on his side of the bed and feel the springs being a bit softer; I sensed him. I would lie on his side of the bed, bury my head in his pillow, and imagine him being there.

I ran my fingers through the inside of his shoes so I could feel the indents his feet had left, and I would imagine his physical presence. I looked at the last pictures taken of him in the house and positioned myself in the same spot as if to feel him. And I did feel him. Years later, I still feel his presence.

Another traumatic experience was going to the cemetery. It took me over a month to go there for the first time after he had died. I did not go to his funeral; it was all very foreign to me as it was not my native country and just too hard to be a part of. I cannot remember being very much aware at the time of the fact that the funeral was going on. It was all a blur then.

The lack of your loved one's physical presence is extremely painful and strange. It is incomprehensible that you will no longer be able to give him a hug. He will no longer put his hand on your shoulder, give you a smile, or lovingly put his hand on your thigh when you are in the car.

I think of our last holiday together and feel extremely sad to realize he will not be standing in the waves at that beach again holding our oldest son's hand and looking at me with a big smile as the waves crash on them. He will no longer get the chance to lie on the lounger all lathered up in sun lotion and ready to fry and say, "Ahh, this is the life!" It is very hard to believe and accept such things are instantly gone forever. You feel cheated and not in control. You may feel an ocean of different feelings, but all are real.

It is also extremely painful to imagine the fact that from then on, you will have to live every day without the person who has passed away. You will have to humbly realize that this is how things are as devastated as you feel.

At the early stages, you cannot even really begin to accept it. It will be a long time before you reach the acceptance stage. The sudden end of a life can be very hard to understand.

In the initial stages of having lost a loved one, you may feel you are in a bubble. Your network seems to increase, but that may not last; people have their own lives and cannot continue to give you the same undivided attention they can for the first days or even weeks.

Furthermore, as time moves on, you will want to reestablish some normalcy and will realize it feels more normal with the number of people and frequency of gatherings at your house than before your loved one passed away.

But in the beginning, it is very important that people are there for you; that will give you comfort. You need an outlet to cry, to talk about your loved one to, and to remember things. You will need others to share your feelings and thoughts with, people who knew your loved one, people your loved one was close to. You need others with whom you can share your grief.

But you also need to have time alone even though it will hurt and you will cry. It is painful to go through it, and you will wonder, *Why do we have to go through the pain of losing people we love?*

You will ask yourself many questions and wonder about your faith and values. You may find your thoughts change as time passes. You may gain insights, and you may feel overwhelmed. Whatever you feel, do not put yourself in situations that will cause you discomfort.

Seek balance, and start doing daily things such as eating, sleeping, driving to the supermarket, and going back to work. It is important to get back to your life. It is okay to push yourself a little with daily routines that are part of normal living; at first, that will feel strange, and you may cry and have many thoughts while you do different things. But it will feel strange and you may cry whether you do it now or whether you wait for two, four, or eight months.

Push yourself a little toward normality so you do not put your new normal life on hold for too long, but do not push too hard; it is okay to say, "No, I just can't do that right now"!

You know yourself best, and if the thought of doing something makes your whole body curl up and it is just too much to handle, wait until you are a little stronger. You will become stronger by taking things one step at a time.

In the beginning, you will feel submerged in a pool of overwhelming emotions, thoughts, and experiences. You will get a glimpse of life again when you feel hungry and have to eat, when you have to pay a bill, when you have to go to the post office, and when you shop for groceries.

Get outside the house and do normal things; you do not want to stay in that pool of overwhelming emotions, thoughts, and feelings because that way, nothing will change. Even if you feel you do not care about that right now, you will eventually care about feeling better, and you can start that by doing normal things again.

Starting to take part in life again makes room for healing to take place. You will slowly let other things into your sphere including healing.

It is very hard, and you may break down in the supermarket, car, bank, or at your friend's house, but it is okay. These breakdowns will happen less frequently over time, and you will have longer stretches when you can breathe and feel you are alive. It is okay that you are alive; you are allowed that! Your loved one wants you to be alive and okay and start living your life again.

## 4. The Future and the Past

Do not worry too soon about the future. Let your thoughts and emotions surface, react to them, and let them pass through you. Allow yourself to take part in life again one step at a time. Eat, drink, drive, laugh, cry, talk, take a shower, read a story to your children, cook a meal, look out the window, think of your loved one, and know that all things you do for the first time since your loss will make you cry. They will probably make you cry the second and third time too, but it will not be as hard.

Just because your crying lessens does not mean you are caring less or forgetting; it means that your body, mind, and heart are showing you that their sparks of life are still there. You can continue your life even though it has completely changed; you can get through this tremendous adjustment.

The body, mind, and heart cannot go on being in deep sorrow all the time. To cope and establish your balance again, your sad reactions to experiences and thoughts will become less frequent and less intense if you let that happen.

It is common in the months following a loss to feel you want to turn back the clock. You may feel it strongly enough that you find it hard to move on. I have sometimes felt time was dragging me forward. I felt I was being dragged because I wanted to go back in time to when my husband was alive and talking to me, playing with the kids, and making plans for the future. I did not want to go forward in time.

You may suddenly feel that you are subject to time, fate, destiny—to something bigger than you, and it may be hard for you to accept that. Taking things a step at a time helps the healing process.

At times, my son says he wishes he were three years old again; I know he too wants to turn back the clock so he can be with his daddy again.

## 5. A Sense of Normality

The first weekend I was alone with the children and our domestic helper, I felt desperately alone, sad, and overwhelmed.

I went to our friend's house; we sat in the den, and I cried and cried. The news was on, and after my crying had quieted a bit, I felt it strangely comforting to realize that the news was on, the studio was cozily lit, and the groomed announcers were talking. That gave me a sense of normality though for only a brief moment before the tears started again. But I thought it was important to hold onto even brief moments of normality and reminders that life goes on, the world still carries on, and I would too.

You will still cry hard and feel despair, fear, anxiety, sorrow, confusion, anger, self-pity, and sadness for yourself, your children, and everyone else touched by your loss.

You may feel sad for the one who has passed as he or she will no longer enjoy experiences with loved ones. You may think of things he or she loved doing and feel sad that he or she will not experience them again. You know how much joy certain things brought your loved one, but he or she has been robbed of that joy.

Over time, you will laugh again. You will get glimpses of the future and not be filled with only fear. You will go to the supermarket, be creative with your children, go to the hairdresser, and take your kids to a restaurant and enjoy it.

Your children will make you strong, and you will want to be strong for your children. They need you! Use that as an incentive to hang in there and move forward. Do things with them too.

If you do not have any children, if you feel you have only yourself to take care of and are tempted to let go of healing—do not! Be strong for yourself and others in your life.

You still have your life to live. Spend time with your best friend; do something together. Even if it makes you cry, you will feel better in the long run for having done something. My sister told me, "We can all support and comfort you and tell you things that might make this easier, but you are still the one who has to go through this." As cruel as it may feel to go through something like this, you have to go through it even when you do not want to.

Nobody wants the pain of loss, but all eventually will experience loss either early in life as was the case with our two sons, in the middle of our lives as was the case with me, or later in life.

We need different branches of comfort, help, and motivation to hold onto so we can move on.

## 6. The Present—A New Normal

One of my and my husband's close friends told me, "We all have to establish a new normal." That is so true. Everything you used to do before as a family of, e.g., four, can be done only by three of you now. Everything my husband used to do with our older son—taking him to the beach, riding bumper cars, getting haircuts—will be done by someone else. And our younger son will never have had any of those experiences with his dad as he was only eight months old when his daddy passed.

Weekends, birthdays, and holidays will be different. I will be the one going to school events with the boys and helping them with their homework.

Routines will of course be different because a key person is missing. This is similar to divorces; usually, the mother is now alone with the children and handles chores and events. Those who divorce go through many emotions relating to loss through death. It is difficult to get used to the fact your loved one is missing from your daily life.

Keeping the memory alive and keeping your loved one alive by talking about him or her and remembering his or her spirit, strength, sense of humor, and take on things will help establish a new normality where your loved one still seems a part of it.

I keep "involving" my husband in various matters. I talk to him, I think about him in certain situations, and I feel connected and get his approval or disapproval (as I know him so well). I think about him when I hear certain songs, I cry when I am in certain situations, and I look up to the sky and ask him, "Did you see that?" when the boys do something cute or funny. I ask for his opinion on things, and it is as if I knew what he would say. I feel a strong sense of gratitude and a deep love for his kind heart.

This type of involvement may be too painful for some, so maybe performing a few more or less formal ceremonies on special occasions could be another way of coping.

## 7. Stages of Grief

Grief is very much an individual matter. We can only try the best we can to share ideas that might help others too. The concept of five stages of grief was introduced by Elisabeth Kübler-Ross in her 1969 book *On Death and Dying*. The road through these phases or stages supposedly takes you to the other end—toward healing.

In brief, Kübler-Ross defined the five stages as follows.

1. Denial and Isolation—we deny what has happened and may isolate ourselves even from our close friends.
2. Anger—with oneself, someone else, or the whole world.

3. Bargaining—we may bargain with God, a deity, an angel, etc.
4. Depression—we may find it hard to find a reason to go on.
5. Acceptance—we accept our loss though we still feel sadness and maybe even anger but not as strongly.

Researchers have moved away from the five stages of grief as defined by Kübler-Ross due largely to the work of bereavement research pioneer George Bonanno, who began studying grief in 1991. In his many studies, he did not find evidence that the stages existed. Nevertheless, many people still lean toward the stages model (wapedia.mobi/en/Grief).

Another source said, "Kübler-Ross herself never intended for these stages to be a rigid framework that applies to everyone who mourns" (http://helpguide.org/mental/grief_loss.htm).

Apparently, in her last book before her death in 2004, she said that the five stages of grief were feelings (or responses) many people have when they experience loss. She said that grief was as individual as our lives were.

## 8. Waves of Feelings and Thoughts

I am not experiencing any stages in a linear way as in one coming after the other. I have found that all stages or feelings can come simultaneously in little portions at a time.

I have found emotions, thoughts, and feelings hovering above me and presenting themselves in glimpses before going away and coming back like waves small enough (albeit extremely painful) that I can process them in my inner world with the help of my very qualified and empathetic psychotherapist, my friends, some family members, and my spiritual mentor.

These same feelings and thoughts come and go, but because I have moved through time, my view may have changed or I may have had a chance to discuss my feelings with someone; it feels like the intensity or contents of the stages change. Maybe it is simply the way I deal with a given stage that changes; maybe as time goes on, new thoughts and perspectives appear because I am slowly moving on.

Though it may take some time to be aware of or care about your feelings and emotions, I found it comforting to identify what I was going through with the help of my psychotherapist and to accept the feelings and thoughts as they were happening. It is okay to be angry about having these feelings as you go through the phases; each is important in the healing process.

Accepting that it takes time to go through the healing of a traumatic experience is also part of healing. If you feel overwhelmed, go to someone who cares and is able to listen to your concerns and thoughts in a serious, helpful, and maybe even professional manner (i.e., a psychotherapist, psychologist, or a religious or spiritual advisor).

Do what you feel you need to do as long as it does no harm to you or anybody else. It is what you need to do right now. Listen to yourself and others who genuinely care about you. Somebody may have a good idea or may present a thought that may feel right for you.

Two major aspects that in particular may stand out after a loss are coming to terms with the fact our special person is gone and getting used to continuing our lives with the voids our loved ones left. How we deal with these aspects is very individual.

## 9. Incentives to Go On

You may ask yourself, *How can I go on living when he [or she] is gone?* I have had that thought. Thankfully, my boys remind me that life must go on. They still have their needs—food, clothing, and so on. They need me to take them to school and play with them. They need me to listen to their stories, and I want to smile at them and laugh with them.

I need to be healed so I can be a mother to them. They need me as I need them. That is living proof that life does go on.

I also want to keep our boys as strong and happy as I can for my husband's sake. He adored our boys. He did everything to ensure their security, comfort, and well-being.

Those of us who are on this planet in the physical form have to tend to all these physical and emotional needs. Those who have passed are fine, I believe, where they are. We cannot see them, but they can see us, and they know more than we do.

We can still connect with them through meditation, dreams, or thoughts. I am still connecting with my husband in all these ways, and I know he is connecting with our boys. I have had and still have so many incidents when this happens that I am way beyond doubting (which I never even did) that there is something after our physical lives here.

If you do not have children and find it difficult to keep going, think of other people who are close to you and need you; let that motivate you.

More important, remember that you need you and that you can help others. Your skills are unique to you, and you can help others with them. Let your skills shine out to others.

After you have lost someone close to you, you may think you will not be able to live normally afterward. But the day will come when you can tolerate imagining the future. The day will come when you can look at pictures of your loved one and smile at something he or she once told you.

The day will come sooner than you think that you will laugh at something somebody says or does, and you may feel guilty about it, but you will laugh anyway. The day will come when you will remember his or her sense of humor and think, *This would have made him [or her] laugh*, and that will make you laugh too! And it is okay.

## 10. Dealing with Grief

Keeping busy can be a very good coping mechanism as it keeps some momentum going even if it is doing simple, everyday things such as shopping and cooking. If you have children, they will keep you busy. Paying attention to things outside yourself can help draw your attention from your pain, and that is fine as long as you pay attention to your pain so you can heal. Again, it is about balance.

Keeping busy helps the time pass, and you will see other perspectives, you will talk to people, and you will understand the world does not stand still. You will have new feelings and thoughts that will help you move through time until you feel you can handle more and more bits of normality again.

Extended periods of inactivity, grieving, and shutting the world out will not serve you or others well. Bringing everything to a halt for a long time will not bring you any new impulses or motivate you to move on. You may have an even harder time finding a reason to go on if you stay inactive and locked in the same position and situation day in and day out.

Your loved one who passed away would not want you to sit around day after day feeling empty, guilty, bitter, drained, angry, miserable, and so on. Think about how he or she kept busy.

Our passed loved ones will not be offended if we start to move on. They know the grief we are carrying and the void we are feeling, and they know our love for them will never diminish no matter what. We must keep a special place for them in us so we will know that no matter what we do, they will be with us.

Friends and family will eventually talk to you about events from their daily lives, and this can help push you to get your feet back on the ground and realize there are still many things for you to do too.

Keeping busy will help keep you grounded and in touch with reality. You may feel you do not want to be part of reality anymore. You may feel alienated from all others, and you may feel alienated from the life you led before you experienced this terrible loss. But keeping busy, being grounded, being with close, compassionate friends and family, and getting back in touch with life in the physical world will help you. In time, you will feel more with it and less numb.

## 11. Creating Time and Space for Grieving

Keeping busy does not mean blocking out the grieving process. You can keep busy and still allow feelings and thoughts to pass through you. Even if those feelings are painful, let them come to you and pass through you. On that note, below is an excerpt from my journal:

> "For a few days I had been so concerned with the whole aspect of the future, financially and materially speaking, and it had given me butterflies in my stomach, and I knew that I wasn't really giving room for the sadness and the 'missing him' inside me … It had been two days with almost no crying, and as I was putting my youngest son to bed, I was holding him and rocking him to sleep, and I started crying so hard I was bouncing up and down right there on the bed. It was as if I had been holding on to a pool of tears and now there was a quiet moment and it all came out. I finally, after a few days of tension, acknowledged what was inside, and once I let it out, I felt a big relief"…

Over the following months after experiencing a loss, you will encounter many situations that will trigger your reaction. Going through something for the first time since your loved one passed away will trigger the strongest reaction. It can be frightening to think about doing some things. You may fear doing them, but in time, they will become easier to do.

Things you did not think twice about doing before may suddenly become a big deal—things like driving, shopping, hearing a familiar song or looking at a familiar painting or photo. Things will prompt you to think, *He will never see this again* or *I will never touch him again*. Those times can be difficult to get through.

You will want to avoid these things; you will want things the way they were, and it feels overwhelming having to do all these things because you know you will cry and it will drain you. But painful as it is, it is still better to go through them and let the feelings out rather than denying them and bottling them up inside.

If you shut out your feelings, you will soon feel you are not living; you will feel empty and start to descend into depression. Even when you acknowledge the feelings that surface in you and you are willing to go through them, you will feel emptiness, despair, fear, longing, anger, guilt, and sadness. If, however, you go through them by screaming, crying, or talking to someone about them, you are on your way to healing. That is because when you acknowledge your feelings, let yourself react to them, and talk about them, they will melt away. They may resurface, but then you can talk about them again and allow them to flow through you so you can heal.

In the early months after my husband's death, I would cry so hard when I was alone in the car, and just feel desperate to have my husband with me again. These desperate feelings are natural to go through after a loss. All imaginable feelings are bound to appear just as ripples are bound to appear in water when an object is thrown into it.

The feelings are there; they are natural however painful they are. After you cry, you will feel relief. Allow it to be easier for yourself the next time you look at a picture or go to the supermarket. It will take time, but it will indeed become easier.

Time is a healer. You are a healer. The river of life keeps flowing.

## 12. Emotional Numbness

I have gone through short intervals of emotional numbness, days when I have been keeping myself busy and have not let reality enter my mind.

I would for example suddenly realize I looked away when I walked by pictures of my husband, or I would push any unpleasant thoughts aside and get on with practical things to avoid the pain.

I would buy something I knew would be therapy for the boys and myself. For example, I bought a piano, which I had yearned to buy for many years, and I bought plane tickets for us to get away for one day. Those purchases would however make me feel guilty because my husband was not there to enjoy them and I felt I should not be spending "his" money on somewhat expensive purchases. Because of the guilt, I would keep him out of my mind.

I believe these examples demonstrate some kind of subconscious coping mechanism for the times that are too much to handle and we want to avoid them.

But continuously avoiding the pain does not heal anything. Loss is painful, and it can be scary to go through, but you will start to heal only when you go through time with the grief. This is why you should seek help from someone you feel very comforted and supported by, someone you can cry with or feel sorry for yourself a little bit with without feeling guilty or ashamed. You will get better over time with support, comfort, and the chance to let out all your thoughts and feelings.

## 13. Becoming Aware of Your Thought Process

When you go through grief, find someone to hold onto and pull you forward when you feel you have no strength. As time passes, you may need help with different things than at first.

The healing process changes. You can let it lift you and move you forward so you do not get stuck. Feeling stuck with your life only adds to the sad situation you are in. As hard as it may be to find something that can add value to your life, it is extremely important to trust in the purpose of your life, to trust you can contribute to your life, and to trust you can contribute something positive to the lives of those around you.

Once you start being part of and taking part in life again, you will be able to reestablish a normal relationship with life and again be able to give to others despite your sorrow!

My psychotherapist validated my desire to not become stuck in a moment. If you find yourself thinking too much of a certain moment or reliving or reacting the same way to triggers, take some deep breaths and remind yourself that you are not there at that moment, that you are here now. Now could be three months, eight months, or two years later for example. Time has passed since the devastating moment, things have happened since then, and you are moving on with time, with the world, and with your life.

One day, I caught myself thinking about my husband and his work and imagined the situation when his colleagues were told what had happened. It made me cry every time I thought about it. I know how dear he was to them all and vice versa. I also think of my husband's family and friends and feel their pain, though theirs comes from a different angle than does mine. But we all feel the loss, the pain, the void in various ways and situations.

When you lose someone close to you, your mind and body tries to make sense of it all; your thoughts may fast-track through scenarios and experiences. Remember though that what you are thinking now, a week, a month or six months later is a thought. You are not really in that same now as you were when you first found out your loved one had passed. You will never be in that same now again.

Keep grounded, feel your body, give your children hugs, feel the physical side of yourself. You are here for you and your children, parents, siblings, friends, and colleagues.

A major catalyst for self-growth is becoming consciously aware of how you go through life, how you think, and how you act. Then you can begin altering the focus of your thoughts and actions.

Becoming consciously aware of your thoughts and feelings can also help you get through painful experiences such as bereavement. It also frees up space in your mind to let in more spiritual or virtuous ideas and experiences.

Moving on does not mean forgetting what happened or minimizing your loved one. It means realizing where you are now and living with the void, the loss, while keeping the memory of your loved one alive while allowing for new to enter your life.

## 14. A Sense of Control and Keeping the Memory Alive

When you lose someone close to you, your sense of control vanishes. You are suddenly forced to surrender to life's circumstances. This can frighten and humble you.

After the initial shock, you may slowly start to feel you want to regain control of certain things in your life. You may want to do certain things, but there will be things you do not want to do. You may put off doing something that seems too final to you.

If you feel something would be too final, leave it for the time being unless it is something vital or legally important or necessary. But leave it for now, and return to the matter when you are feeling stronger.

Keeping the memory of your loved one alive is very important; it is in a way creating a new type of relationship with your loved one for yourself and others.

You can keep your memories alive in many ways. As time passes, you will develop ways that suit you. I put up photos of my husband on our refrigerator and console. I planted a special flower for him in our garden, and when I buy new flowers for the pots in our garden, I plant them with him in mind. On the first anniversary of his death, I lit candles at breakfast and dinner for him.

I do different things at different times now, but I always include him in my thoughts when I have to decide something or make some changes. I share songs with him on the radio, I think of him, and I talk with him.

Those are just some of the things we all can do when we have lost someone close. Keeping them as parts of our lives in healthy and non-obstructive ways can help us move on. We will have to learn to live without our loved ones, but we will never forget them.

It may scare us or overwhelm us with sadness when we think about not having the physical presence of our loved ones around anymore. We may feel we do not have much left of them. In the physical sense, that is of course true. But this is why it is important to keep their memories alive through other physical things such as treasured mementos or by remembering their essences and allowing them to be one of the many aspects or little ceremonies of our new lives.

## 15. Spiritual Beliefs as a Coping Mechanism

Our faith and beliefs may be tested when our loved ones die whether we are strong believers or atheists.

You will search for your loved ones, wonder where they are, and sense their presence. Even if you require scientific proof before you accept a theory, you will consider the possibility that there is something out there other than our physical reality.

I do not see how you could not at least wonder where the energy, the essence, the spark of life of the deceased has gone. Imagine that when people die, their life energy lives on albeit in a different form. Highly spiritual and intuitive people including me sense that we are all energy and that there are gross and subtle forms of energy.

Gross energy is a physical manifestation of a person living in the physical world. Subtle energy is the manifestation of a person in a spirit realm. According to those who are spiritually aware, this means we are still alive as energy but in a spiritual rather than a physical realm. Life goes on but in a different form.

I think when you lose someone, unexpectedly or not, your mind has a hard time comprehending the loss and you wonder where the person has gone. *He was just here!* Maybe you can still feel them; maybe you feel their presence above and around you, and it seems a veil of invisibility has come between you and them.

Your contact with them suddenly becomes nonphysical, intangible. Your contact with them becomes real only through different channels—your thoughts, intuition, sensations of a sudden chilly or warm feeling, or visual or physical signs.

I felt the presence of my husband very strongly after he had passed away, and I can still feel him to this day though not all the time anymore. I am very receptive to picking up energies and vibrations; I am also, probably because of this sensitivity, a longtime believer in the spirit realms. I have, however, over the years also been looking for proof for my beliefs, and I am still amazed at the signs I have received and keep receiving. I am in no way doubting if I even ever had doubted.

My belief and trust in the spiritual world and in fact the evidence of it I keep receiving helps me get through the loss.

My belief and openness help me heal physically as well as spiritually as they provide answers to my questions. It is not that my belief fits the answers I want to hear as skeptics may argue, no; I feel it is in fact the other way around. The signs come first, and then I consciously notice them and see how they do not just randomly fit.

The connection is helping me function and move on in life with him even if he is in a different state. I am moving on with my life and those of our boys. I feel a great respect for our children because they are part of him, and I want to give them security, comfort, and positive experiences. Believing that my husband is aware of this and is there too helps in that process.

*Marriage, birth, and death are all destined to be.*
—Anubhaa Sharma

## 16. Spiritual Tools

I have become more aware of the spiritual tools that work in the healing process. Examples of these spiritual tools are meditation, dream therapy, Reiki and other forms of energy healing, angel guidance, tuning in to your loved one, clearing your mind by spending time in nature, past-life regression, and being open to and aware of sensations and information received through inner guidance to mention a few.

I believe we all find the pieces to our jigsaw puzzles of life; we keep the pieces we accept and let those that do not fit our puzzles go.

Whether you are religiously inclined, are more into spirituality, believe in nothing special, or hold onto other beliefs, if your beliefs help you move on, they are right for you.

## 17. Spiritual Beliefs—Or Not

Those who do not believe in the afterlife, the spirit realm, and the angelic realm will argue that those who do believe in those things are simply using them as mental or emotional Band-Aids to calm and comfort themselves so they can cope.

Yes, it certainly is comforting to believe our loved ones are still around and always will be, and it is comforting to believe we will again be together and our children will join us eventually after we pass from this physical realm. Whether our minds are playing Band-Aid tricks will become a hundred percent confirmed.

Belief in the spiritual world is an individual matter. Millions of people, including me, have had all sorts of afterlife encounters and so-called near-death experiences. Numerous books have been written on that and similar subjects. People alone or in groups are tuning in to the spirit realm, to angels and guides and loved ones who have passed. They receive information and comfort that will perhaps help them move on, find their way, and become more aware of their purposes.

I find comfort and pure sense in the notion of another reality and other realms. However, the concept of an afterlife is another of life's big mysteries with proponents and opponents. I believe that among our purposes for being here are

- to define and melt away our shortcomings,
- to get better at overcoming challenges in a way that does not hurt ourselves or others,
- to spread positive ripples wherever we go, and
- to help others for the highest good of all.

These virtues and deeds become more engrained in us the more we tune in to the spiritual side of life and the less we are preoccupied with materialism and vanity.

## 18. Signs from the Spirit Realm

We all can learn to tune in to signs and guidance from the other side as well as from our higher selves. We can choose to be an open channel. One of Doreen Virtue's excellent books is *How to Hear Your Angels*; it has all the information you need to start becoming consciously aware of the guidance and signs around you. Her books have supported my experiences.

My spiritual mentor and dear friend Anubhaa Sharma has reminded me many times that we are all energy and that though we cannot see our deceased loved ones, they are still around us and we can connect with them through meditation or by being open to communication and signs from them. Below are a few examples of literally hundreds of such communications I have experienced and that I see as signs from beyond the veil.

While driving in the early months after my husband had passed away, I would often break into tears. Suddenly, I would get a hunch to turn on the radio. And I would hear a song that sounded like words of comfort coming from him and exactly on the subject I had been thinking about.

Three days after his death, I saw a huge butterfly; I had never before seen this particular butterfly in the country where I lived. My husband and I sometimes talked about signs from the other side and that butterflies were a beautiful way of sending a message. In the following weeks, I would see the same type of butterfly again and again circling me and our boys when we were in our garden. Even now, I occasionally see other kinds of butterflies at times that coincide with me thinking of him and often when the boys and I are out in nature. It is as if he is saying he is okay and he is with me and our boys.

I have sensed him near me many times when I suddenly think of him. I get a tingling sensation, and I feel his presence as if he were physically in the room or the car with me.

Days after his passing, I saw on several occasions a bird—a sparrow or a pigeon—that would land on the table I was at with a friend or on our windowsill and look in at us. The bird would come just as we were talking about my husband, and it would sit quietly there and just look at us. The experiences even made my friends feel tingly.

I have had many more experiences and continue to have them. When you have experienced moments like these, you can tell them apart from other moments in which you feel no contact. You just know, feel, sense, see, or hear something that makes you aware. It is not frightening. On the contrary, I find it very calming.

## 19. The Planets and Us

Just as the moon affects water on earth, it also affects many people. They feel particularly vulnerable or agitated during a full moon. Others, also myself included, feel the influences of the planets.

In earlier times, only royalty, aristocrats, and other upper-class people hired astrologers to help them figure out the most favorable time to take certain important actions. Today, astrology is for everybody; some believe in planetary influences while others do not.

I often read horoscopes written by a renowned and my favorite but now sadly passed-over astrologer. I am always amazed at the accuracy and the timing of his interpretations.

After my husband passed away, I kept reading his horoscope as well, and I noticed how the essence of my husband's horoscope continued to fit for a while after he had passed. In my search for answers, I wrote the astrologer, who kindly replied to me and pointed out that the planets influence us as long as we inhabit this physical realm of our solar system and until our spirits or energy bodies move on to the spirit realms.

I kept reading the horoscope and eventually found what was written no longer seemed to match my husband's situation. I imagined that my husband had then begun to move away from this realm and into the next one.

## 20. Testing One's Beliefs

I believe in the spiritual realms and that all life is energy. I do however also occasionally feel a need for earthly, tangible, visible, or scientific proof before I can accept something. I have found that my belief in the spiritual is sometimes put to the test.

More than ever, I feel connected to the energies, but more than ever, I also feel the need for some kind of proof that the other realms actually exist because my husband has passed away and is on the other side.

A big part of me knows he is still around as an energy form, but I think because we are also human and physical, our sense of reality sometimes depends a lot on our using our physical senses to understand the world.

However, the more accustomed to our spiritual senses we become—even when major events like death happen—the easier we will accept a greater reality.

Labels like supernatural, paranormal, dangerous, crazy, and so on have been put on spiritual and extrasensory experiences throughout time. These labels may have caused many to believe that these experiences are not normal; people who have had these experiences may be deterred from sharing them out of fear of being labeled as not normal. This has been going on for so long that many have forgotten to trust their experiences and consider them real.

Nowadays, however, many people share their spiritual experiences with others in centers and institutions or at group meetings, seminars, and so on. The concept is becoming more normal than paranormal or supernatural.

## 21. Questions

I think most if not all people who have lost loved ones will ask some of these questions.

- Why did he or she have to die?
- Where is the justice in this?
- Why could we not have had more time together?
- What about us who are left behind? How can we go on?

We may also think about it from the departed's viewpoint.

- He or she had so many plans and was so full of life! Why could he or she not have had more time with loved ones here?
- Why did he or she have to be ripped away from his or her children, spouse, parents, and friends?

We may look upon death as a punishment, but if we look at it spiritually and imagine we are eternal spirits having a physical experience, maybe we can see everything happens for a reason. Maybe we will see that only much later on in life.

Nevertheless, our loved ones had a purpose while on earth. Their deaths may have happened for reasons we cannot yet comprehend. But we can trust that we and our children still have reasons to be here. Our loved ones do not mind that we keep at it.

We all have something we can bring to others. We all have gifts that can brighten others' lives. Our purpose is to learn as we go through life and find our unique skills that will benefit others. One day, we will surely rejoin our loved ones.

Giving advice and support to your grandchildren, providing guidance, teaching, being a counselor, helping others get physically fit, giving others thrilling experiences, running a daycare, healing others, providing others with food or shelter, clearing away other people's waste, helping others reach their potential, and helping others look and feel good are ways of helping others. And we all have something we can give and share because we are all important.

## 22. Changing Your Perspective

After losing someone you love you need time to get your feet back on the ground. You need time to evaluate your new position in life.

However, you also need time to realize you are meant to go on with your life. You were connected with your loved one on earth and lived together until the day came that he or she had to go. But realize your loved one would not want you withering away in misery.

So many aspects of life, so many other people, places, or things around you would benefit from your presence, and you will see how many if you let yourself look for them!

Your loved one would not want you to be unable to live your life after his or her passing and be the cause of that by his or her death. As hard as it is, it can help to see it from that perspective. It may help you out of an unhealthy rut. Learn to ask for help from friends, relatives, or professionals who match your needs. It is okay to seek help to get through all your feelings constructively.

Become part of an exchange. Even if you are at the receiving end now, you will later be at the giving end helping others. But to help others, you need to be okay first.

## 23. The University of Life

You can feel angry and irritated among many other feelings as you go through loss. Sometimes, I ask myself, *What am I supposed to learn from this? Why do our children have to grow up without their father? What is their lesson? Why couldn't we just have learned our lessons with both of us here? Why do we have to go through this terrible experience?*

My husband adored our boys. He did everything for them, for us, and for our future. That made it much harder to accept and understand he would not be around to see them grow up. We even talked about how sad it would be for us to not see them grow up!

Though the death of a loved one may seem at first a punishment, I do not see it that way after living through many months of grief, soul-searching, and pain. I see it as a lesson, a gift from a higher spiritual level, a glimpse of a lesson revealed in time.

I have for example found myself with a more humble feeling about life and creation including the cosmos and our planet. I also see more clearly that we are energy whether in physical or spiritual form.

When you start thinking about these bigger questions, you embark on a journey that is hard to stop. You will become more thirsty for knowledge and answers, and the questions will keep coming to the forefront of your mind. I see this quest for knowledge as growth if you put the knowledge to positive use.

Life is a continuous learning process. We should all get help where we can in ways that feel right for us be it through prayer, asking angels for guidance and support, talking to friends, keeping open minds, listening to music, reading, spending time in nature, having a quiet moment alone, and keeping our bodies healthy to maintain clear minds.

# Chapter 12

···················································

# Nurturing Dreams
# and Aspirations

···················································

*To the degree we're not living our dreams, our comfort zone
has more control of us than we have over ourselves.*
—Peter McWilliams (1949–2000), writer

Do not worry if you sometimes or often feel you do not know where you are going. Once you learn to listen to and follow your heart, you will see your path. Listen to your intuition, follow your urges, and keep it positive.

Do not regret the past. You will eventually see that whatever you did in the past was meant to happen to bring you where you are now. You needed your past lessons to get to where you are now. Be grateful for the lessons. Some of your past choices may have led to something that looked like mistakes, but once you learn to accept that you did the best you could at that time, you will be able to draw something positive out of the event. Make your choices with the help of your heart and mind. Focus on and describe to yourself your dreams and desires to manifest and then materialize them.

Create the space, time, and conditions you need to calm your body, mind, and soul. That will help you realize your dreams. If your dreams and aspirations reflect what is right for you, opportunities will arise naturally. Look for and embrace your opportunities!

If you have a positive trait you have not yet nurtured but would like to bring out, nurture it and give it your attention. That trait could be respect, compassion, or empathy for others. Focus on it and let it grow.

*If you follow the promptings of your higher self, you will see things
realistically and find harmony within yourself and others.*
—www.fromthestars.com/page46.html

When you work on achieving your dreams and aspirations, you are looking for fulfillment and a purpose for your life. You are looking for that feeling you get when you have done something good for yourself or others. Feeling good about doing good for others is fine. When a good deed is received positively, that means a positive exchange has taken place. It does not mean you are selfish just because you feel good about it.

When we stay true to ourselves and pay attention to positive guidance from within, material abundance will come to us in whatever way we need.

One way to make ourselves feel valuable and significant is to use our hands or bodies to create something.

Kelly Lambert (*Scientific American Mind*, 19[4], 2008) pointed to studies that showed important neurochemicals were boosted when we did things that were meaningful be they working with wood, knitting, sewing gardening, cooking, and such.

> Our brains … derive a deep sense of satisfaction and pleasure when our physical effort produces something tangible, visible and … meaningful in gaining the resources necessary for survival.

Our brains also derive satisfaction and pleasure when we do what we enjoy such as painting, writing, and playing music. Whatever gives us satisfaction and pleasure will bring us a sense of purpose and fulfillment especially if it reaches others as a positive, needed, and appreciated service.

In some societies that are referred to as nanny states, many aspects of day-to-day living are surrounded by rules and regulations to a degree that they stifle imagination, living conditions, and lifestyles. That could leave some feeling inadequate or too pampered to the point they feel no responsibility or liability. In addition, to some, having to find out only what rules they have to live by could leave them feeling lazy and unmotivated about their situations.

We can feel a great sense of achievement when we have thought about a problem, asked others for help and advice on it, allowed our imagination free rein, and finally achieved success.

We may sometimes feel that we are kidding ourselves or that we will never reach our goals or dreams. We are all here to learn lessons on a personal level, and we may well think we have learned a lesson only to find out we really did not. We feel we have come to a dead end—*I'm back to this again?*

We might find ourselves in a negative situation and cannot figure out how we got there. This happens to us all; we all learn continuously but in phases.

Sometimes, it is hard for us to see how we are doing; we think we are heading in a good, healthy direction, and we might think we are doing something good for others and ourselves until somebody says something that makes us realize we are maybe not as good as we think. That can be devastating especially if we were convinced we were on the right path.

But we were on the right path even if it turned out to be a wrong direction. We were on that path to learn something. Suddenly, we realize what we are doing wrong or what we ought to be doing, and we alter our actions or thoughts.

Nobody knows how to handle every situation in the most positive and constructive way. Nobody knows how to handle all types of people. We can all make the same mistake more than once. If we were perfect, there would probably be no need for us to be on earth going through all of life's challenges.

Even if we sometimes feel down about our dreams and aspirations, we can get up again, decide what we can do differently, and decide if we have been listening to our egos or hearts.

> *Life itself is prone to sudden change. And it's still something*
> *to be deeply glad of. Fill your life now with hope, not fear.*
> *Stability you can never have. But joy is always on offer.*
> —Jonathan Cainer, author and astrologer

# Chapter 13

## Choice, Responsibility, and Accountability

*Behind every Choice, there is a Reason. Acknowledge the reasons behind Your past choices—and recognise the reasons for the choices You make from now on.*
—Marianne Johansen

## 1. Your Choices

Your situation was influenced by the choices you have made. Focusing on the choices you have made can give you useful information about yourself and your circumstances.

If you do not like where you are, you can choose how to fill and influence your days to come. That is often easier said than done, but you may be amazed at how focusing on the moment can make a big difference in your life.

Choices that come from our minds alone are unbalanced. Balance is achieved when we use mind, body, and heart in unison. A balanced body creates a quiet mind, and a quiet mind hears the heart. We have an infinite number of futures based on our choices.

In 1957, Princeton physicist Hugh Everett was the first to propose the many-worlds interpretation of quantum physics (Wikipedia: "Many-worlds interpretation and self-prophet.com"). He argued that many possibilities and outcomes are present every moment and are awakened by our choices. He wrote that we collectively respond to any given time in history through all our individual choices.

I read another interesting article (on a website that no longer exists—www.selfprophet.com) that talked about how an infinite number of futures exist at all times. The article theorized, "The choices you make and the actions you take determine which future you breathe life into. Once you breathe life into a certain future, all the other potential futures collapse."

Wikipedia's definition of a self-fulfilling prophecy is "a prediction that directly or indirectly causes itself to become true, by the very terms of the prophecy itself, due to positive feedback between belief and behavior." Sociologist Robert K. Merton is credited with coining the expression *self-fulfilling prophecy* and formalizing its structure and consequences.

The theory holds that if we believe very strongly in a certain outcome, our actions may become so greatly influenced by our belief that the event actually happens. This would naturally work for both positive and negative outcomes. The 2007 movie *Premonition* starring Sandra Bullock and Julian McMahon comes to mind. If we hold onto an image and perhaps a feeling of a certain event we would like to see happen long enough, by reverse engineering, we can backtrack and determine how we got there.

Look at the future you are breathing life into now; is it the future you want? If not, imagine the future you desire and how you got there. You are not to hurt anybody or anything along the way because you want to arrive feeling good knowing you have accomplished all in a positive way.

All the positive we can imagine exists. Trusting this, lets us find the key to the door to let all the positive in.

It is in fact all about the choices we make. We can choose to be adulterous, drink too much, tell lies, betray a friend's trust, go back to an abusive spouse, hurt a partner, or say something hurtful to another.

On the positive side, we can choose to be loyal partners, treat our children like dear friends, help the elderly and friends in need, be compassionate toward our partners, or cheer someone up.

## 2. When Feelings Make Us Choose

Most of us have experienced our feelings come on like a tidal wave and take control of us. This can happen when we fall head over heels in love with somebody or get a boost of energy from something we do, witness, or experience. When we feel that volcanic surge of emotion, we can make choices that in hindsight we think we should not have made. But we learn as we go along; it is all part of being human.

At times, our choices may not be fully compatible with our true selves and true purposes, but as we harvest knowledge from our experiences, we tend to get better at making positive choices.

## 3. Consequence and Responsibility

We can benefit from advice and encouragement, but when someone is telling us how to live, deal with situations, behave, or think, that can stop us from using our free will and common sense. It may also interfere with our learning how to become humane human beings and how to take responsibility for our actions. It may also prevent us from realizing everything we do has consequences for ourselves and others.

With free will comes responsibility. When we use our free will and take responsibility for our actions, we will notice how our actions have consequences for ourselves and others and will appreciate positivity spreading around us like ripples in water.

We must take responsibility for our lives and deal with the consequences of our choices. Think about a judicial system. It can be a safety net that catches people heading in a negative or destructive direction. This net might catch those whose emotional intelligence does not allow them to care for others' feelings.

It might catch those whose self-esteem is so low that they do not care what happens to them. Some people are unable to tell right from wrong or good from bad due to mental illness, a handicap, or trauma. Such people and their victims can be helped by a judicial system that makes them aware that their actions have consequences and can affect others.

However, those with good mental health and emotional and interpersonal intelligence should not consider laws and rules as substitutes for their own ability to feel responsible for their actions. Again, the nanny state comes to mind. Too many rules that do not allow people to use their moral standards and humane values and creativity may have an adverse effect.

## 4. Responsibility and Accountability

The above points out that your choices may have a deep impact on others. With life comes responsibility and accountability. Blaming others for where you are today will only give you the illusion that you had nothing to do with it.

The world can seem very confusing and complicated if we let ourselves be disturbed by the plethora of events, happenings, and information that circulate globally every day. If we feel we must keep up with everything and have an opinion on everything, we will find it difficult to keep our minds focused on simple things. But it is possible; with awareness and consciousness, we can learn to focus on what makes us unique and helps us benefit others.

Here are excerpts from Christine Comaford-Lynch's book *Rules for Renegades— how to make more money, rock your career, and revel in your individuality.*

> I've wrestled with self-doubt. I don't have what it takes, I don't know the right people, I'm poor, I'm scared, I'm unpopular, I'm dweeby and lack social graces ... Do any of these sound familiar? This is fostering destructive illusions.

> Here's what I've learned: you will stay small, and your life will stay small, until you drop all that emotional baggage. Dumping baggage is hard work, and I don't want to minimize the challenge.

> Please forgive me if I proceed to give you a compassionate kick in the pants. I wasted a lot of time and energy battling these demons and would like to spare you the same suffering.

> Dump your baggage; abandon your destructive illusions. If you want to race toward your dreams, it helps to travel light.

> Like most people's childhoods, mine wasn't perfect.

> When my dad told me that he wished I'd been a boy, and that as a girl I wasn't smart or pretty enough, I took it to heart, I embraced this destructive illusion, morphing by turns into a controller, rescuer, and manager.

> I was obsessed with proving my worth so I wouldn't get tossed out of the boat. It took me decades to figure out how to reframe things; my dad's criticisms were my motivation to find my own value, to convert pain to action to results.

To a great extent, my self-sufficiency and skills for motivating others and accelerating businesses were born from my dad labeling me as deficient.

I had to find my own worth, bring it forth, and show myself I had more value than I'd been told. And as I did, something super cool happened: over time, I realized that my father didn't mean to discourage me at all. His intention was to toughen me up, to prepare me for the world. Eventually my father became a trusted advisor.

More often than not, our destructive illusions can be turned into something empowering. (Reprinted with permission of the author)

## 5. Our Choices and Actions Influence Others

One day, I saw about ten seconds of a TV program from the 1940s or so. It was showing children being "treated" by what looked like doctors—men wearing white coats.

The children were hanging upside down in scary-looking contraptions. The device was supposed to alleviate spinal defects. Seeing the faces of the children left me horrified. They were petrified and crying. They received no comfort, supporting words, or calming touches from the so-called doctors. I thought, *People probably did not know much about human psychology at that time. Life was more physically challenging and tougher than today, and compassion and empathy were not always an integral part of people's lives.*

That horrible incident showed me how important it was to realize that our choices and actions can influence many others' feelings and that we have to at least notice how others react to our actions and balance and calm them. That should be a given.

## 6. Moving Up in a Spiral—Encountering Similar Events

In his book *Fractal Time*, Gregg Braden wrote that everything in the universe came in cycles like the seasons, but he also suggested that scenarios or "seed events" returned in cycles.

To illustrate his theory, we can imagine a tree with healthy roots in healthy soil growing bigger each spring and building on what it has achieved. Just as a tree can grow bigger every spring, we can also grow every time our lives have taken us around the cycle.

We can build on what we have achieved and add to what we have experienced. We can also prune the branches—possibilities that are no longer growing.

Braden explained how everything moved in an elongated spiral taking us past the same point repeatedly. Every time we pass that same point, we have gone through a lot in between, so we have a different foundation to build on and different situations behind us; that lets us make different choices the next time around.

Earth goes through seasons, and we go through cycles in our lives. If we start noticing, we will see we sometimes feel we are repeatedly facing the same situation. The place, time, and people may have changed, but what we feel or perceive will be the same. The people may be the same, but we may feel differently about them. It depends on what we are supposed to gather from the experience.

It is somewhat like the 1993 movie *Groundhog Day*. Phil, the main character played by Bill Murray, relives the same day over and over until he learns from his mistakes and how to be a decent, selfless, considerate guy. In this movie, the people, places, and events are always the same, so Phil eventually can predict what is coming round the next bend. But even with this foreknowledge, he still struggles to get things right because of the chain of events provoked by each of his actions.

We (unfortunately?) do not know what is coming round the next bend, but we know and can start noticing more how we feel and how we perceive what happens to us. With this attention to our feelings and thoughts, we can make conscious changes to our negative scenarios, stop unwanted patterns, and instigate positive ones.

# Chapter 14

## Coincidence? Synchronicity?

The previous chapter leads me to the concept of coincidence. Looking back on people in my life as well as events and situations gives me the outline of what looks like a master plan. When you start noticing things in the past, you realize everything that has happened is connected to choices you have made.

You have gathered experience and knowledge directly from every situation you have been in. How you use that experience and knowledge is up to you, but you have more choices to make every day that will always be based on where you are right now.

Look at your choices as opportunities and conscious ways to take you where you want to go. Whether you make choices consciously or subconsciously (based on habit or not really thinking about them), things meant to happen in your life will happen.

When you use your free will to make choices that are in tune with and guided by your intuition (your heart and soul), you are bringing the whole you—body, mind, and soul—to the present rather than only your mind or heart.

You may have had the experience of hearing a song on the radio and suddenly something makes you say, "Aha!" Someone may have lent you a book, or you coincidentally come across a book, or you somehow stumble upon an article on the internet that will provide you with exactly the information you need right then. A friend might one day mention something he or she has experienced that will make you see your situation in a different light. You may even coincidentally meet someone who changes your life.

You may overhear a conversation between strangers, or your eye may wander to a certain newspaper headline that casts a new light on your thoughts. If you start noticing and being open to these things, they will seem less and less coincidental. You will start to see that these events were meant to happen and that they are just what you need to move on.

You may have the same signs or synchronicities presenting themselves to you in regular intervals, but they might escape your notice because you are not open to change or are using your energy on something that clouds your ability to look for a way out of a situation.

Try instead to be in a state of readiness to move on. Be ready for something to come along that can help you move on. Go with whatever seems too coincidental to be true.

If something feels like a sudden impulse or a flash of guidance, if it gives you a positive feeling in your mind and heart and if your action will hurt nobody—go with it.

# Chapter 15

......................................................
# Common Sense and No Sense
......................................................

*Your vision will become clear only when you look into your heart ...*
*Who looks outside, dreams. Who looks inside, awakens.*
—Carl Gustav Jung

When you use your common sense, you draw on your knowledge as well as that passed on by peers, parents, and others and you draw on real-life experiences that make you see or feel the consequences of your actions on others so you can make a sound judgment in a positive direction the next time you are faced with a similar experience.

Common sense is often defined as that which is most harmonious with the laws of nature including human life. Our common sense is based on an innate, intuitive feeling of what is right or wrong or positive or negative for others and ourselves.

Sometimes, we act contrary to common sense but see things come out better than expected; however, that is risky. When things turn out fine in such situations, we might feel a strong sense of self-confidence or pride because we were able to handle something that others would hesitate to try.

## 1. Examples of Common-Sense Scenarios

- If you run into a burning building, you might suffer injuries.
- If you eat lots of fats and sugars, you will likely put on weight.
- If you go boating in stormy weather, you could end up in a life-threatening situation.
- If you go somewhere with someone you do not know, you could end up in a bad situation.

- If you try strong drugs, chances are you will become heavily addicted and could end up losing control of your life.
- If you throw garbage on the streets and in nature, disease can spread more easily and the natural habitats of many plants and animals will become threatened.

But on a positive front,

- If you go on a holiday, you will have a valuable life experience.
- If you learn about different foods and nutrition, you will likely be concerned about living healthily.
- Breastfeeding your baby gives him or her comfort and a healthy start in life.
- Spending positive time with your children gives them a great foundation to build on.
- If you learn to listen to your body's distress signals and act preventively, you can lower your risk of illness and chronic conditions.

## 2. A Pool of Common-Sense Practices

We all build up pools of common-sense practices just by living. When we do something that has a negative impact on something or somebody, we could imagine that experience entering our collective pool of common-sense practices as an example of how to do or not do things. We could imagine the same with our actions that have a positive impact. Over time, we learn to trust our ability to make judgments.

Using our common sense will help us in many situations and can even give us a satisfying feeling of responsibility and a feeling of having followed choices we made based on our knowledge of situations and surroundings. Using our common sense can even bring about a grounded feeling and a feeling of being interactive with our surroundings as I will explain a bit later.

## 3. Barriers against the Use of Our Common Sense

Unfortunately in our busy world, people are often left with fewer invitations to use their common sense. What is of special concern is that younger people are part of this trend also and may carry it into adulthood.

Many are too busy with artificial events such as time-consuming jobs that leave them with little time to experience more-natural things. And some rules, laws, and regulations may rob people of the use of their common sense. Marketing tactics also play a big role in shaping the way we think.

Too many rules and regulations could prevent some people from thinking of the moral and humane consequences of their actions. The laws may seem like a last barrier to some people's ethical and moral boundaries.

Some people may stop doing something only if they know they could end up before a judge. They let somebody else define the consequences of their actions and thus do not take responsibility for their actions for whatever reason, and there is always a reason.

## 4. Trends vs. Use of Common Sense

We innately want to follow others and be accepted by them. Certain marketing tactics—for instance, the trend phenomenon—make use of this trait. Following a trend can sometimes be a substitute for using common sense.

People of all ages follow the latest fashion, food, diet, exercise, and vacation trends, but I have always been confused about who exactly defines these trends and how they do it. Do the trends actually come from people gradually changing their habits, or are they driven by companies that simply want to make money? Maybe certain industries detect hints of tendencies in small groups and consider them potential investment opportunities.

It seems to me to be the chicken-or-egg question. We cannot be sure if what we see is what 7 or 7,000 out of 10,000 people are doing. For all we know, only a small percentage of people may have for instance bought property in a certain area, but because it has been mentioned in the media a number of times or vigorously marketed, many more people may be tempted to buy there, and reality suddenly matches the advertisements. A little bit like self-fulfilling prophecies as discussed earlier.

Either way, the marketing or the media coverage will have an impact on many people who tend to follow trends. Sometimes, following trends might interfere with their common sense, their situations, their possibilities, and their lives.

Positive inspiration is great in various doses and from various sources, but we should not let it cloud our judgment on how we want to live. It is not common sense to buy something beyond our means and thus jeopardize our finances.

## 5. Fill Your Pool of Common Sense

People of all ages spend a lot of time on their computers, smartphones, iPods, or other electronic gadgets. Computers and the internet are great for entertainment and gathering knowledge, but sitting in front of a computer does not make you street smart or teach you how to handle real-life situations with people.

Working on your computer for a large portion of your day will not make you aware of your natural surroundings outside. Your body will not be in contact with the wind, sun, cold, warm, or rugged terrain, which are all important factors in making you feel grounded and in touch with the natural world.

Sitting at our computers can be very isolating even when we are chatting with friends. Actually being in the same room with others is far more interactive and positive because we learn from seeing each other's expressions and body language, we learn from listening to each other's tone of voice, and we can feel something special when we make others smile.

We learn to use our common sense by experiencing things physically by trial and error, by being out there, by feeling the consequences on our bodies, and by making mistakes or misjudgments only to see their negative effects and learn to alter our actions. We also learn to use our common sense by seeing the effects our positive actions have.

## 6. Know Your Habitat

Another way of building up your personal pool of common sense is by gaining geographic and biological knowledge of your surroundings. Animals examine their natural habitats. They know their areas, they know what lives there, and they know how to sustain themselves.

Animals use their instincts, which are much like common sense. Animals are instinctively aware of their surroundings and their neighbors. It is as useful and natural for us humans to want to be aware of our surroundings.

Being aware of the arrangement of the different continents and having at least a general knowledge of geography, topography, people, and societies of countries gives us a valuable feeling of living on earth and belonging here. I cannot stress the significance of this enough.

Knowing about the history of your country as well as that of other countries gives us a sense of belonging and understanding if it is presented in the right way.

I will go deeper into history in a separate chapter about the importance of fitting all the pieces of the world puzzle together.

## 7. No Sense

When we use common sense, we can see how many things make no sense. For example, it does not make sense that

- heavy industries pollute the air, land, and sea and potentially harm biological life,
- food products contain chemicals that have proven to negatively affect the physiology of humans,
- body-care products contain chemicals proven to negatively affect the physiology of humans,
- organic food is so expensive especially considering that before modern times, all food was organic and was the natural way of using our resources,
- we destroy forests and wildlife habitats around the globe creating a global imbalance in nature, and
- a great percentage of the televised news, other media, and Hollywood movies creates fear in people.

The list goes on. Easily accessible information is filled mostly with topics that create fear or at least uncomfortable feelings. But when we choose to go beyond and do our own research, look for other sources, and use our eyes, we will find many positive stories and events in the world on which we can focus and even help create.

Whatever causes negative effects on nature and people does not make sense. It can lead to feelings of hopelessness. Some people may think, *Compared to the negative effects industry has on the environment—and this is even allowed by the government—does it really matter if I throw my soft drink can out the window?*

Yes, that does hurt the environment. If we all thought about it and felt a sense of responsibility for the environment, we would have a cleaner world in no time. We can help by thinking about what we do and taking positive steps. The term *mass consciousness* comes to mind. It makes no sense that so much of the information we encounter is negative and creates fear.

People like thrills and adrenaline rushes—many people thrive on them—but we should choose such thrills, not be influenced by fear. I am talking especially about children, who are influenced negatively by an array of TV programs, computer games, and movies that show violence, fighting, disrespectful conversation, and rude behavior. It does not make sense to expose our children to such negative concepts.

Common sense tells us that children copy what they see and hear, so why not produce movies, games, and TV programs that teach them positive, constructive, and sensible behavior?

Fortunately, there are many funny and educational TV programs that teach children compassion, care, and respect for others, but so many TV programs and games are violent. It is up to us to choose what our children learn from.

Studies conducted by the Television Violence Monitoring Project show that more than half of American TV programs contained some violence and that three out of four programs contained violent scenes with no immediate punishment or condemnation of violence (www.safeyouth.org/scripts/faq/mediaviolstats.asp, 2008; now: safeyouth.gov).

The same source said this:

> There is now solid evidence to suggest a relationship between exposure to violent television and movies and aggressive behavior. Researchers have found that children are more physically and verbally aggressive immediately after watching violent television and movies. It is also clear that aggressive children and teens watch more violent television than their less aggressive peers. A few studies have found that exposure to television and movie violence in childhood is related to increased aggression years later, but further research is needed in this area.

Think about why violence in those quantities is allowed. Think about what would happen if we focused on the positive and stopped using so much energy to invoke fear.

# 8. Common Sense and the Professional Life

One day, a friend and I were writing down a list of countries we would like to live in and those countries' good and bad sides. That was supposed to help us pick our favorite country.

I thought of decorating each item I had written with either a smiley or a sad face—very simple but effective. My friend, however, did not agree with the faces and suggested, "Let's make it look professional."

In my mind, we were not creating a professional list; we were just daydreaming about other places. But I understood he just wanted to make it look smart and inspiring in his own way.

However, something clicked in me, and I built on the thought and wondered if maybe in general, the "professional" life needed more breaths of humor, humanity, and common sense.

When I think about my time in professional life, I think back on structures and routines that did not always seem logical. We need routines and structures to help things run smoothly, but it is healthy to stop and evaluate our routines to see if we are still following the best practices we can.

Some people stuck in their habits wake up and realize how much time and energy they could have saved if they had only adjusted some of their work practices. Thankfully, many companies and businesses have reevaluated their practices because of fierce competition. Fierce competition can make the work environment more stressful, but that is another matter.

In my work in the environmental sector many years ago, I saw how talks and negotiations were often impaired because people did not have a mandate to wholly express the opinions of the people from their areas or regions. At unofficial dinners and meetings, many opinions were expressed freely and agreed upon across the table, and it was easy to see that achieved political agreements that did not always reflect common sense.

Think about how things could be more enjoyable for many if humor, common sense, and in many cases more respect for others were part of the daily work routine at all levels.

Ironically, we humans are generally very resilient and adaptable. No matter how harsh the conditions may be, there will always be someone who can make light of a situation. So even if we are working under negative conditions, something or someone is bound to shine some light on our daily lives.

On the other hand, many managers could learn more about being inspirations to their staffs and not let their personal shortcomings overshadow the way they treat their employees.

Many still believe in ruling by the rod rather than by the heart. In the end, it is more fulfilling to be a knowledgeable manager with a heart than a manager everybody fears. Managers with hearts will be rewarded with respect and loyalty from their employees. Some managers will take advantage of the kindness offered and will not return it, but they have their issues to deal with—jealousy, bitterness, anger, or fear.

The corporate world has become increasingly harsh and hardcore over the last decade. People in many professions and jobs feel they never have a weekend without a work-related phone call or email. They feel they must be on standby even when they are on vacation. All this stems from the fear of being pushed out and replaced by others who are willing to or feel they have no choice but to give up a large part of their spare time. The pressure in many lines of work has become so great that mainly only young people can survive with their health intact.

Most people's lives naturally progress toward marriage, children, and family time, so it would make sense to make sure they have time to enjoy those stages of life.

We all naturally progress toward old age and retirement, and that stage ought to be honored and enjoyed.

# Chapter 16

........................................................................

# Power of the Mind

........................................................................

*Allow yourself to have a positive life.*
—Marianne Johansen

*All that we are is the result of what we have thought.*
—Buddha

Our mind is a powerful tool. The idea that our thoughts create our reality is becoming more widely accepted. Many are beginning to realize the huge potential we all have to create positive changes for others and ourselves.

Our brain—the mind's tool—can help us deal with everyday issues and insignificant information. It can also help us look at the world more broadly and become open to new ideas and theories. Our minds also help us gather and formulate the information we receive from our hearts.

## 1. All Is in Us

Many believe that we possess all abilities and that it is only a question of us using our minds and bodies to nurture and practice them.

Great personalities such as Louise L. Hay, Dr. Wayne W. Dyer, Deepak Chopra, Neale Donald Walsch, Oprah Winfrey, and Doreen Virtue offer powerful tools and ideas to help our minds as well as our spirits to work in our favor. They and many more inspire millions to learn how to harness the power of their minds to steer their lives in positive directions.

To an increasing number of people all over the world, living positive lives means making things more positive not only for themselves but also for others.

Living conscious, positive lives requires being aware of our actions, thoughts, and feelings and actively changing unwanted and negative patterns

135

in ourselves. Affirmations are among the many powerful ways to achieve that. (More about affirmations later in the book.)

Use your mind for something positive. With practice, patience, determination, and humility, you can achieve your goal.

## 2. That Powerful Mind

By consciously unleashing the power of your mind, you are (allegedly) able to do just about anything. Below a few examples of how the power of the mind can challenge the laws of physics.

- An Indian yogi was able to consciously slow his heart rate.
- A Tibetan monk was actually levitating.
- The popular fire walk requires people to spend a day or two preparing mentally for the physical challenge of walking on hot coals.
- We can raise the temperature of cold hands or feet just by use of visualization or affirmations. Cold hands or feet often indicate stress, so by making our hands or feet warmer by using the power of our minds, we can actually reduce the physiological and emotional effects of stress.

## 3. Your Contribution

If thought equals creation, all seven billion of us on this planet are creating many things and events all the time!

Imagine we are all part of creating everything that occurs on this planet, and think about how you are contributing to it. If you subscribe to the idea that thoughts manifest into physical reality, you are not far from believing you can change reality with your thoughts. Perhaps not instantly as things are not yet always that fast here on earth, but with perseverance and focus, it is possible that you can change your reality.

Imagine a lovely green meadow with a stream running through it. You are lying on the warm ground amid all the grass. Above you is a blue sky with a few white clouds, and the sun is warming your face and body. You hear birds singing and see butterflies fluttering about.

Were you able to concentrate on the image, or were you interrupted by other thoughts? How many negative thoughts about your life entered your mind as you were trying to hold onto that image?

Now, imagine that the world around us was not as full of negative things as it is. Imagine how much easier it would then be for us to hold onto positive thoughts. Intend whatever you want.

For positive creation to emanate from us, we need to keep making room for calmness and positive thoughts. Someone might argue that many creative geniuses did not have calm minds, that they often had extremely active minds that would interfere with their skills in other areas such as social skills or mathematical skills. Some also suffered from insomnia. But often, creativity would find its way into their conscious minds when they were walking, showering, enjoying nature, and at other times.

We are more aware of the importance of calming our minds so we can function on several levels at the same time. Meditation for example is an excellent way to quiet our minds and access creativity and wisdom.

I came across an interesting claim about how we can change what we want to change.

> Bad moles, indentations, piercing, scars marked, lines, and even the shape of your face can change over time, meaning your fate can alter through the years. You can utilize your Own Power, the Earth Power, to neutralize the Heaven Power. Ultimately, when you change your heart, you will change your face; when you change your face, you can change your fate. (chinesefacereading.blogspot.com)

I have not yet gone deeper into the theories behind the above statement, but I am intrigued by it and mention it here to present another aspect of our physical presence on earth.

# Chapter 17

······································································

# Your Relationship with Others

······································································

*Goodness speaks in a whisper—evil shouts.*
—Tibetan saying

*Do good and don't worry to whom.*
—Mexican saying

## 1. When We Click or Do Not Click with Others

It is okay to be critical about choosing friends. If a relationship with someone seems to be hard work, sacrifice, and compromise and does not fill you with positivity, that person is probably not the right person for you to be around.

Similarly, if social events with certain people leave you feeling empty or drained, it is time to seek different social events with different people.

Joy and love are at your core, and if you feel that others are putting a lid on that, they could be in your life to show you what you do not want. That can help you define what you do want.

Do not be ashamed to admit it to yourself if people around you do not give you positive feelings. There can be many reasons for feeling like that, but if you are true to yourself and act on your gut instinct, you will feel much better and find friends who will leave you feeling positive and fulfilled and vice versa.

When you click with people, it will be a positive exchange and you will feel energetic after spending time with them. They will feel the same, and you will both find you can help each other through difficulties and negative feelings.

Have you noticed that at times when you introduce a friend to another friend, the two often do not get along? You may wonder why as they are both friends of yours.

Think of it like this. There are so many aspects and sides to each human being, and you and your friends bring out or see some things in each other that make you click and like each other. Your friends whom you introducing to each other may mirror other aspects in each other, but these may be aspects that you do not notice because they are not in you. It could be that your two friends mirror aspects in each other they are not ready or willing to deal with at the moment, so they will clash because they do not like seeing that side of themselves mirrored in the other.

We also find aspects about our friends that we do not like, but they probably have many aspects we do like, and they are why we regard them as friends.

Not clicking with someone often happens on a subconscious level. You and that person just feel a dislike of or an indifference to the other. We cannot always pinpoint what makes us feel uncomfortable about that person. We can remove ourselves from the situation or the persons, or we can deal with whatever has been triggered in us. We can consider it a challenge and work on it.

Sometimes, a side of us is actually blocking our growth in an area. Other times, the lesson could be that we have to make our boundaries clear to others by for instance just walking away.

If we are feeling rejected by someone for reasons we cannot see, it could be a lesson for us to find approval from within, in which case we would not be in a rejection-or-approval scenario.

Our lessons are many, and if we choose, we can use them as ways of finding our core of joy and love and growing beyond our current blockages.

When we are in tune with ourselves, we will know what to do.

## 2. Protecting Ourselves from Others' Dramas

Think about how you felt when someone said something bad about you behind your back. Think about when you have done that. Think about why you said it and how you felt after saying it. What did it give you? Was it worth it? Did you think about it and maybe even regret it? Did you find that you were hurt and possibly angered by it? Do you feel that was time and energy well spent?

Some people thrive on creating drama and observing from a distance or through gossip how others handle it. They may even add fuel to the fire by creating new stories and thus more drama. Sometimes, it may take a while to realize who those people are. They may be in your circle or even friends of friends.

Nevertheless, you can learn not to get entangled in intrigues. You can learn to become unconcerned and choose to imagine you are sending love to that person and protection to yourself.

If you ignore such people's behavior, their interest in you will eventually fade, and as you imagine sending out healing to the situation and to that person, the situations will eventually melt away because you chose not to get involved in their games.

This is not the same as avoiding conflict or karma because you are actually choosing to actively heal the situation or the dislike from the other person with love. The more you try this, the more you will see that it works and that you can positively influence others at least on the level they are subconsciously letting it work!

We should always be aware of our actions, thoughts, and feelings. We may not always be aware of what causes our reactions to others, but we may sometimes feel triggered by certain people or situations and say something we would not normally have said had we been calm and harmonious. But we can certainly work toward achieving that state.

I am certain that many times in your life, you have been triggered by something someone said or did and you snapped, erupted like a volcano, yelled, cried, or had other similar outbursts. These are just some of the reactions we may have when we feel trapped like a mouse in a corner. Whatever reaction comes out is coming from deep within us, and it may even be related to a past event. But with awareness, we can learn to identify it and to focus on more-positive ways to express feelings of hurt, shame, guilt, pressure, and injustice.

Putting words to what happens can help us become aware and think about our actions the next time we sense the same feeling bubbling up inside us. We can see anger as a poison for a visual aid. We can also ask our angels, guides, or God to help us release our painful memories or situations so we can feel unburdened by them.

Many label or judge others by external values such as gender, race, social status, and even gossip. The best way to learn about others is by considering their internal values—their mind-sets, attitudes, actions, and personal histories.

There are compassionate, empathetic, and generous people as well as negative, selfish people on all levels of society and of different genders and races. Many factors play roles in the lives of human beings including culture, background, and social circumstances.

What also matters is the degree to which people use their inner strength and ability to find harmony. Imagine that we all come here with a core filled with positive qualities. Imagine that we all have our share of difficult circumstances and issues we have to work on to get us wherever we want to go.

Why do we have a difficult time learning to master positive traits such as forgiveness, patience, unselfishness, tolerance, generosity, surrendering to the flow of life—traits that come from trust and from the heart? Is it because our egos, the home of our selfish traits, are that powerful? Are we here to learn how to let our egos work in unison with our hearts? To learn to surrender ourselves to our hearts? To find the way to our hearts and use our minds and bodies to manifest what is in our hearts?

I very much believe that.

## 3. We Walk Different Paths ...

Some people seem to have it all together even at an early age. We meet these people in school, at work, and at social events. They always seem to be ahead of others. They wear nice clothes and have cool friends.

They seem to end up with the right partners and the right jobs. They may be financially on top and free to do as they please long before others have figured out what they want to do with their lives.

Many of us know such people, and we could end up feeling jealous, spiteful, and bitter. We might ask ourselves, *Why couldn't I be like that?* and focus on our negatives. We can easily fall into that trap when we compare different life circumstances, paths, and uses of personal capabilities.

If you find yourself feeling jealous or down because of how other people live, realize that they do not lead perfect lives; they too have struggles and challenges because everybody does. Some people have more than others do in some respects, but they will have challenges in other areas.

We all have negative and positive experiences that match where we are on our soul journeys. If we looked closely at those we are jealous of, we would see their internal turmoil. Maybe they are not happy inside. Maybe they wanted something different. Maybe they feel they did not choose their paths.

When you do not know somebody, you cannot tell if his or her life is better than yours in comparison to your desires. Maybe wearing nice clothes and having all the luxuries are the cause of their problems. It is easier and more constructive to focus on defining your values and desires that come from a balanced inner self, a calm mind, and an open heart. Realize that with self-awareness, you too can have what you want right where you are.

We all have challenges. We all have to work for something. We all go down different routes in life. If we feel down about how well we think other people's lives are, we are not focusing on and living our own lives.

What do you want? Whom do you want to be with? Where do you want to live? What are you doing with your life? What would you like to surround yourself with? Define these things. Dare to ask yourself these questions to help you move on; look objectively at what you need to conquer externally and internally to get where and what you want. Learn about yourself by looking at the people you surround yourself with.

## 4. ... but We Are All Connected

Earlier in the book was an illustration of the Mandelbrot fractal. The concept behind it is that whether you zoom in or out, the image is made up of the same components. You will see how the small parts are replicas of the bigger version of the image, much like a hologram, where each little piece of the hologram contains an image of the complete subject. If you are not familiar with the concept of the Mandelbrot fractal, looking at the picture may help you understand what I convey next.

Imagine we are all part of each other and not separate from earth or the universe. We have emerged from somewhere in the universe, are interconnected, and are all part of something bigger.

If you do not believe this, try at least to entertain the thought that there are no coincidences. That everything happens for a reason. That our fates and destinies are intertwined at some level. That synchronicities—not coincidences—are signs that let us know we are in tune with our path.

We are all at the same place at the same time in the universe. The people who surround us are connected to us but at different levels; some are physically near while others are far away.

We are emotionally close to some people and not to others. Some people remain acquaintances we may or may not become close to. We encounter others just briefly, but we may leave a big impact on them and them on us.

You and I are intertwined but at a distant level. We do not know each other, but we may still have an impact on one another. My book may stir something in you; you may contact me and write something that will have an impact on me and so forth.

We all come from the same source, the universe. Just as the planets are part of a solar system, our solar system is one of many in our galaxy, and our galaxy is one of many in the universe, so we are all part of something bigger than us.

Our natural world on this planet was formed from materials from the universe, so how can we not see ourselves as part of it or nature? That leads me to one of my favorite proverbs: "The more we are separated from nature, the unhappier we get."

I would even say we become more unhappy if we are separated from nature because we get confused regarding our roles and places here. So a connection with nature is of utmost importance for us to feel grounded and connected to the universe, galaxy, solar system, and earth.

## 5. We Are Influenced by Others

When we were children, we were very alert to everything and everyone around us. We were like magnets that attracted and digested information about our world and the people close to us. We did not think so much about what and whom we attracted; we were just in our natural state with all the hardware and software we came here with.

When we were teenagers and young adults, the circle of people who influenced us expanded. It included people we had just heard about through the media in addition to our friends and families.

Many teenagers want to look and live like the celebrities they see on TV and in magazines and movies. They see celebrities in chic clothes trotting the globe and indulging in luxuries and parties while looking happy and carefree.

Teenagers also read about how some of their role models are substance abusers who endanger their and others' lives through their thoughtless behavior. Some will argue that it is all part of being young. But we all choose our paths based on what we let influence us. That is why we—especially children and teens—need loving guidance to help us see our value and walk positive paths.

Millions of teenagers around the world live in war zones, impoverished countries, or religious states that do not allow certain media. Though their circumstances and influences differ greatly from those who live in Western[1]* countries, these teenagers will have the same feelings, dreams, and aspirations teenagers everywhere have. However, they may have to find alternative ways of channeling what goes on inside them.

The key is to find your inner self and be at peace with it. This is what most of us spend our lives aiming at, and this is what can be especially difficult when we are teenagers and young adults.

No matter how teenagers go through these often difficult years, having supportive parents or teachers around them can be very crucial for them.

As we get older, most of us have an idea of who we are, what we want, what our strengths are, and so on. This inner knowledge comes from the numerous positive and negative experiences we encounter.

Some people are very good at learning from their experiences and influences and keep improving their lives. Others may need several attempts to get over their hurdles that tend to come in different disguises even if the theme is the same.

As adults, we are influenced by others, but as we mature and become more in tune with ourselves, we tend to stand our ground better, be less sensitive about what others think, and resist temptations that go against our deeper values, things that can be hard to do when we are younger.

We are of course also influenced by ourselves, and as this book suggests, we can change our lives. If we start living more consciously and intuitively, we can significantly improve and heal our negative traits, even those that are deeply ingrained in us.

---

[1] *Western* is a term I find inappropriate and imprecise as it and *globalization* seem to be more illustrations of a mentality and social status rather than a geographical location.

## 6. Other People as Mirrors

We observe others' character traits and consciously or subconsciously weigh these traits against ours to define ourselves. Until we rest comfortably in our worlds and find internal peace and approval, we tend to compare ourselves with others. Do we feel as good as they do? Do we feel better or worse than they are?

When we are aware of ourselves and become interested in personal growth, we look at others as mirrors of ourselves. We know that what we see in others reflects what is in us. So with that and being honest with ourselves, we can learn a great deal about ourselves via those around us—friends, family, and acquaintances.

When we see a negative in others, we may sense a nudge inside that tells us we have that same negative trait, but we can work on that and heal it.

If you would like to explore yourself and do some work on a personal level, define the feelings a person wakes in you and the circumstances that triggered those feelings. Observing yourself in a nonjudgmental manner can help you pinpoint where that negative trait comes from and work toward healing it and letting it go.

We all possess negative traits, but sometimes, they are not as deep seated as we think. Once we acknowledge our negative behavioral or thinking patterns, we can start releasing them.

## 7. We Influence Others

Most of us have a feeling or urge to positively influence others. We may take care of somebody because we feel we can. We may want to impress others so they will like us. We may be nice to somebody so a positive exchange of energies take place or just because we want to.

We may also want to hurt others because we think they deserve it or because we feel insecure and want to take that out on others. We may want to control somebody to fulfill our egos' lust for power.

Whether your interactions with others come from your ego or your heart matters. You can discern the difference when you listen to your feelings, thoughts, and inner voice. The soul speaks through your heart and gives birth to peaceful and loving thoughts.

My desire to write this book had its roots in my wish to influence and help others—you, dear reader—in positive ways so you will find ways to bring light to your life and radiate it to others.

Whatever we do to others good or bad has its roots in ourselves. Our conscious and subconscious actions are rooted in our inner core. The good we do can be a reflection of balanced virtue in us when we do it from our hearts.

On the other hand, when something in us needs healing, chances are that some of our actions or behavior toward others could be in need of some improvement as well. We all still have a lot to work on. But with perseverance and an interest in improving ourselves, we can make that happen.

Changing our way of thinking, gaining a bigger perspective, balancing our bodies, and opening up to our intuition and inner and outer guidance are ways to overcome our negative traits.

## 8. More on the People in Our Lives

Some people want to be friends with everybody and are frustrated if they feel some people do not like them. It may leave them feeling ashamed, less confident, angry, or even spiteful.

I have long ago come up with what I have noticed are four categories of people in our lives.

1. people with whom we feel an instant bond that is significant to us and them and makes us want to spend time with them
2. people we do not take to at first but who over time grow on us as we meet them at class, at work, or when exercising for instance
3. people we are at first attracted to but that feeling fades because we turn out to be too different
4. people we do not want to be around because we clash or it does not feel right no matter how many times we encounter one another

This last category has two subcategories in my mind—those who are in your perimeter but have not had any impact (yet) on you, and those who represent something in you that you are not willing to face and needs healing.

You may find it hard to acknowledge category three or four if you feel you are showing kindness to everybody so you think everybody ought to like you, but that is not always so.

This does not mean you are not a kind person or your actions are not kind; it could mean that some people are just not ready for you and your actions. They may in fact be jealous of you, or they may view the world differently and have different values and standards.

Keep doing the kind and friendly things you do, and appreciate the friends and acquaintances you have. No one is everyone's friend.

## 9. Competitiveness

Competition fills a need of the ego. When we compete and win, we get an instant surge of satisfaction; we feel good about ourselves and our achievement. I think we momentarily get a kick out of feeling better than others and being in a sense on top of the world.

While winners have great experiences and positive feelings, they may not think about how the losers feel. The winners shake the others' hands, pat them on the shoulders, and may briefly empathize with their disappointment, but they then go back to feeling elated.

Our innate need for accomplishment and success can push us in a desired direction. It can have a positive impact on us and give us a boost. Then, however, we may be talking about our life spark, our drive, which I feel is not the same as the competitive fire in our egos.

Competition has become somewhat glorified in the name of money. The amount of money involved in sports (tennis, golf, football, baseball, etc.) and activities such as dancing and singing is astounding and in my opinion not common sense. Performance-enhancing drugs have entered the scene, but why is there such a need?

Though the combination of money and sports has good and bad aspects, sports and games are here to stay because of our natural desire to push ourselves beyond our physical boundaries and because most of us are curious about how far we can go.

However, I think that as people gravitate toward less ego and more heart, competitiveness driven by the ego and resulting in big money or only personal gain will either evaporate or at least take on a different form.

# 10. Marking Our Territory against Aggressors: Boundaries between Lands

In the animal world, alpha males mark the boundaries of their territories to inform trespassers of dangerous consequences if they try to take over the area and the females.

Despite the markings, there will always be some males who will invade the territory to gain control and power. An intruder is sure to get into a fight with the current alpha male. If he fails, he will have to search for another territory to invade.

In the human world, the alpha people—the rulers—mark their territories with borders and through agreements and treaties with rulers of other countries. They also mark their territories by having armies ready to crush intruders. Whoever has the strongest army or bargaining point gets what he wants.

But in spite of treaties and agreements, some countries will have less and want more. Rulers want land for many reasons.

- to grow crops
- to access the sea for fishing, transport, and trade
- to develop resources such as minerals, gems, and oil
- to gain strategic advantages
- to access spiritual and energetic values

Generally, those at the top want whatever makes them rich and powerful and lets them live comfortably. But those wants can have a negative impact on many other people.

## Boundaries between People

Taking relationships on a grander scale, for instance those between rulers of countries and their peoples, we sometimes find aggressors who are not out to invade a land but to gain control by invading the thoughts, beliefs, values, and boundaries of others.

It is important that we mark our territories against these people and let them know when they are invading them.

When people feel others are walking all over them, invading their space, or trying to control them, they may respond in assertive or aggressive ways. Others seem to capitulate; they bow their heads and take the blows and sometimes even feel ashamed or at fault. But we do not have to get aggressive or feel at fault.

This is easier said than done because we often react from deep within as we do when hurtful experiences from our past are triggered. Our behavior is deeply seated in us, but we can change things around by becoming aware of our patterns and interactions.

We can set up loving boundaries to show others how far they can go, but we must first learn how we feel when others go too far so we will know when a boundary is being crossed and let others know where our boundaries are.

Below are a few suggestions on affirmations to actively change a negative pattern in your relationships with others. Recite these mantras when an undermining situation arises.

- I will let people know in a friendly way what I like and dislike.
- I will remember that people do not know how I feel unless I tell them.
- I will not let anyone make me do things that make me feel uncomfortable.

As with any type of healing, it may get worse before it gets better in the sense that when you start reprogramming your behavior and responses, you may trigger new or suppressed feelings you will then have to deal with.

Nevertheless, look at whatever comes up as a positive thing; see it as something you have released from within that is bubbling to the surface where it may boil for a while. If you let it, it will evaporate like steam. Be grateful that it has been released and that it left a space in you that is light instead of dark. Sometimes, visualizing situations like this can help negative feelings and blockages disappear and heal.

Maybe like me, you often need time to reflect on a certain situation and digest the facts to find out what is going on in you so you can take a healing approach to the situation. Giving yourself space so you can respond in a positive manner rather than resorting to spiteful and angry behavior is a better solution. Resorting to retaliatory behavior comes instinctively, which is why it is necessary to become aware of your reaction so you can change the underlying cause or emotional dilemma.

If you argue with others whom you feel keep invading your boundaries, tell them you need to discuss the matter later if that is an option. That will give you time to regain balance before you talk about the matter again.

If the situation has more of an urgent or destructive tone, just walk away—remove yourself from the dispute. It is best to avoid situations that could spiral out of control due to flaring tempers. Then, take time to think about what you can do to heal the situation and yourself.

We are bound to encounter the same types of situations until we have learned to handle them in a positive way. Again, the movie *Groundhog Day* has a lot of truth in it; Bill Murray learned over time to become a better man and handle situations in a positive way.

In his book *Fractal Time*, Gregg Braden wrote about how all events and situations move forward in spirals and take us back to the same type of event only at different points in time.

If we learn to define our boundaries and not be afraid to stick to them when pushed by others, we will eventually not encounter that particular type of situation anymore. Our internal dilemma will be healed; we will have learned that lesson, and the need for similar situations to arise will simply vanish. That is how the universe works.

People who instigate trouble usually do so because they carry around hurt, embarrassment, despair, anger, shamefulness, guilt, or other emotional imbalances and blockages within.

You might realize this about yourself the next time you find yourself showering somebody with negative words or abuse. Think about what triggered that behavior in you and how it makes you feel. Is your verbal aggression a sign of desperation because you do not know how else to handle it?

How about catching yourself just before you start shouting at someone and thinking of ways to expend your energy positively?

## 11. Communication Is Key

Throughout life, we will encounter numerous difficult situations when dealing with others be they our parents, siblings, spouses, friends, and so many others.

When we are with certain people, we have a great time; we laugh, we support each other, and our conversation flows. We leave each other feeling recharged, and we want to meet them again.

But other people may leave us feeling dominated and controlled, and others may seem to trigger a dominating side in us. Certain people may bring out jealousy in us or make us feel manipulated; somebody may hurt our feelings, or someone may hurt us physically.

## When We Have Feelings We Find Difficult to Meet in Others

Be glad when you notice a negative feeling or reaction somebody brings out in you; that means you are becoming aware of what you need to heal in yourself. A negative feeling or reaction is triggered in you because of something that has happened earlier. Sense what that is, or just define the feeling it brings out and then "wash away the layers" (see chapter 10 "Your Thoughts and Feelings", section 2, Healing Visualization I).

Have you ever recalled a situation with a certain person and suddenly you feel uneasy, angry, and ashamed? The feeling just surfaces and makes you remember a negative experience with this person. You may even start to imagine future situations with this person and feel uneasy, angry, and so on.

I can relate. One morning many years ago, my train of thought took me through different past events, and I was suddenly feeling angry and sad about a certain person. I acknowledged the feelings but did not know how to deal with the anger and sadness or stop those feelings from reoccurring. The specific issue had been going on for years with the same person.

I mentioned it to my husband, and we discussed what might be the causes and solutions to this very uncomfortable issue. I pinpointed the main feeling or the underlying feeling as disapproval or judgment of me; I had a very strong sense of the person disapproving of me and my actions.

As my husband and I were talking, something he said suddenly made me realize that I showed my disapproval of people who acted in ways that went against my values or beliefs. If I was in the company of someone I did not enjoy being with for whatever reason, I was unable to hide my dislike very well. My face and body language would reveal my feelings, and I would realize the other person was picking up what I was sending out. That other person most probably felt my disapproval and left feeling angry, sad, or ashamed just as I did.

It became clear that since I was showing my judgment or disapproval of others, which left them with a negative feeling, I was inviting those same feelings into my sphere (see illustration).

Since then, I have been very aware of my reactions to people whose behavior or actions I do not sympathize with. I try not to judge or disapprove of them; instead, I remember they have reasons for their behavior as we all do for our behavior.

You will attract into your life whatever thoughts and feelings you focus on.

What are you attracting?

What can we do to change the cycle of inviting negative feelings and reactions into our lives? First, we have to define the underlying feeling. In my case above, I found out that my anger and sadness came from a feeling of disapproval.

Second, we must eliminate the underlying feeling. In my case, I had to remove disapproval from my sphere; I had to stop leaving an open invitation for it to enter my life by not showing my disapproval of others. This is my issue and something I have to deal with. I became aware of that, so then I could change it. I cannot easily or at all change the people who show me disapproval, but I can change what is in me.

When I now am in the company of people I dislike, I do not stop disliking them; instead, I work on not showing them my dislike because that provokes a bad feeling in the other person, and there is no need to make anyone feel bad.

My task with this issue is to remember that all others act as they do for a reason, so instead of showing dislike, I radiate neutral and nonjudgmental behavior if not kindness and healing!

When I stop sending out disapproval and making others feel angry, sad, or ashamed, I no longer have disapproval in my sphere and thus no longer attract it.

The outcome may not show immediately, but give it time to manifest. In the meantime, stick to your new resolution; you will see results.

> *Love someone the most when they least deserve it,*
> *because that is when they need it the most.*
> —Unknown

## 12. When a Relationship Is Not Working

You could be in a relationship with someone—your spouse, a friend, or a relative—that is just not working. You may have tried to resolve some issues with your best intentions, but still, you seem to move in different directions.

We all experience difficult relationships, and we should work them out the best we can, but we should not stay in them to the point that it drains our energy and leaves us feeling depleted. If that is the case, we need to remove ourselves from the scene for some breathing space and look at it from a distance.

Over time, we may be able to return and solve the difficult issues, or maybe we realize that a break is what was needed to let something more positive into our lives.

Breaking off a relationship that is not working may serve both parties better particularly when children are involved. You cannot stay in a relationship only for the sake of the children; they are very much attuned to moods and atmospheres around them. Witnessing a withered relationship could give them a distorted idea of what a loving relationship ought to be.

Even if you do part ways, you may encounter the same kind of issues with the same person or with another. But the next time around, you may more easily identify whether you are inviting something into your life.

Notice how people and situations make you feel and react. Observe how you make others feel. Look at these situations and issues as opportunities for you to work on yourself. Do not be discouraged when there is something about you that needs work! We all have something we need to work on.

We choose to be with someone when it feels right. The path that our choices take us down may not feel right in six months, two years, or even sixteen years, but we can make a new choice that will take us in the direction we feel is right at that time.

Life involves making choices, growing, healing, using our sense of humor, learning, and expanding our horizons.

Think about criticism from others, and be honest with yourself. Can you make a change in your behavior that would help heal you and your relationships? Look at it from others' perspectives too.

## 13. Jealousy

Some people may feel that others deserve what they have, and some people may feel that others do not deserve what they have. Have you ever found yourself feeling bitter or resentful toward someone for having something good?

You may want something that somebody else has so badly that it creates negative vibes in you. But jealousy does not get you what you want; it may only blind you and destroy your ability to work toward creating something positive in your life.

You may become aware of your feelings of jealousy, and when you do, you can track down the origin of the feeling and the place in you to heal it. Find where the feeling is in you and how it makes you feel physically. Do any thoughts come up that are clues why you feel jealous of others?

Everyone is on a different path. The person you are jealous of has walked a path that has led him or her to a certain place in life. He or she has obtained that certain something you want. However, that does not mean that person has everything else you want as well. He or she may not be entirely happy with life. And you might in fact have something that he or she wants, or you might have something somebody else would love to have. However, whatever you want but do not have is just not right for you at this moment; otherwise, you would have already obtained it.

The path you are on has not led you to it yet. The path you have taken so far has led you to where you are. If you want something else, strive for it, but feeling bitter about what others have will not give you what you want. Think of it like that and consciously define what you need to do to get where you really want to go and achieve.

You can change your life. You can work with what you have; you can gather all your positive abilities and work positively to achieve whatever you desire. When you look at it consciously like that, you will have a good chance to help yourself heal whatever negative feelings you hold toward other people's achievements.

# 14. Forgiveness

Being able to forgive others is important, but how exactly do you forgive? What do you do to forgive those who have made you feel hurt, ashamed, or angry? Do you just forgive them in your mind? Do you have to do or say something to them? And how do you know when you have been healed of your feelings of mistreatment? How do you know you have let go of your anger or desire for revenge?[2]*

It is often a case of trial and error. We may not always know ourselves as well as we think. We may be surprised when we realize we are still feeling angry, hurt, worthless, or ashamed about something somebody did to us. We may find that we still cannot look a certain person in the eye and be calm.

I believe that if we still hold these feelings, we have not yet healed and need to try again. Forgiveness is connected to a place in us where we keep our emotions. If someone has caused us hurt, shame, pain, or other negative feelings, those negative feelings are still there in need of healing and release.

Some may consider revenge the only way to get over what others have done to them, but revenge does not heal feelings; it only creates more negative feelings.

Instead, focus on healing your hurt, shame, or pain. Imagine sitting next to yourself and seeing yourself; how would want to protect and care for yourself? Think of yourself as valuable and important; think of how you want to release all your hurt and angry feelings and how you can make yourself feel better.

Looking at ourselves in this manner does not make us a selfish; sometimes, it is helpful to view ourselves from the outside, see our mistakes and dark sides, and decide we want to take care of this person—ourselves. Visualizations like these can be a big help when we want to heal our layers of emotions and feelings.

When you actually want to take care of yourself and your feelings, you are on the way to healing yourself, and the more you heal yourself, the better you become at dealing with different situations.

---

2  *I am not talking about major criminal incidents; they would need a more elaborate discussion than what I offer here.

# 15. Other Practical and Spiritual Ways to Forgive

If you are into meditation, you can meditate on the situation by asking your angels or God to release your negative feelings about the person or situation. You can also visualize healing light (white, violet, green, gold, silver, pink) surrounding your feelings, yourself, and even the other person involved.

Some people might prefer to come face to face with their opponents. This is of course a great solution if the purpose is to heal the situation and not just get even. The success of this solution depends on if the other person also wishes to reach an amicable solution.

You cannot force something on others; you can do things only in a positive way. If the others fail to respond positively, you will know that at least you tried; it is then out of your hands and up to those people to heal whatever they need to heal.

Look at it this way—the person who caused your negative feelings has done you a favor though it may not seem that way. It has given you a chance to heal something in you. Maybe you needed to learn a lesson about forgiveness or how to look inside yourself. Maybe you have learned how you influence others. The fact that the feeling was awakened in you means you can accept and heal the feeling and then release it. This is personal growth that helps you move on and face the world, yourself, and the other person again with a new perspective.

We all regularly experience minor incidents when we can practice forgiveness. I can get irritated at other drivers, but I have come to realize I am being tested in such situations.

I melt away my irritation and impatience by sending a wave of understanding to other drivers. They probably have reasons for driving the way they do. When think about those possible reasons, my irritation disappears. In some cases, other drivers are unaware of the reactions they have caused in me, so it is very clear that I am the one who has to deal with it.

In other minor cases when someone is blatantly annoying us, we should also send out forgiveness or neutralization, understanding, and acceptance of where they are at that moment. Then we will be free to walk away.

If we have responded to a trigger in an angry or insulting way, we should apologize whether at that moment or later. We can sometimes find it easier to apologize by doing something generous before saying, "I'm sorry that I ..."

The more we practice forgiveness, the more natural it will become to apologize for our thoughtless or rude behavior.

## 16. Still Feeling Negative?

One way to check whether you have cleared your resentment, anger, or bitterness toward another is to think about how you feel when you think of that person. How do you feel when you see that person? How do you feel when you imagine meeting that person unexpectedly?

If you still get an uneasy feeling when thinking about this person, try again to focus on letting your negative feelings toward the person go. Imagine the feelings leaving your body, going up in the air, melting away in the sun, or being blown away by the wind or washed away by rain—whatever image works for you. Such visualization can give great results!

Eventually, you may get back on good terms with that person, talk about what happened, and possibly resume that friendship. You may also just peacefully keep going your separate ways, and so be it. Your karmic interaction has ended.

## 17. Manipulation

Manipulation is a widespread phenomenon that can be a very strong trait in humans. Some people use manipulation consciously to gain something, while others may not be aware that they manipulate others and have a negative impact on them.

Manipulation is closely linked to marking our territory as I described in an earlier chapter. It is up to us to set our boundaries in a neutral or friendly way, and it is up to us to enforce our boundaries and not let anyone manipulate them.

The concept of manipulation also ties in with common sense as I discussed in a previous chapter. If something feels wrong, listen to your intuition, trust your gut feeling or your experience, and walk away from the situation.

Manipulation can be overt or covert, direct or subtle. It can be done instantly or over a longer time. You may not always realize you are being manipulated, but again, if you feel uneasy or uncomfortable about someone's agenda, think before you agree to go along with it.

We should teach our children to build up trust in their intuition. That will increase their self-confidence and teach them to trust their positive behaviors and actions. This will give them the upper hand with bullies or anyone trying to convince them to do something they know deep down is not right.

## 18. Influence—How You See Others and How People Can Help Each Other

Your experiences influence who you are and how you react to different situations and people. Think about whom you influence and how you do that. Think how much more positive your influence could be if it came from an even more balanced you mentally, emotionally, and spiritually.

## 19. Family Ties and Influences

Many people feel they are with the right immediate family. They feel they fit in, and there is a certain rapport between the members of the family.

Many others find that they have chosen a path that is completely different from those the other members of their close families are on. They may feel they fit in better with friends' families for example. You may wonder why that is.

We need to learn certain lessons from our immediate families. Because we spend so much time with those people, we are very much influenced by them during our young years just as our parents were influenced by their families when they were young.

You may want to delve deeper into those speculations and think about the interpersonal exchange happening in your family and how it has influenced you negatively and positively. You will find motives for much of your behavior there and can then work on those patterns in you that you do not approve of.

You may find that your present position is largely influenced by the atmosphere in your family, but of course, your present situation is also largely influenced by your choices.

Maybe the positive influence of your family has encouraged you to go in your desired direction. Or maybe you have succeeded in breaking away from what you may have seen as negative influences and have found your own niche.

Negative influences happen in every family, but at times, things that seemed negative may turn out to work in your favor. We often see how certain experiences we thought were negative at the time actually made us stronger. What may have seemed as tough parts of our early years have maybe helped us deal constructively in other situations later on, and this earlier adversity will then appear as what we needed to learn and move in a different direction. Looking at things in a broader perspective can often inspire us to deal with our situations.

Think about how the people in your life who had a negative impact on you did not know how to handle their negative circumstances. This may help you forgive them and allow you to move beyond their influence.

The more we help ourselves, the more we can help others. When we fill ourselves with positive energy, it will flow into our surroundings.

## Stereotypes

The way we interact with some people is influenced largely by how we view them, and that is often based on which group they belong to. Some of the major groups on which we base our often biased observations are nationality, religion, and skin color but also profession. We should remember that all groups give only a general picture of some of the common traits shared by those in that group; no group can reflect all traits and characteristics of those belonging to it.

We find generous, compassionate, and inspiring people among Muslims, Jews, Somalis, top executives, Indians, teachers, Germans, and so on. We will also find greedy, extremist, and stubborn individuals in those same groups.

We unfortunately tend to extend our judgment of some people in a group to all the people in the group. That has been and still is the root of many clashes, conflicts, and wars.

We sometimes blame hundreds for something only a dozen in a group are responsible for. Why this collective judgment that at times leads to taking revenge on innocent people? Is it innate, an instinct? Did it originate in humanity's early days when people needed to observe, judge, and even hurt others as they could be potential enemies? Or is it a behavior we have learned? We often have preconceived ideas about how other people are and what they comprise based solely on external factors. This often keeps us from seeing every human being as an individual.

The societies we live in influence us as do our religions. But a more appropriate grouping would be based on our relationship skills and internal qualities rather than outside factors. We should learn to see others for who they are behind any external factors.

## 20. Unfolding Higher Levels of Each Other

Visualize all your qualities on levels like an expandable ladder ready to be unfolded. Imagine all your positive traits and qualities and those others have as well. Then imagine how to unfold these levels or qualities in others and yourself. Imagine how you can unfold positive responses and actions in others and how you can let others unfold positive qualities in you. Allow others to bring out your positive qualities.

This image may be another tool for you to see your and others' existences from a different perspective. Listening to your recurring thoughts and noticing the visions, ideas, or signs you encounter will helps you open your inner self.

## 21. Caring about Our Purpose

Imagine that one of our purposes here was to become more light and become positive through our experiences tough as they may be. Imagine we were here to become more focused on being joyful and spreading joy.

However, before we can really know, become, and spread joy, we need to know and feel the other side of joy. This is maybe why we go through much hardship and complex situations.

We could just shrug and say that we don't care about what our purpose is, that we just want to get on with it and not think too deeply about it. Many people think that way, and they may do just fine up to a point. It is not until we actually start to care that we realize how important balance between our minds, bodies, and souls is that we can truly feel we are creating something positive.

When our minds, bodies, and souls are in tune with each other, we use them simultaneously to make decisions and choices. We sense we can do something positive. We sense new doors opening. We think about how to nourish our souls, and we know what our minds and souls want. We mirror the powers around us.

Those who are familiar with meditation will know the feeling I mean—the connectedness with the energies or powers around us we can feel during meditation that brings about awesome and inspiring feelings of bliss, harmony, and wisdom.

It also brings about a strong sense of purpose.

## 22. Helping Others

I came across the website www.spiritualdove.com/are_you_an_empath_. htm a while ago and found a view on how best to (or maybe rather how *not* to) help others.

It refers to the unconscious empath who with the best intentions tries to help remove somebody's baggage but in reality ends up depriving that person of a learning experience and causing that person to become angry.

According to Yona Jyotiananda, the author of the website, the receivers become angry because they have to recreate the problem again so they can work through them with their own insights and abilities.

As I have mentioned, we each come here with certain issues and lessons we have made a pact with our higher selves to work through during this lifetime, so maybe we do feel upset or angry if we feel somebody has snatched away the essence of a lesson. We may feel cheated that we did not have the chance to feel victorious through our efforts.

Much depends on how such assistance is provided; we often do need a push, a hint, or some encouragement from our friends or relatives to wake up and work on a specific issue.

When the push, hint, or encouragement is offered in a positive and empathetic way, that helps us get past a roadblock or out of a dead end; it is thus valuable and will not make us feel cheated or angry. We get the help we need to reach the finish line on our own. That will make us feel we have accomplished something with the help of someone close to us.

That kind of help is something to be grateful for.

# Chapter 18

## History—A Perspective and an Influence

*Not to know what has been transacted in former times is to be
always a child. If no use is made of the labors of past ages, the
world must remain always in the infancy of knowledge.*
—Marcus Tullius Cicero (106–43 BC)

*The mind of man is capable of anything—because everything
is in it, all the past as well as all the future.*
—Joseph Conrad (1857–1924)

"History is boring." Many people, especially young people, will say that.
Many seem to connect dusty old books and unimportant and irrelevant facts
with history. I have many times heard, "We had such a boring history teacher,
so I never paid attention." That is a shame; history influences our lives even
if we do not think so.

It all depends on how history is presented. If it is presented in a way
that enables you draw a line from the past to the present so you can see how
the past influences the present, then it becomes interesting, alive, and relevant
to your life today.

Feeling the relevance of historic times will give you a feeling of
connectedness with the world and with what is happening; it will give you a
sense of belonging to the world and a sense of having a place in history.

However, many people say they do not care about history and say,
"History is the past. You cannot change it. We are living in different
times."

This may of course be true; we can maybe(?) not change the past, but
we can learn from it and avoid making the same mistakes again by drawing on

others' experiences. Why shouldn't we? It is all there laid out for us. So many things, situations, and scenarios have already been played out. The people, times, circumstances, and places vary, but if we dissect history, we can find common motives and reasons behind much that is happening today.

## 1. Gaining Perspective through History

I have talked about our common quest for improvement. Look at some examples from history and see how that quest for improvement has led many of us to where we are today.

## Surgery

Blunt tools and painful operations with minimal or no chance of survival have given way to today's highly skilled surgeons, high-tech equipment, and high recovery and survival rates from many illnesses and traumas that formerly would have meant disabilities or even death.

## Hygiene

From housing with no toilets, running water, or sewage and with garbage dumps nearby resulting in illness, we have moved to homes with fully equipped bathrooms, kitchens with running water, drain systems for waste, and refrigerators.

## Transportation

People used to rely on horses, camels, donkeys, and other animals for transportation, but we have progressed to ships, cars, trains, airplanes, and many more-efficient means to get ourselves around. And this is not to mention rockets and space shuttles.

## Communication

The dramatic changes in this field have certainly had an enormous impact on many. We went from word of mouth and words written on stone and parchment to the printing press, telephones, and radios all the way to the internet, which has had a profound effect on the way people communicate.

Knowledge can be expressed and shared in ways no one would have imagined just forty or fifty years ago let alone a hundred years ago.

## The Industrial Revolution

The Industrial Revolution involved mechanical inventions and contraptions that later gave way to electronic machinery, computerized plants, and giant power-generating plants. The Industrial Revolution brought about positive as well as negative changes. Much work became a lot easier as heavy or tedious work was taken over by machines. But machines took over to such an extent that many men and women lost their jobs though others were created. This revolution took a lot of adjusting to.

The above examples show how seeing things in a historic context can bring about a feeling of awe for all the inventions that have come about, and it can bring about a sense of gratitude toward all those who have shared their ideas, imagination, and knowledge with others to improve humanity's circumstances.

We should be grateful that our quest for improvement along with a growing population have made acquiring food and drink easier. We no longer have to hunt for food and skins to wear, head out to pick berries or nuts, or go to streams for water and fish. People learned to farm and domesticate animals, and they started bartering for whatever else they needed.

As people gathered in towns and cities, the chores of daily living were naturally divided; some would tend to crops, others would tend to people's health, some would produce clothes and household items, and others would take care of and teach children.

Nevertheless, for centuries, people relied on the food nature provided in a natural form. Now of course, most people rely on supermarkets.

## 2. Bartering, Swapping, and Money

Before the concept of money came about, people would barter and swap items and services. In feudal times, people would get access to land for the work they would do for the landowner, and some learned crafts. People swapped services and products, but then as now, because of human nature, many ended up being taken advantage of and ended up with the shortest straws.

The concept of money was invented because some wanted to make more of it. Then as now, those with money lent it to those without, at an interest. . This concept was the foundation of our global economy. Money is a great business idea if you are on the right side of the fence.

My older son asked me one day, "Why don't people just swap things instead of having to buy them?" He was interested in a specific toy and wanted to know how to get the money to buy it.

I had thought about that myself—why don't we just swap as we used to? Since my son asked me about that out of the blue, I started thinking that bartering must be the most natural and satisfying way of exchanging goods if it is done fairly.

Why are there differences in the price for the same goods depending on in which country you buy it? I can see the complex reasons behind it, but I still feel it is not logical that the same T-shirt costs $7 in Australia, $9 in the US, $2 in Thailand, and $1 in the Philippines just as an example of my point. How have T-shirts come to symbolize how well or how poorly a country is doing? Logically, it doesn't make sense.

When you look at it from a child's perspective, you see how much politics and economics are behind the state of the world.

## 3. Going backward or Going with the Flow?

Due to the way society and civilization has developed and perhaps more so due to the size of the world's population, bartering would maybe be difficult to recommence.

The size of the population has meant that many of us have the same kind of services to offer. Food is naturally at the top of everybody's list of goods in demand, but urbanization for instance has meant that not everybody has a piece of land to grow crops or raise livestock.

I will not go deeper into the global economic and political situation; I am just raising a few pointers to support my argument that history is very much alive today and is influencing our lives.

Things develop, and we develop as well; circumstances change, and we change with them or at times against them, but to gain some perspective on today's world, it is sometimes helpful as well as a good idea to look at how things used to be.

## 4. Same Personalities but Different Settings

The history of humankind seems to be made up of repetitive issues albeit with ever-changing scenery and social environments. Our history holds terrible images of wars and conflicts. However, it is also full of good deeds, kindness, sharing, love, empathy, positive ideas, amazing talent, and other positives.

Through the media, we can witness conflicts and see how greed triggers most of them—greed for wealth, control, and power over land and people.

Nevertheless, we can also witness big and small positive things every day if we look for them. We can see smiles, helpfulness, care, compassion, kindness, and generosity. The majority of people can let these virtues shine through, and we can bring them out in each other.

## 5. Learning through History

You can look at almost any topic with a historical perspective to learn more and become more grateful for some of the positive inventions and modern amenities most of us have. Consider these elements to see if you feel things have improved.

- **Food**. In early times, the Middle Ages, and the recent past, what did people eat? How did get and prepare food?
- **Spirituality**. During the times before established religions, in the Middle Ages, and in the recent past, how did people perceive the scenery around them? How did they understand the universe? What happened to the flat-earth theory? How did they treat nature including animals and each other?
- **Children**. In early times, the Middle Ages, and the recent past, what role did children play in families? What role did grandparents have? Did anyone listen to children's needs? Were children respected? Who took care of them and taught them? Who were their role models?

The possibilities are endless. But comparing the past and present gives us a useful snapshot of where we are today and how we got here. This information can inspire us to look ahead as well.

# 6. Ancient History

It is interesting to explore how old myths, stories, and pagan beliefs developed from natural surroundings. Many indigenous peoples still revere nature in the way they perform their daily chores and routines. They live with nature.

In many old myths and stories, individual gods represented a basic natural element such as the wind, earth, sky, water, trees, sun, moon, or certain animals.

Also, natural phenomena such as earthquakes, volcanic eruptions, thunder and lightning, floods, and eclipses were considered signs from the gods that something important was happening.

The next time you read about ancient myths, substitute the names of the gods with the element they represent and you will often find that the story makes much more sense bearing in mind also how people at that time perceived the universe.

The world has a plethora of ancient places of particular attraction, energy, and mystique. Some of the more popular ones are the pyramids in Egypt, Machu Picchu in Peru, Ayers Rock or Uluru in Australia, the Grand Canyon in the US, Stonehenge in the UK, the ancient Lascaux caves in France, the Nazca plains in Peru, the lands of the Hopi and other native American tribes, places in Iraq (sometimes called the cradle of civilization and where the Sumerians lived), the mountains of Tibet, Mount Fuji in Japan, the temples of Cambodia, and many others.

We can find fascinating places all over the planet. Are there any places of special attraction in your area? Do you ever wonder how towns and specific places got their names? Do you wonder why a town is in a specific place? Do you check out places or towns from the Bible or other religious scriptures?

The back garden of one of my childhood homes led straight out onto what used to be an ancient trail where Roman soldiers once walked. The trail on this particular stretch is still a gravel road that stretches for hundreds of kilometers through the Danish landscape. Much of it is now tarmac countryside road, but a great stretch of the trail is still a popular route for walkers.

I find it exciting to know I lived right next to a trail Roman soldiers used to walk. It has inspired me to read up on the Roman invasions and learn more about their incentives, strategies, and so forth. I find it exciting because I know I have shared the same trail, and I am sure that is no coincidence.

## 7. Early Knowledge

Many believe that many secrets can be found in the first, sacred, enlightened texts and teachings on for instance how to use the energies that surround us for positive purposes.

Texts on Hinduism, Buddhism, Ayurvedic healing, and the ancient prophesies of the Hopi, Mayans, Aztecs, and Tibetans are very interesting. We can also find perplexing hieroglyphs and drawings in many caves in Europe, North and South America, and Australia.

In addition, we can wonder if they have all been found, explored, and interpreted and if they are connected. There is still so much left to study.

The people who lived thousands of years ago had different frames of reference; they lived in tune with, in awe of, and in harmony with nature and natural events.

Although we live completely different lives now, we are still human beings living on the same vibrant and living earth, and one day, everything we do will be ancient history to our descendants.

## 8. Think Out of the Box

People still possess the same virtues, urges, egos, ethics, and morals (or lacks thereof) as they did in the past. But a big difference is that a greater percentage of the population is taking the step into more-enlightened times.

Imagine taking a time machine to medieval times. Your world is suddenly limited to your town and the neighboring towns. Your social interaction and thus your frame of reference is minute compared to what it is today. Your level of education if you have one at all is limited to very basic, strict and probably religious teachings. You are most likely not allowed to express any concerns or queries regarding your education.

Yet since you went as your present you, your thoughts would probably revolve around the same big questions of life as they are today. But in the Middle Ages, you would maybe have to keep these thoughts to yourself out of fear of being punished for being a heretic, a troublemaker, or a lunatic. And your thoughts would take longer to flourish and develop.

Intellectual watchdogs would curb your ability to express yourself; thus, your personal growth would be inhibited. Your range of physical movement would be limited as there would be no modern forms of transportation, so your range of influence would also be smaller.

Today, we find societies in which people still feel an iron grip, but in many of those societies, people are finding alternative ways to express themselves or discuss matters. Setting somebody free is still the best way to get the best out of people.

The future changes every day.

## 9. Basic Call to Consciousness

Below is a message given by the Iroquois Confederacy to the United Nations in September 1977. The message carries valuable insight into what happens when natural ways of living are disregarded. Having always felt a deep connection with native people in general and Native Americans in particular, I feel the injustice done deep within me.

> To the Non-governmental Organizations (NGOs) of the United Nations … The Non-governmental Organizations had called for papers, which describe the conditions of oppression suffered by Native people … to be given to the commissions. The Hau-de-no-sau-nee, the traditional Six nations council at Onondaga, sent forth three papers which constitute an abbreviated analysis of Western history, and which call for a consciousness of the Sacred Web of Life in the Universe …

> Christianity advocated only one God. It was a religion which imposed itself exclusively of all other beliefs. The local people of the European forests were a people who believed in the spirits of the forests, waters, hills and the land; Christianity attacked those beliefs, and effectively de-spiritualized the European world …

> The Native people were ruthlessly destroyed because they were an unassimilable element to the civilizations of the West …

The Western culture has been horribly exploitative and destructive of the Natural World. Over 140 species of birds and animals were utterly destroyed since the European arrival in the Americas, largely because they were unusable in the eyes of the invaders. The forests were leveled, the waters polluted, the Native people subjected to genocide. The vast herds of herbivores were reduced to mere handfuls, the buffalo nearly became extinct. Western technology and the people who have employed it have been the most amazingly destructive forces in all of human history. No natural disaster has ever destroyed as much. Not even the Ice Ages counted as many victims.

The air is foul, the waters poisoned, the trees dying, the animals are disappearing. We think even the systems of weather are changing. Our ancient teaching warned us that if Man interfered with the Natural Laws, these things would come to be. When the last of the Natural Way of Life is gone, all hope for human survival will be gone with it. And our Way of Life is fast disappearing, a victim of the destructive processes.

The majority of the world does not find its roots in Western culture or traditions. The majority of the world finds its roots in the Natural World, and it is the Natural World, and the traditions of the Natural World, which must prevail if we are to develop truly free and egalitarian societies.

The traditional Native peoples hold the key to the reversal of the processes in Western Civilization which hold the promise of unimaginable future suffering and destruction. Spiritualism is the highest form of political consciousness. And we, the native peoples of the Western Hemisphere, are among the world's surviving proprietors of that kind of consciousness.

We are here to impart that message. The crystallization of centralized executive power serves to separate civilized societies from primitive societies. It is immaterial whether such controls are located in a feudal castle or in the executive offices of the capitals of nation states. The appearance of the hierarchical state marks the transition of food cultivators in general to the more specific definition contained in the concepts of peasantry. When the cultivator becomes dependent upon and integrated in a society in which he is subject to demands of people who are defined by a class other than his own, he becomes appropriately termed a peasant ...

A peasant is not a member of a true community of people. His society is incomplete without the town or city. It is trade with the town or city, an economic relationship, which defines the early stages of peasantry. As trade becomes more necessary, for whatever reasons, the tribesman becomes increasingly less of a tribesman and more of a peasant. The process is neither immediate nor is it necessarily absolute, but to the degree that a tribesman becomes dependent, he becomes less of a tribesman ...

It is the market, in one form or another, that pulls out from the compact social relations of self-contained primitive communities some parts of men's doings and puts people into fields of economic activity that are increasingly independent of the rest of what goes on in local life. The local traditional and moral world and the wider and more impersonal world of the market are in principle distinct, and opposed to each other ...

The European invaders, from the first, attempted to claim Indians as their subjects. Where the Indian people resisted, as in the case of the Hau-de-no-sau-nee, the Europeans rationalized that resistance to be an incapacity for civilization. The incapacity for civilization rationale became the basis for the phenomenon in the West which is known today as racism ...

The European legal systems had, and apparently have developed, no machinery to recognize the rights of peoples, other than dictators or sovereigns, to land. When the Europeans came to North America, they attempted to simply make vassals of the Native leaders. When that failed, they resorted to other means. The essential thrust of European powers has been an attempt to convert "... the Indian person from membership in an unassimilable caste to membership in a social class integrated into Euro-American institutions" (Ibid.) ...

The Europeans landed on the shores of the Americas and immediately claimed the territories for their sovereigns. They then attempted, especially in the case of France and Spain, to make peasants of the Indians.

The English, who had already experimented with the enclosure system and who thus colonized North America with landless peasants which were driven by a desperation rooted in their own history, at first simply drove the Indians off the land by force ...

Their reasoning is patently medieval and racist: "Civilization is that quality possessed by people with civil governments, civil government is Europe's kind of government; Indians did not have Europe's kind of government, therefore Indians were not civilized. Uncivilized people live in wild anarchy; therefore Indians did not have government at all. And THEREFORE Europeans could not have been doing anything wrong—were in fact performing a noble mission—by bringing government and civilization to the poor savages ...

Many Western institutions are in fact colonial institutions of Western culture. The churches, for example, operate in virtually the same manner as did the feudal lords.

First, they identify a people whose loyalty they wish to secure in an expansionist effort. Then they charter a group to conduct a "mission." If that group is successful, they become, in effect, the spiritual sovereigns or dictators of those whose loyalty they command. That process in organized Christianity may actually be more ancient than the process of political colonialism described here ...

Modern multi-national corporations operate in much the same way. They identify a market or an area which has the resources they want. They then obtain a charter, or some form of sanction from a Western government, and they send what amounts to a colonizing force into the area. If they successfully penetrate the area, that area becomes a sort of economic colony of the multi-national. The greatest resistance to that form of penetration has been mounted by local nationalists.

In North America, educational institutions operate under the same colonial process. Schools are chartered by a sovereign (such as the state, or the Bureau of Indian Affairs,) to penetrate the Native community. The purpose in doing so is to integrate the Native people into society as workers and consumers, the Industrial Society's version of peasants.

The sovereign recognizes, and practically allows, no other form of socializing institution for the young. As in the days of the medieval castle, the sovereign demands absolute fealty.

Under this peculiar legal system, the Western sovereign denies the existence of those whose allegiance he cannot obtain. Some become, by this rationale, illegitimate.[3*]

We all need food, drink, and rest. We all absorb, process, and feel. We all wonder about our surroundings. We all wonder why we are here on earth and what is beyond our physical reality.

Ancient myths and history have formed and are still forming the world we live in today, and they carry a lot of truth! We are living in historical times now; every day is history in the making. One day, today will be ancient

---

[3] *Excerpts from *Basic Call to Consciousness* edited by Akwesasne Notes, Summertown, TN, 1991.

history. Old proverbs and sayings from cultures around the world often carry wise but forgotten truth. Most of them can help us process situations even today. Human personal and relational issues are universal and timeless. The settings vary through the ages, but the internal feelings, inner journeys, and aspirations of people remain the same.

> *It is easy to be brave from a distance.*
> —Native American Proverb

# Part 2

......................................................

## Spirit

......................................................

*Wonder is the beginning of wisdom.*
—Greek saying

*I Salute the Light within Your Eyes where the whole Universe dwells. For When You are at that Centre Within You, and I am at that Place Within Me, We shall Be as One.*
—Teton Sioux Chief Tashunca-Uitco, Crazy Horse

# Chapter 1

· · · · · · · · · · · · · · · · · · · · · · · · · · · · · · · · · · · · · · · · · · · · · · · · · · · · · · · · · · · · ·

# A Spiritual Life

· · · · · · · · · · · · · · · · · · · · · · · · · · · · · · · · · · · · · · · · · · · · · · · · · · · · · · · · · · · · ·

Throughout my life, I have always believed in something higher and deeper than what meets our physical senses and minds. Over time, I have grown to trust in my coexistence with this higher reality and have made it part of what I do as a clairvoyant energy reader and intuitive healer.

I have grown to be aware of my possibility, responsibility, and accountability for the direction and the contents of my life.

## 1. What Is Spirituality?

What is a spiritual being, and how do you lead a spiritual life? Spirituality is about living in respectful harmony with everything around you. Spiritual living is taking all aspects and observations of life into consideration including the physical, spiritual, and the materialistic. Spiritual living is allowing everything a place in your worldview.

Spirituality is sensing the energies in and around you, your fellow beings, your planet, and the universe.

Spirituality is accepting and trusting everything you experience. You accept that life is a learning experience; you observe what you go through and learn to deal with it as lessons you learning to keep evolving.

- You keep an open mind as to what your purpose and that of others could be.
- You at least consider new thoughts, discoveries, and philosophies as being possible.
- You live in awe of beauty and positive ways.
- You live in respect for all life and your surroundings.
- You live in balanced humility.

- You wish to help others.
- You listen to and follow your intuition in all areas of life.
- You connect with other beings in a deeper sense.
- You believe in yourself and in your immense and in many cases still-undiscovered abilities.

Many people who have gone through some sort of crisis or trauma come out the other end and claim to have seen the light. They say they feel as if they have gone through life-altering experiences that put everything in a more spiritual perspective.

They have gone through something that has changed them; they have become aware of what really matters in life, and they have become aware of what they want to pursue. Some may suddenly realize what their purpose in life is.

The things that stand out as being most important to them now are always positives such as these.

- love and support from a loving family and friends
- meaningful conversation
- sharing positive experiences with like-minded people
- humor
- a sense of belonging and respect
- nature experiences and perhaps a newfound sense of wanting to be in balance with nature—a grounded feeling
- a newfound sense of purpose

Most people tend to become much more attuned to and respectful of virtuous things, but some become bitter and seek revenge for something that happened to them. They need love, assurance, and comfort to help them heal the trauma they have experienced.

Those who come out the other end in a lighter way suddenly see that things such as war, greed, jealousy, bickering, and material things do not produce long-term, satisfying results.

This does not mean that they suddenly display angelic behavior at all times; they will still have many other issues and lessons to go through and to heal.

Having seen some sort of light does not mean they now wish to or should abandon all material things because they can offer spiritual comfort and support. But it means they have realized that living in harmony with themselves, others, and the material world and meeting their needs and purposes in sustainable and unselfish ways and helping others is the best way. They will try to reach a state of harmony and love in themselves.

It is tempting to think that the state of being we are in following a trauma big or small and when layers of greed, ego, and status suddenly mean less or are gone is the true nature of our core. Often, it does not take a full-blown trauma to help us get closer to our core and our spirituality. Small-scale events and positive events can also suddenly open our eyes to something bigger.

Have you ever read a new book, heard a song on the radio, or had a conversation with someone that made you say, "Aha!"? You suddenly had an epiphany; something inside you clicked, and you saw the bigger picture of something. If you let that epiphany become a natural and integrated part of your life, spiritual awareness will opens many doors, and the more open you are, the more you will see.

Your spiritual growth depends on how ready you are to register signs and synchronicities and how ready you are to turn all that into something useful in your life. Spiritual growth cannot be rushed. It is as it is, and it happens exactly at the pace that is right for you.

Living spiritually is about using our minds, bodies, and souls simultaneously. When we help others and serve the highest good, we are living in tune with spirit.

> *Searching, means having a goal. But finding means*
> *being free, being open, having no goal.*
> —From *Siddhartha—An Indian Tale* by Herman Hesse (1922)

## 2. Other Definitions of Spirituality

Margot Adler wrote in 1986 that some women in a modern-day coven had shared with her their definition of being spiritual. To them, spiritual meant "the power within oneself to create artistically and change one's life," and she wrote that they equated things of the spirit "with the need for beauty or with that spark that creates a poem or a dance" (Pete Jennings, *Pagan Paths*).

Spirituality and creativity seem to be very much connected. With creativity comes manifestation; when we create something, we manifest our thoughts and ideas into something we can perceive with our physical senses. It can be a painting, a piece of music, a useful gadget, an educational book, a novel, or a product that makes our lives easier for instance. Creativity comes from the heart, which is the seat of the soul.

An attempt to define paganism—one of many spiritual paths—has been done with these three principles, which are widely accepted among pagans worldwide (Pete Jennings, *Pagan Paths*).

- a love for and kinship with nature; reverence for the life force and its ever-renewing cycles of life and death
- a positive morality by which people are responsible for the discovery and development of their true nature in harmony with the outer world and community often expressed as "Do what you will as long as it harms none"
- the recognition of the divine that transcends gender and acknowledges both the female and male aspects of deity ("What is Paganism?" leaflet, The Pagan Federation, 2000)

Spirituality forms internally while we consider external things. It is closely connected to trusting that our experiences are real and that there are no such things as coincidences. That is often difficult for many to accept as free will is sometimes mistaken for things happening by coincidence.

Millions of people live in harmony with established religions, and they are content with that; it brings them a sense of spirituality and purpose. But others piece together their own pictures of spirituality maybe through one or more teachings across cultural, traditional, and national boundaries.

## 3. Spirituality of Indigenous People

> Aboriginal people were perceived to be "primitive," atheistic, pagan, immoral "wretches" who required "saving."[4]

Upon the first encounters between "civilized" man and indigenous man all over the world, many people had the above perception of indigenous peoples. Sadly, many still hold that perception today often without knowing about or understanding the rationale behind the way of life of indigenous

---

[4] *Aboriginal Spirituality and Cosmology*, by Penny Tripcony, 1996. Oodgeroo Unit, Queensland Univ. of Technology, (www.qsa.qld.edu.au/downloads/approach/indigenous_read001_0708.pdf).

peoples. We are all through our ancestry in fact indigenous people, but many of us have just become too civilized to remember this.

Many people today still honor and live by the same standards and virtues their ancestors did. But that is difficult for many because their lands and lifestyles have been encroached upon over time and civilization has taken over.

Indigenous peoples on all continents have had experiences with colonization, including Native American Indians, the Sami in Lapland, the Inuit and other peoples of the Arctic, peoples in the Indian subcontinent and Africa, the aborigines of Australia, the Maui of New Zealand, and people living on Pacific islands included.

Mayans and later Aztecs experienced violent and abrupt changes of life. Christian missionaries entered every continent in search of indigenous people they could assimilate and transform into civilized people. *The Mission* is a brilliant but heartbreaking movie that portrayed gruesome events that took place.

The indigenous people portrayed in this movie and hundreds of other indigenous peoples all over the world were living with old traditions and cultural norms in sustainable harmony with nature, but the missionaries quickly changed that.

> The realm of Spiritual existence is not divorced from the material world, but embedded in it. People and nature are one, whereas in Western thought these are separated. (Sutton, 1988)

Here is a definition of aboriginal spirituality.

> Aboriginal spirituality lies in the belief in a cultural landscape. Everything on the vast desert landscape has meaning and purpose. Life is a web of inter relationships where man and nature are partners and where the past is always connected to the present. Through their painting, Aboriginal artists are paying respect to their ancestral creators and at the same time strengthening their belief systems. (Central Art, Aboriginal Art Store, Alice Springs, Australia)

Again, we see the noteworthy connection between spirituality and creativity.

## 4. More about Paganism

Paganism existed long before the world religions such as Christianity and Islam. In his book *Pagan Paths*, Pete Jennings wrote that paganism was a collection of earth-based folk religions.

The word *pagan* comes from a Latin word meaning "of the countryside." Pagans revered all aspects of nature and believed everything had a spirit. They worshipped many gods, goddesses, and deities in relation to nature and in relation to everyday life including events such as craftsmanship, war, death, reincarnation, and others. Many wonderful books and websites offer information about this very early way of life that by the way thousands still live by.

## 5. Society's View of Spirituality throughout the Times

The classic period of witch hunts took place mostly in Europe and North America between the fifteenth and the eighteenth centuries. The last witch burning of that period happened around 1750.

I believe these witches were simply people who had developed special healing and psychic skills but lived in societies that weren't ready for them.

In indigenous cultures, shamans and witch doctors were and still are respected. It is believed they can contact the other side for knowledge and advice. The shamans also have great knowledge of herbal and plant medicine, human psychology, and various illnesses, and they have an innate, spiritual way of looking at life in a bigger perspective.

People who demonstrate special powers, who actively use their spiritual connection and intuition, have always been viewed with a certain sense of awe and wonder but often ridicule and fear as well.

In many societies throughout time, spirituality and extrasensory powers have been considered dangerous, harmful, ridiculous, coincidental, unimportant, abnormal, or heretical by people who did not understand the concepts or even wanted to.

Even in many movies, spiritual people or those who use their special powers are often portrayed as eccentric, ridiculous, or just plain strange. This portrayal has become ingrained in the minds of generations, and it still influences many.

Some do use these skills—which we all possess by the way—to direct the energies into something dark and negative, but millions of others use these skills to tap into the universal energies to heal and for other positive matters.

People who actively or inactively use their extra senses are often confused by their abilities and often find them scary until they learn to use them in positive ways.

People often feel ashamed of or shy about their special experiences or skills. The fear of ridicule holds many back from sharing their experiences with others. It can be very difficult to come out of the spiritual closet. But thankfully today, tens of thousands of healers and intuitives are stepping forward and talking about their beliefs in something besides our physical reality.

Many people share their out-of-world experiences and how they found new meaning and purpose in life through them. Many people are becoming more conscious and aware of themselves and their surroundings in a more enlightened and spiritual way. Many try meditation or alternative healing, and others visit psychics and tarot card readers or explore their own powers. These avenues of self-exploration may still be frowned upon or ridiculed by many, but they also have found a strong foothold in many places and cultures.

In some cultures, the spiritual side of existence is still very much something not openly discussed, but in other cultures, individual spirituality is perfectly accepted and practiced. Places including India, Tibet, Egypt, and Peru to mention a few seem to be infused with spirituality and spiritual beliefs.

Paganism, the indigenous spiritual belief of the West, was almost annihilated with the arrival of the new religions, but it is going through a renaissance and becoming an object of curiosity and interest among many people.

## 6. Spirituality and Your Relationship with Others

You are a member of a family and probably have a circle of friends small or large. Maybe you have colleagues or classmates; but in one way or another, you are a part of one or more groups.

For any length of time, each of your groups seems to be harmonious and symbiotic; you give and you take, you provide input and you receive input. You may feel stimulated and energized after spending time with the people around you, and they have similar positive reactions to you.

But over time, you may slowly start to feel not a part of this or that group anymore. You may notice your mind wandering when you spend time with certain members of a group. You may feel empty or even negative after being with them for reasons you do not know. Maybe you do not really laugh at the same jokes anymore or find the conversation uninspiring if not mind numbing.

If that happens to you, realize that you are just on different paths and levels. Some move faster than others; there is no right or wrong pace. You may have each grown spiritually, mentally, and emotionally at different rates, and one day, it will hit you. You may slowly start spending less time in a group. Eventually, you may even drop out of the group and turn to new acquaintances and friendships that have blossomed in the meantime.

Because different people seem to be in our lives for different reasons, we all have at least one person we feel comfortable with in every way, and the relationship lasts from the day we met whether that was in our childhood, our teen years, or adulthood. We seem to grow at the same speed, and we keep stimulating one another. We take the relationship to higher and higher levels because we bring out the light in each other.

Once we realize that any development in our relationships with others is okay, we will no longer feel the need to hang onto somebody because we used to be best friends with them or used to have so much in common. Since we all walk different paths, it is very natural to grow apart.

## 7. Picking up Vibes

Some of us have the ability to pick up vibes from a crowd. It can sometimes be difficult to remember to shield ourselves from the negative energies that emanate.

Sometimes, we may feel the atmosphere in a room is filled with so much negativity that we wish we were somewhere with more friendliness and compassion.

We should remember to use all the tools we have been given so we can handle such situations in positive ways. Sometimes, the best cure is to simply walk away and spend some time either alone or with a trusted friend.

*True love brings peace of mind and fire in the heart.*
—From the movie *The Notebook*; author: Nicholas Sparks, 1996

## 8. Can You Find Your Spirituality?

Behind most spiritual beliefs, groups, cults, and movements are sincere individuals who are positively interested in guiding and helping others. But other groups are managed by people driven by selfish, negative values such as the desire for money and power. We have to listen to our intuition and go with whom we feel is right for us. And we should not beat ourselves up if we go with something that turns out to be not right; it is part of our learning curve.

Some of the main religions incorporate forms of individual spirituality. One thing, however, that I do not agree with is the concept of a God who punishes us if we do not adhere to certain principles; that creates an element of fear, which can be detrimental to the use of our free will, creativity, spontaneity, self-confidence, and innocence. It can, however, also be a driving force for some, who get even more determined than ever.

I believe in consequences from our surroundings and within us according to our actions. This creates a sense of responsibility and accountability, but this just shows two perceptions of the same concept I suppose.

Many find and create their own spirituality by finding information from different sources that fits them; they cut and paste this information into their own spiritual puzzles. I have done this myself.

Maybe the way you feel about your spirituality is more important than where you find it. But your belief should feel right for you; it should harm no one or thing, and it should help move you forward in the direction you choose.

If you follow your intuition, you will be able to focus on whatever feels and seems right—and thus *is* right—for you. Listen to what goes on inside you, and pay attention to your dreams and daydreams alike.

Those who meditate can reach a state in which they allow their thoughts to flutter around, come and go, and after a while, they reach the essence of themselves—their souls, inner voices, intuition, higher selves, and inner guidance. That is when they discover what is really going on inside them and realize they are part of something bigger.

That is where they find answers to all their questions.

# 9. Living Consciously with Spirituality—Keeping Spiritual Focus in the Physical World

Those who become more aware of and attuned to the spiritual aspects of life feel less attracted to the unnatural, plastic, and overly materialistic life.

They want to get more in touch with nature. They start to notice that they sense things. They feel their consciousness expanding. They can look at their existence from a higher perspective. However, that may challenge them to incorporate their newfound spiritual sense in their jobs, their worldly and physical desires, and their everyday routines.

Make a habit of thinking how you can spread love, comfort, and light to those you know and love. What do they appreciate? What do they need? How can you support them? Would it give them comfort to know that you are thinking of them right now?

My spiritual mentor and dear friend told me that she wanted to serve as many as possible, so she wanted to fit her yoga class schedule around everybody's needs. If somebody could do a yoga class only at 8:00 p.m., she would gladly change her schedule to suit that.

Our conversation rang some bells in me. I have always wanted to help others. Since my husband's passing, I feel it even stronger in the sense that I feel connected to him and sense him helping our boys and me from where he is. I feel he knows and is letting me know that it is all about helping each other and serving the greater good the best we can wherever we are.

We all have skills that come so naturally to us; when we put them to use, they make positive changes in others and inspire them, as well as ourselves.

## 10. Getting on the Right Track

But what if we have not really found our unique qualities yet? How do we combine our physical and spiritual realities? How do we live our busy lives in a spiritual way?

There are many tools along our spiritual path to help us find our inner selves whenever we are ready to including aura readings, past-life regression, Reiki, quantum healing, akashic records readings, meditation, counseling, writing books, teaching yoga, tarot card reading, life coaching, NLP, art, and many others. Many ways can help us shift our focus and perspective on our lives and the world around us.

We will always have bad days when we feel inadequate and not sure of our abilities or ourselves. But talking to like-minded friends who understand what we are going through and who are able to give us a little push can get us back on track.

## 11. Taking Time to Be Spiritual

If you want to become more spiritually minded, you have to take time to meditate, practice yoga, have an energy session, read, study, take a course, or talk to a friend or mentor. You can be creative, play an instrument, or take a walk in nature. Whatever spiritual tool you feel comfortable with that helps you connect with your inner self and everything around you will help you become more spiritually inclined.

You can surround yourself with people who give you a sense of a positive exchange—you feel good around them, and they feel good around you.

You can spend more time doing whatever gives you that positive feeling; that will benefit yourself and others.

As you let spirituality into your everyday life, your mind and soul will open up to letting in more intuitive guidance, which will direct you to a more spiritual life in all areas.

## 12. From Seed to Fruit— Spiritual and Personal Growth

In his book *Pagan Paths*, Pete Jennings wrote,

> [Paganism] is still going to be the province of independent intelligent free-thinkers with a love of the natural world and a self-motivated desire for spiritual and personal growth.

I often found it difficult to deal with my desire for growth in this physical world because things can be very negative here and it takes a continuous effort to focus on the positive.

Here is another conversation that rang bells in me. After meditating with a friend, my mentor, and the father of my mentor, we all talked about our experiences while meditating. The meditation focused on grounding and sealing, and I had experienced some resistance in my root chakra, the chakra that links us with the physical world.

The father of my mentor is like my mentor very intuitive and spiritually evolved. I told him I sometimes felt that I was tired of all the negativity and hardship here on earth but that I wanted to be here. I sensed a strong desire for both.

My mentor's father explained to me that he saw between the lines my statement that I was showing him that spiritually speaking, I was evolving from seed to fruit—the image of a tree came to my mind.

He said that positivity was the ultimate core of us all and that I would probably find it very difficult and draining to be in this world of illusions and negativity, the seed part of us, since I was on a higher spiritual plane and wanted to spread positivity—my fruits.

We all have to deal with illusions and negativity, but how we deal with them and how long we want to spend before we start blossoming is up to us.

After we spoke, I felt a wonderful sense of validation and peace with my feelings. It was as if he had just described in a single sentence how I felt about my existence! It suddenly seemed normal and okay again. No matter how spiritual we are, we are still human beings with a range of feelings and needs.

The need to feel that our newfound feelings, emotions, and thoughts are okay is normal. Sometimes, it helps to get validation and support from the outside when it harmonizes with our perceptions. That helps us move in the direction we are heading. And remembering to be grateful helps us stay on our right path.

## 13. Visualizations That Help Illustrate Spirituality

If you are a visually oriented person as I am, the following visions could help you look at your life on earth in a spiritual way.

## 13.1 Beings of Energy and Light

Imagine everyone as energy. Do not see the physical bodies; notice human shapes of energy.

Imagine our planet and all other objects in space as spheres of energy.

Imagine us as energy beings floating around this planet and constantly emitting and absorbing energy and light to and from one another. We are affected by the energies around us.

We can determine what kind of energy we wish to emit and absorb—positive or negative.

With our free will, we can transform ourselves and become positive energy and light.

This visualization helped me focus on the higher levels and higher perspective of our existence. It helped me remember to focus on attracting, noticing, and sending out positive energies.

## 13.2 Absorbing and Emanating Light

I had the following vision after my husband had passed away.

Imagine yourself in your current shape but as a being of light. You are moving forward in open space filled with all life and everything there is. It is filled with all the light and dark you can imagine. As you move forward, you absorb light or dark—positive and negative—knowingly or unknowingly.

The more positive light you absorb, the more enlightened you become, the more light you emanate, and the more you light up your surroundings so you can see more of what is around you.

If you absorb—are more occupied with and spend time on the dark—negativity, your positive light dims, you do not radiate as much light, and you are not able to see as much.

The more time you dedicate to positive thinking or doing, the more you enlighten yourself and your surroundings and get more out of your existence.

Think of how a firefly lights up its surroundings depending on how much light it allows itself to absorb.

## 13.3 Enlightening Our Planet and Ourselves

Some years ago, I had a vision of earth emanating light (as when a Universal Pictures movie starts!). In my vision, however, the earth was covered in a thick crust, but with our effort, with our spiritual enlightenment, we were all able to spread light from within to penetrate the crust and melt it thus making the world a lighter and brighter place.

Imagine every positive thought and prayer sends out beams of light. Then imagine the globe beaming with light coming from the inside and penetrating land and sea and radiating into the universe. Think how we would be able to heal this part of the universe if we all focused on it.

In this vision, the light comes from within us and lights up the macro cosmos. I felt this vision portrayed us as micro-cosmos beings; the light penetrated our shells, our negative layers. We have the light inside us, but we have to let it out and melt our crusts, our negativity.

In line with the three visualizations above, imagine you are pulling in light, love, peace, and all good things from the other side—from angels or energies in the other realms around us. Imagine that we are on earth to make this part of the universe a positive place and that the tools we have to do that with are our minds, thoughts, and ability to create thus manifesting it here in a physical form.

Being open to out-of-world experiences expands our consciousness and awareness of reality as we know it.

If you have ever watched *Horton Hears a Who*, a children's movie, you can identify with the concept of how everything is part of something bigger. The main characters realize that their big world turns out to be merely a dewdrop in somebody else's world.

I watched a movie many years ago in which in the end, you realize earth is a soccer ball about to be kicked by a boy. The movie stops there and leaves you with the idea of a disastrous outcome for those on earth. (I cannot find the name of that movie.)

Most of us at times wonder what the universe really is. Are we all—including the planets, galaxies, and the rest of the universe—one living organism? Does what we do affect the whole organism? Are we cells of the universe just as our bodies are made up of cells? Or are we something bigger than that?

# Chapter 2

......................................................

# About Us

......................................................

All I have read, thought, seen, heard, felt, and experienced leads me to believe that we are vibrating energy (spirits, souls) that have entered earth in a physical form. I believe we can influence and change the energy in and around ourselves and around others—all living things. I believe we can learn to make this influence or vibration positive.

I believe in the law of attraction—we attract what we send out via our thoughts, feelings, and actions. If we focus on and act positively, we will attract positive things, but if we think or send out negative thoughts or give too much attention to negative things, we will attract exactly that.

## 1. Interpreting external conditions

I believe we do not take in only air; we also take in colors, sounds, moods, thoughts, and vibes from others. We take in energy from nature and everything else around us.

I believe in the concept of *feng shui*—the state of our houses inside as well as outside reflects what we hold in ourselves and what we will attract. I also believe that the clothes we wear and their colors reflect many things going on inside us.

I believe the vehicles in which we physically move forward in life—cars, bikes, motorcycles, jets, boats, and even if we do not have a vehicle—is a reflection or symbol of how we go through life.

And the way we use our vehicles gives us away. Do we drive recklessly? Bump into other cars, lampposts, or cement pillars? Do we have dents on our bumpers or sides? Do we cushion our car with furry blankets and teddy bears? Are we considerate drivers? Can we anticipate what other drivers might do? I think this and more tells us something about how we go through life on other levels.

Some TV shows point out that what we surround ourselves with reveals who we are. A professional lifestyle expert is able to tell in detail about somebody based on the house he or she lives in, the décor, the car, the food in the fridge, the type of furniture, the state of the garden, and so on. Even if we do not always think about it, our physical product is a reflection of who we are inside and what goes on inside us—harmony or imbalance, mess or order, and so forth.

Animals, plants, crystals, rocks, water, and other things are also energy in physical or manifested form. Crystals, for example, are a particular type of energy in manifested form. I experience these different types of energies in my daily interaction with crystals.

We all emit and absorb energy; we have that power. But we have conscious minds and egos that can make it harder for us to follow the energy we are inside.

With our minds, we can create bliss or create adversity. Are we good or bad? Is everything basically positive and sustainable? Does the way people react to negative events determine whether they live in a negative, dark way or in a positive, light way?

## 2. Nature and Us

I compare us to nature and the state of our planet as we are all part of nature, the base of our existence here. If nature were left to its own devices, it is perfectly capable of keeping a healthy and positive balance to sustain healthy living conditions and growth for everyone and everything living in harmony with it. But if exploited and abused the way humans have done and continue to do, the natural balance is disturbed and so our balance is disturbed and we have to work harder at reaching that balance in us to manifest it around us.

Everything living in that nature will subsequently have to adapt to the new and unbalanced circumstances. When we create a toxic, sick, and unbalanced natural environment, we are making ourselves toxic, sick, and unbalanced. And vice versa.

Nature does whatever it takes to stay alive, and so do we. I think we are basically positive, healthy, and interested in staying alive in a positive and sustainable way in a positive and healthy environment. So why are we not all living in positive and sustainable ways? Why are we not living in harmony with the nature that nurtures us? What determines the way our lives are?

First, I believe our core is basically good, positive, and healthy and sickness and negativity are destructive but in a transformative and thus often positive way.

So why are we all not living happy, healthy lives? Why do we have to deal with pain, suffering, troubles, and issues? I believe we come here with some sort of spiritual or psychological luggage we can learn to rid ourselves of through experiences and interactions with others.

We are experiencing duality here. We see the good and the bad. We see light and darkness. We see greed and generosity. We see love and fear. Maybe it is all up to what we choose to focus on that determines our lives.

When we learn to open up to our hearts and our souls and see the bigger picture, when we care of the greater good, when we declutter our physical, mental, and emotional bodies, we are ready to let more light into our lives. With more light inside us, we can dissolve the dark, the negative sides.

When we see darkness, we appreciate the light; when we experience heartache, we learn about love. How we see the negative and deal with it can help us stay on a positive path.

Second, I believe we can change our surroundings and ourselves into something positive and sustainable by changing our attitudes, focuses, and actions. To do that, we must learn to trust our abilities and inner guidance.

Third, the way nature's resources are managed is not conducive to the natural wealth or health of the planet or us. Economy seems to come before ecology; that naturally creates a twisted and illogical world. But nature has its own power, and it is strong enough to eventually shake off whatever negative energies threaten its existence through quakes, eruptions, floods, and storms, which is of course exactly what is happening.

Last, connected to the greed and fear I mentioned earlier, we have been players in, witnesses to, and victims of countless wars and conflicts that caused poverty and hardship for millions and robbed them of the chance to live decent lives, a major obstacle to positivity for them.

## 3. Where Are We?

I believe we are on different levels spiritually speaking and have different things to learn. We have circles of people—family, friends, and so on—whom we need to further our and their personal spiritual development though we may not get along with all of them. Through them we see sides of ourselves we can work on be it low self-esteem, insecurity, arrogance, patience, gratitude, being less judgmental, and others. We may also have these people in our lives to show us what we do not want or accept.

When we have identified the reason certain people are in our lives and when we have healed, we may find that the people who represent those issues vanish from our lives. I feel it makes a lot of sense to look at your life this way.

# Chapter 3

............................................................

# Types of Guidance

............................................................

Help sometimes comes in unexpected forms, so notice things like the following; they could be signs for you.

- when you suddenly start noticing a song's lyrics
- when you feel attracted to a certain book
- when you feel an impulse to look for something on the internet
- when you hear snippets of a conversation
- when receive a call from someone who has some useful news
- when you bump into a friend
- when something enters your mind and makes you think, *This feels right.*

Notice these things and take action on them. Go with what you feel if nobody including yourself will be hurt. That could lead you to new opportunities, experiences, and epiphanies.

The more you follow your hunches, the more you will be reassured that these hunches can lead you to where you are supposed to be.

## 1. Numbers

Millions of people call Doreen Virtue the Queen of Angel Therapy. If you are interested in angels, archangels, guides, and divine callings, her books are must-reads.

One of her books is about number sequences of the angels. She explains how you may suddenly start to notice how you see the same number combinations on your watch or clock such as 11:11, 5:55 or 0:07. Or you may suddenly realize that you notice the same numbers on license plates, road signs, or house numbers.

I started noticing number combinations on my mobile phone clock many years ago, and I am astonished by how much information and guidance I have received by those numbers over the years. I was amazed to find that the more I got into it, the more precise the information became.

I started checking out the house numbers of places I had lived previously; I checked out road numbers and even license plate numbers. They all added up to a certain number that signified something special was going on in my life. With each shift in lifestyle or major change, the numbers changed.

I have never deliberately looked for number combinations; I have never waited for the clock to get to 3:33 for instance. It would happen out of the blue; something was telling me to look at the clock or a license plate in front of me.

I may have already passed fifty cars and not had the inclination to look at any of the license plates, but I suddenly notice one, and that number combination adds up to something that gives me an answer to a question I have joggled around in my mind. That is baffling, amazing, validating—and always comforting!

## 2. What about Angels, Guides, and Spirits?

A survey performed in Denmark showed that 43 percent of the people asked believed in angels. Surveys conducted in for example the US and Australia often show that around 50 percent of those asked believed in angels and guardian angels.[5*]

There are thousands of testimonies from people around the world and throughout time who have seen and communicated with angels, guides, or spirits. The testimonies are from people from all walks of life including royalty, celebrities, and politicians, and they speak of encounters with and help from someone from beyond.

Many people claim to see and communicate with angels. Some see the outline of a brightly shining figure—sometimes a color; some see sparks, and others see shimmering and hovering white or colored light. Yet other people feel or sense a presence or just *know* that something or someone benevolent is there for them.

---

[5] * Further information can be found on the internet; search word: "angel survey."

I have had many different experiences and visions, and I believe in the presence of benevolent energies that are here to help us if we only ask and let them. Help and guidance always come when we ask, and it is always comforting.

It has become second nature to me to communicate daily with angels and other benevolent energy forms for support and guidance on small and big issues. Rest assured, something positive and helpful always comes right back!

*You are never alone … You have a whole team of angels and*
*guides just waiting for you, to ask them to help you.*
—Doreen Virtue

## 3. Noticing Details and Sensations in and around You

Maybe you too observe and notice details such as numbers and want an overview of everything. I have always zoomed in and out on things I experienced. I must have driven my mother mad when as a child I would ask her, "Can you die from this?" even if I had suffered just a minor cut or a nosebleed.

I think many children with sensitive dispositions ask their parents this question. I asked it because I wanted a clear picture of the effect of what was going on; I was curious about how things worked and what happened when I did this or that. I have built up an internal experience book from which I learn.

I have an innate thirst for acquiring knowledge and sharing everything I have noticed, absorbed, and processed. This book for instance is based mainly on my experiences and observations.

## 4. Using Our Observations for Growth

Noticing details and sensations in and outside ourselves can help us move up mental, emotional, and spiritual ladders. We sometimes subconsciously notice details about physical life and our physical surroundings, others' behavior and its effect on us, and how others handle things vs. how we handle things.

When we notice what goes on around us, we use that information to find out about ourselves and our situations; we get inspired or turned off. We find out through observation and our experiences what we do and do not like or want.

Our lives are made up of many bricks, and we may not always be able to see what we are building. But we should believe that whatever we are building will be strong and just right for us.

## 5. Opening up to Our Senses

Consciously opening up to our senses including our clair senses and intuition is a fantastic way to find out more about our surroundings and ourselves.

For example, many of us can sense positive or negative vibrations other people are knowingly or unknowingly sending. We can pick up on the atmosphere between individuals or in a group and can pinpoint its essence.

We can sense imbalances in others' energy or in the energies around us, and we can create balance. We can see or feel life areas where people invest too much or too little energy. When we realize we are finely tuned to these energies, we can use the information for the benefits of others.

As we get more and more in tune with our intuition, we get epiphanies— we suddenly see or understand something on a grander scale.

# Chapter 4

..................................................................................

# Be Grateful

..................................................................................

Gratitude is a spiritual virtue. Once you start being grateful and put words on what you are grateful for, you start letting more things into your life for which you can be grateful.

It is like opening up a door to the universal flow; as soon as you start noticing what is behind that door, you will see other new doors. They have always been there; once you open the first door, you will see them.

Being grateful is actually equivalent to living consciously. When you are asked to find something to be grateful for, you are forced to think about your life and situation, and that alone may help you focus on areas that need improvement.

Even if you feel you do not have much to be grateful for, find at least one thing to be grateful for. Find that feeling inside you about something, someone, a place, or an event you feel happy, relieved, and relaxed about. Think about it often, and feel the gratitude often.

If you do this, very soon, you will have one more thing, person, place, or event to be grateful for, and very soon, you will have many things to be grateful for.

Gratitude is like a magnet and a stone you throw into a pond that spread ripples.

Why not try it? Faith can move mountains.

## Chapter 5

·············································

# Get Connected—Meditate

·············································

With so many negative and confusing events taking place around us, I have found that whenever I meditate, I feel more whole, real, balanced, and connected and better able to deal with everyday situations that are stressful.

Meditation is a tool that can make you feel full and harmonious. It charges your battery; it leaves you feeling balanced and ready to face the world. And when you are charged, you can give your energy to others.

Even long after you have finished a meditation, you can recall the experiences and feelings, and through those feelings, you can find comfort, peace, and love within.

During and after a meditation, your thoughts are met with answers; it is as if meditation creates a wall of knowledge and inner wisdom off which you can bounce your worries, fears, and anxieties.

When you meditate, you realize that your higher self holds all the answers and that you can access them with your calm, relaxed, and openly conscious self.

Meditation clears your mind, provides answers, and connects you to your inner self. It releases hidden feelings, thoughts, and emotions, and it acts like a mental and emotional vacuum cleaner. Meditation is as vital as dreaming.

# Chapter 6

............................................................

# Laughter and Joy

............................................................

Laughter is the best medicine. When we laugh and have fun, we feel good with our whole being. We often feel relief from and a release of negative energy after a good chuckle.

Having a sense of humor can help us through tense or disastrous situations especially if we share a laugh with others. There are now laughing events that gather thousands who just start laughing. Laughter is so contagious that soon everybody is laughing at nothing and at everything. How awesome is that?

Having someone in your circle who is always ready for a good laugh is worth gold. Even in difficult times, it is okay to laugh. We may sometimes feel guilty for finding something funny in an otherwise grave situation, but we need that outlet, and we need a sense of humor to get through life, which is all about experiencing joy.

Have a laugh with your children, your spouse, and your friends. Have a laugh in an awkward situation with a stranger you meet. Call a friend who always makes you laugh. Laughter connects us with our inner child, our innocence, wonder, and awe for life!

A laugh can brighten up a moment and make it last a long time!

# Chapter 7

# Balance Your Energies

Through my work with energy healing, meditation, Reiki, soul readings, benevolent light beings, and so on, I have come to feel that a balancing of our chakras—our bodily energy centers or vortices—can help us feel grounded, calm, and full of energy much as meditation, music, yoga, gardening, or making love can.

An energy healing treatment is a spiritual cleanser and a transformer; the effects of a proper treatment can be felt deeply in and beyond you.

Meditation or balancing your chakras shines a spotlight on some of your negative traits or anxieties. Imagine how afterward you can shed these negative layers because they are now apparent to you. With your awareness, you are in a much better position to address and heal the negative, which leaves room and time for you to spend on the positive.

We are spiritual beings having a physical experience here on earth. We are going through the school of life to learn from everything that happens to us. If we can accept those theories, we may be able to consider that our core is essentially light, goodness, and positivity but that we carry negative layers in the form of ego-based traits such as greed, jealousy, manipulation, vanity, excessive materialistic values, fear, shame, and so on due to our previous lives and experiences.

We are here to learn to heal and dissolve these ego-based traits so our true, positive cores shine through for the highest good of all.

## 1. Our Positive Core

To demonstrate that our true core is in fact positive, think of how most of us evolve in a positive direction through life. We are all trying to shed our negative layers so we can get back to our roots, our core. In my mind, this makes sense.

As we become older, we do not seek to take on more layers of negative thoughts and behavior. As we become older, most of us become wiser, kinder, deeper, and more spiritual. Our vision reaches further, and we are better able to see the bigger picture and value the positive much more.

Most of us intuitively know that the more layers we can shed, the closer we get to our true inner source or core of compassion, empathy, and forgiveness—in short, love.

Meditation and other ways of balancing our chakras and regaining equilibrium can help us reach our inner positive core and let it come forward.

Imagine that you continuously aim to fill yourself with healing golden light or any color you feel is right. When your body is full, the light starts to spill onto your surroundings.

To get to that point, we can use our spiritual as well as our physical senses. We are in the physical world now, so we have to use the three tools available to us here in unison—our minds, bodies, and hearts.

# Chapter 8

·············································

# When It Feels Like Our Spirituality Is Being Tested

·············································

A belief in the spirit realm can be comforting, but we might still feel our faith is being tested especially after a traumatic and emotionally challenging experience.

After my husband passed away, I felt that my sense of spirituality, my belief in the existence of the other side, and my belief that life is vibrating energy were being challenged.

I often wanted proof that my husband was actually still around me and our boys. As in the movie *Ghost*, I wanted my husband to pick up a coin or help me mold something out of clay. I needed physical, visible, tangible proof that he was still around. I needed proof of the veracity of my other nonphysical senses.

Because we are in a physical world, it is easier for us to rely on our physical senses. I think it is a very normal craving for validation, and I think it also stems from a longing for comfort. It is part of growing to accept the fact that our loved ones are no longer with us in the physical sense.

I now have had so many experiences that I know he is still around in some form or another. I have had that feeling of oneness with everything, which is hard to explain; I feel at one with everything around me and realize that reality is so much more than what I normally perceive.

A traumatic experience can be a test for you to see if your faith and trust is strong enough to keep you believing there is a reason for your experience, there is a lesson to be learned, and you are not being punished. It can also be a test to see if you can believe and trust that everything is as it is supposed to be and that something new and good is waiting for you.

After you experience a loss, your future is suddenly different from the one you had imagined, but you still have a future.

It can sometimes be difficult to keep the faith when we are facing challenges or feeling down. Using our connection tools such as meditation, yoga, Reiki, music, or reading about spiritual topics can make us feel better. Being of service and helping others can make us feel better too.

Our egos may fight our faith by ridiculing it or making us feel useless and purposeless. However, when we actively fight back with the aforementioned tools or other tools we find useful, we can feel the change. Our outlook and perspective change, and we can see the bigger picture.

After an hour or so, we may feel down again and unable to find a meaning for it all. It may seem we are living two lives—one that is very spiritual and one that seems tied to negative patterns—but then we can reconnect with our positive feelings and thoughts.

It is hard work. We may feel like we are on a seesaw and playing the part of both riders. (The negative part is often the subconscious part; the positive part is what we should become more conscious about.) When we connect within more often, we find it easier and easier to connect; it becomes second nature, and the effect lasts longer and longer until we are almost permanently connected.

I believe that besides my two boys, true friends, family members, and counselors, my faith is what has kept me going since my husband died. I have faith in the positive, in a bigger plan, in the beyond. I believe that our lives have purpose. I have faith that thought is energy. I have faith in our ability to influence our lives. I have faith in our ability to channel positivity.

This takes me to next chapter on overall purpose.

# Chapter 9

## Is Exuding Love and Light Our Real Purpose?

One day when my younger son was a baby, I was holding him when it was time for his nap. He was a bit restless, and I could not calm him down. I asked angels as well as my husband, who had passed just a short time prior to that, to help my son settle down and fall asleep as he was very tired. Almost instantly, his eyes started to close and he fell asleep.

Whenever one of the boys is restless or cranky, I ask the angels and the boys' dad to surround them with support, comfort, love, protection, healing, guidance, or whatever I feel they need. Alternatively, I may ask the angels and my husband to help me bring about a sense of protection and healing.

And it always works. Immediately after I have asked for it, I feel them calming down, snuggling in, and lying quietly. Soon after that, they usually fall asleep. I also ask for it if I feel they need extra comfort or if they seem especially unhappy, moody, or cranky.

I can almost hear skeptics say, "Ah, but the children feel that you are trying to project calmness, so it reflects onto them." Yes, I believe that whenever we focus on being calm and exude calmness and support, those around us pick up on that. But sometimes, we cannot calm them down because we are full of worry or are not completely focused, so the positivity we are trying to send out is tainted by our feelings or thoughts.

Once we focus on exuding compassion, comfort, support, and love by expressing our wishes to someone—our higher selves, angels, and so on—we are immediately able to do it.

So is someone doing it for us, or are we just more focused and tuned in to our inner wisdom and higher selves and thus able to do it? I believe it is a combination of both.

Once you have asked the benevolent energies around you for guidance and support, you will not doubt the help being offered. When you believe in it and ask for it, you will know. Through contact with your higher self, you connect with benevolent energies around and in you and thus attract that energy.

That day as I was sitting with my baby, I did wonder, *Why do I feel I have to ask for help to give them these feelings of comfort, love, and protection? Why doesn't it always work when I consciously convey these feelings to them?* But sure enough, as soon as I call for help from the angels and guides around us, it works instantly. I think we are here to learn how to draw in and exude the positive feelings that are so abundantly around and in us.

Is our purpose to connect with our core and other benevolent energies around us to manifest positivity? Maybe we are supposed to learn to focus on the love, light, and healing around us and within us, the positive that is the essence of our existence. Maybe we are supposed to learn to draw on it and direct it wherever it is needed. Maybe our purpose is to help others and ourselves.

That day, I felt that very strongly, and I consider that to be a wonderful purpose for us.

## 1. Visualize Sending Out Love Energy

Imagine that various types of cosmic energy are manifested into us, the planets, and everything beyond our solar system. Imagine one type of energy called love floating around, through, and in us.

Maybe you sometimes suddenly feel a stream of love rushing through you. It could come from music you hear that takes you to an elevated state and you feel full of bliss and love that you want to share. Hold onto that feeling, that state.

Imagine that we can draw from that mother essence and direct it to where we want it in our physical realm on earth. Imagine we can send it to those who need love and positivity including ourselves.

Many of us are already doing this whenever we physically help somebody, smile at somebody, give way to somebody in traffic, give a word of encouragement and support to somebody, hug somebody, make love—this is passing on the energy of love.

We can channel whatever positive feeling we want to pass on. By channeling love, support, comfort, insight, and wisdom, we can inspire others to make positive changes in their lives.

By channeling love, we become love.

## 2. Feeling Good about an Exchange of Energies

Is there such a thing as a selfless deed? Is there something you can do for others that does not just satisfy your ego's need to feel good about itself? Is it wrong to feel good about doing something good? Are all positive deeds selfish because they make you feel good?

If you do something with good intentions and it is accepted with gratitude, you feel good because you see the positive effect your good deed has on others. It is okay to feel good about that positive exchange!

On the other hand, if you do someone a favor and he or she does not appreciate or accept it, there is no positive exchange. Your intention is still positive, but the intended receiver was maybe not ready for your good deed or did not want it.

If that offends you, be glad for your positive intention and think that maybe the receiver will appreciate your action or the action from someone else at another time.

When we see someone in an awkward or sad situation, we can imagine that person wrapped in pink light and ask angels to surround the person; we will see the effect of that on the person. The person may not consciously know where the comfort is coming from, but he or she will feel it.

So when you feel good about having done something for others and you acknowledge the positive outcome it had on the recipients, it is okay to be happy about it and acknowledge the positive exchange that has taken place.

# Chapter 10

· · · · · · · · · · · · · · · · · · · · · · · · · · · · · · · · · · · · · · · · · · · · · · ·

# Mockeries and Myths about
# Spiritual Experiences

· · · · · · · · · · · · · · · · · · · · · · · · · · · · · · · · · · · · · · · · · · · · · · ·

We all have different perceptions of the physical world and different approaches to encounters with the spiritual world.

Some people need only one or a few concrete spiritual experiences to be convinced something is beyond physical reality. Others may have repeated experiences but dismiss them as coincidences or imagination. And some do not notice having spiritual experiences at all.

Many people will buy only theories that have been scientifically proven in the form of computed and tangible proof. They often dismiss spiritual experiences as

- a figment of the imagination,
- a fabrication,
- mass suggestion,
- a malfunction of nerves in the brain, or
- as something that could be otherwise explained biologically or chemically.

Is it innate in us to be afraid of or at least wary of the unknown, the inexplicable? Or is it something we have been taught?

Even in our information age, many turn away from things they find strange or try to make them go away. They make fun of those who live by it and those who are willing to explore and perhaps accept new possibilities and realities.

Throughout history and in many cultures and societies, those who have openly admitted to having experienced something strange via their psychic or other special abilities have been ridiculed, mocked, and even disowned by their families and communities due to fear.

In the face of life-threatening danger, fear can be a lifesaver. On the other hand, fear can also be a very powerful and negative hindrance.

## 1. Flower Power

In recent times, we have seen people with beliefs that differ from political and societal norms being ridiculed or not taken seriously. In the 1960s, thousands of young adults were part of the hippie movement that saw people in the Western world protesting against the established society, red tape, nuclear power, inhumane acts by governments against people, and other wrongs.

We may remember seeing footage of students being dragged away from sit-down strikes at universities. But how many of us actually know what they were demonstrating against?

We may assume that their motives for protesting resided mostly in their political and societal frustrations. We seem to remember mostly the long hair, Make Love Not War and Flower Power slogans, music festivals, uninhibited use of marijuana and other drugs, and frivolous sexual displays.

However, the movement paved the way for changes in and more acceptance of cooperative businesses, healthy food concepts, multiethnic living and clothing styles, respect and acceptance across religious and cultural boundaries, and more respect for the ancient art/science of astrology among others (Wikipedia: "hippie").

Spirituality may not always consciously have been behind the motives of the hippies, and there are many more aspects to the hippie movement, but I mention the movement here because I believe these people may have experienced an awakening cosmic blast of compassion and respect for other people and nature.

They saw the way the corporate world was going, and they wanted to hold onto a more basic and natural lifestyle much in line with the spiritual beliefs of native peoples around the globe.

It seems that now, we are seeing another wave of discontentment with the greed of the corporate world.

# 2. How the Energies Are Used

When we do not know what we are dealing with, when something seems a little scary, or when something makes us uneasy, our natural reaction is to push it away or turn from it. It is also a natural reaction for us to alienate those who go along with any new idea or concept. But some people welcome change easier than others do.

The use of spiritual energies has often (mostly in earlier times) been written off as heathen, pagan, witchcraft, or even as the work of the devil. But spiritual powers and energies are just there; it is up to us use them in positive rather than negative ways; the powers are not negative or positive in themselves.

# Chapter 11

·················································································

# Music

·················································································

*Music is the mediator between the spiritual and the sensual life.*
—Ludwig van Beethoven (1770–1827)

*He who hears music, feels his solitude peopled at once.*
—Robert Browning (1812–1889), playwright, poet

One day, many years ago, I was at work and listening to the same piece of music repeatedly the entire day. It was a beautiful instrumental piece featuring a keyboard, a weeping guitar, and some male chanting.

That tune took me to a state of elevated consciousness and happiness that allowed me to relive a wonderful experience I had had the night before. That day at work, I felt I was lighting up the room sitting there in my bubble of musical bliss.

That tune became so special to me that I subconsciously did not allow any other event to be dedicated to this song until I wrote this paragraph! The tune came to me, and I felt it was okay to play it again and again.

Listening to it brought back the memory of that special night and filled me with the same bliss and elevated consciousness it had that day at work.

Music is a mood creator that can bring out our feelings. If I am driving and listening to music with a rhythmic, deep drumbeat and maybe some electric guitar or even strings, I tend to accelerate because my mood is elevated.

When you are in an elevated state, you like to move fast, and you might get some good ideas about how to handle something that needs doing because you feel a surge of energy.

On the other hand, if you listen to soft love songs, you might suddenly feel sad about someone who was special to you, or you might feel that the soft music sweeps away sadness and fills you with acceptance of a certain situation.

Part of human nature is to create music to suit any type of human emotion and feeling. Music is an expression of emotions and feelings, and it generates images as well.

## 1. Feelings Can Be Relived and Accessed via Music

When I was working as a TV sports anchor, I used to listen to a certain song to help get me more upbeat and in a happy mood before I took the bus to the TV station. That song would be with me when I arrived and prepared for the program; it helped me stay in a good mood.

Music can be like meditation; it can connect us to something higher and elevate our moods and consciousness.

## 2. Music as a Liberator

A dear spiritual mentor and friend explained how drums could bring out and release negative energies in us. I had asked her why I felt a surge of positive or dynamic energy when I listened to hard rock or heavy metal especially with drums, bass, and an electric guitar when at the same time I was so into spiritual living, inner harmony, vibrations, meditations, and Reiki.

I thought such music did not match up with my spiritual side, so I was relieved when she said that hard music could release negative energy, feelings, and thoughts stuck in us.

Her words validated my feelings of release and the surge of positive, productive energy I experience while and after listening to that type of music. I felt that even if we live spiritual lives, we are still learning and picking up and emanating negative energies that we need to release. Music is a way of doing that.

So when you stomp your feet, tap your fingers, shake your head, or move your body, you could actually be releasing negative energy and making room for positive energy. You could also just be vibrating with the music and letting in joy and love. Either way, music is a healer!

Interestingly, our chakras are said to correspond with certain tones. Going from our base to our crown, some say the root chakra connects with the tone C, our navel chakra is in tune with D, our solar plexus chakra with E, our heart chakra with F, our throat chakra with G, our third-eye chakra with A, and our crown chakra with B.

This could explain why we seem to have an affinity for certain songs at certain times depending on their composition as the use of tones have an effect on our chakra system and therefore on our whole being.

Maybe some music tickles our chakras and makes us like that particular piece of music. Can we get an indication of which chakra or chakras need to be recharged or cleared via the music we listen to? I have not formally investigated this, so I will leave that for you to think about.

When you like many types of music, you can easily find some music to match your moods and thoughts. And if you want to create a certain mood, you can find some music that will reflect that mood. You may end up listening to something entirely different and feel your mood has changed. The music is partly responsible for changing how you feel.

If you listen to the same kind of music for long periods, do you become understimulated in some areas (chakras) and feel off balance or as if something were missing? I lean toward that idea.

If you incorporated other types of music and gave them a chance, could you recharge some of your other chakras and consequently feel something awaken in you—an inspiration, perspective, or idea? Music inspires, helps, stimulates, soothes, and calms emotions, feelings, and thoughts.

## 3. The Great Masters of Music

Beethoven (1770–1827) is one of my favorite composers, but other composers from his era including Mozart, Chopin, and Bach fascinate me as well. They composed heavenly music involving dozens of musicians and instruments at a time when composers and musicians relied solely on handmade instruments. How skilled they must have been!

Everything was much more basic then. There were no computers, synthesizers, or other electronic equipment to enhance the sound, so think of the genius it took to create such intricate and harmonic music in those days.

These composers created music that millions today still enjoy listening to and feel inspired by.

(*Note: A wonderful way to get an insight into European lifestyle at that time is to watch the brilliant movie "Copying Beethoven" (starring Richard Harris and Diane Kruger – or you can watch *"Amadeus* Mozart", starring Tom Hulce).

## 4. Music and Our Senses

Think of how privileged we are to have visual and auditory facilities with which we can explore the world of sound when we compose music or listen to it in ways that were unimaginable just last century.

We can see the music we listen to on our computers via media player visualizations, and we can see the bars on our stereos move to the rhythm of the music. Seeing music in such ways opens another dimension of the world of sound—it opens our senses.

When we are at a concert, we can feel the sound waves from the bass or the drums and feel alive and in tune with the sound; it can almost take us to a trance.

It is of course no coincidence that shamans listen to rhythmic drums to get into trances and reach a realm where they can access information and advice for the benefit of their people.

Movies and TV programs are brought to life with music. The next time you watch a scary movie, turn down the volume, and it will suddenly not seem as scary. On the other hand, listening to the right type of music for a scene can bring about tears, laughter, and other emotions.

*Music is a universal language that creates*
*understanding across any man-made border.*

Since time immemorial, man has made music. Drums and wind instruments are among the oldest instruments. Music is used in rituals, ceremonies, celebrations, and memorials to create moods and atmospheres.

Music can make us feel elated or calm. It can be comforting. It can create images in our minds and help us forge bonds with others. It can help us be imaginative, creative, and productive. Music can help us accept things in the face of difficult times and show us that life goes on.

Music is a natural healer.

# Chapter 12

........................................................................

# Nature

........................................................................

*The frog does not drink up the pond in which it lives.*
—Native American Proverb

*When all the trees have been cut down, When all the animals have been hunted, When all the waters have been polluted, When all the air is unsafe to breathe, Only then will you discover you cannot eat money.*
—Cree prophecy

Many seem to forget we are all part of nature. The lives and lifestyles of many are connected only remotely to the natural world. Many do not think about the natural cycles of life; they seem to have forgotten to appreciate and respect nature; they seem to have forgotten that nature is the basis of their lives on earth.

Without the natural elements, we could not live here. Earth is breathing and alive, so how can we think we can treat it without a care in the world? How can we disregard the fact that when we pollute our planet, we pollute ourselves?

# 1. The Indigenous Way

Indigenous peoples all over the world have always appreciated and respected nature. They have always lived in harmony with it. They understand the cycles, they understand the real value behind the term *sustainable*, and they know to think ahead to ensure there is enough for their children too. We all innately understand the cycles and sustainability, but many have forgotten to live by this knowledge.

Many people live in ways that are not at all natural and sustainable. However, caring about our planet and the natural ways is vital to our planet and ultimately to us!

Maybe we feel that our small contribution to for instance recycling carries so little weight since many major industrial polluters do so much damage. But if we all pollute and disregard the environment, we are creating a dirty pond for ourselves and will have no clean areas for comfortable living.

All indigenous peoples who live by their old ways in harmony with nature and its cycles deserve a big salute! If we all lived out the same respect for and protection of nature, the world would truly be a different place.

# 2. Mother Earth—Our Natural Provider

Everything we can buy or get on this planet comes from this planet. Everything we have and use is here on this planet. We have to take everything we need for our basic survival such as food, water, and medicine from this planet. Everything we need to build housing and infrastructure for all is right here on this planet. The state of our planet very much influences our well-being.

Over millennia, thousands of plant and animal species became extinct due to our ignorant exploitation of the natural resources. Forests are cut down, animals are subjected to poaching and becoming endangered species, people are living in polluted areas, rivers and seas are polluted, and the air and soil is polluted—for what?

There must be other ways to make enough for everybody on the planet without all these polluting industrial plants. Ironically, they are called industrial or power *plants*.

When we look at the exploitation occurring, we can easily recognize the imbalance of it all. When we exploit and starve Mother Earth, we make it harder for ourselves to live here. We are disrupting the balance, and we know we are doing that.

However, Mother Earth knows how to take care of herself and will eventually rid herself of whatever is disturbing her balance. She does that by being in harmony with the universal flow of sustainability and productive growth.

## 3. Disturbing the Natural Balance

According to an article I read around 2011 in *New Scientist* (www. newscientist.com), about 15,000 of the 50,000 types of plants in Asia, Africa, and Eastern Europe are in danger of becoming extinct due to excessive harvesting, pollution, and the emergence of new plant types. Some of the medicinal plants threatened are potentially natural cures for a number of diseases including cancer and malaria.

Many things happening around the world are not in harmony with nature. When did this imbalance start? With the Industrial Revolution?

Maybe the size of the world population is a problem. Are we in fact too many for our planet to sustain, or could the planet hold and sustain more of us? Should we trust that everything is in divine order and that we are supposed to be this many people at this time? Opinions on this are divided.

Thankfully, millions all over the world are concerned about and thinking about the environment and are taking proactive measures to alleviate the problems in spite of political barriers that can be hard to overcome.

## 4. Littering

Think about litter—scraps of paper, cans, plastic and metal products, bikes, batteries, old medicine, scrap from construction sites and heavy industries, and so on. Think about how much is produced daily.

Many countries have recycling plants; many people have become aware of the need for environmental protection and separate dangerous waste from organic waste. Many companies and industrial plants are recycling their waste and scrap.

However, we also see the opposite in many countries. People throw things out of their car windows without thinking about where it will go after that. Do they think about who will pick up after them? Do they throw garbage around in their homes? This planet is home to us all.

Many young people are thoughtless about our environment because they were not taught they were part of nature too. They are being taken farther and farther from the natural world.

## 5. Lack of Environmental Education

We cannot really blame the young people, but we can take time to guide and inform them. We parents are responsible for this as are our educational systems and the government.

Education about our environment is extremely important, but unfortunately, it is not often on the agenda in schools for long enough to make a lasting impact on children and young people.

## 6. Recycling

We did not invent recycling; the concept has always existed. Nature has forever been recycling. In nature, whatever an insect, a bigger animal, or a plant discards is put to use by someone or something else. In natural, undisturbed habitats, nothing is wasted. Every living thing has a purpose and helps everything coexist.

In times of war or natural disasters, people start using and reusing what would have normally ended up in the garbage. When resources become scarce, we start to appreciate them more.

People who do not have the luxury of a very materialistic life recycle as much as they can; it is second nature to them because it is necessary. When you do not have much, you make the best of what you have.

When you have a lot or too much, you tend to become careless and value each thing less. You quickly end up throwing things away that may have been put to better use again. You may think, *Oh well, it was cheap. I'll just buy a new one.*

We can change that behavior by stopping the excessive production of material things and by becoming more aware of our actions and thoughts in this area.

## 7. The Media

The media could offer information and guidance on how not to pollute, and it could reach millions with that message.

Companies that want to sell products use marketing strategies that speak to our subconscious and conscious minds in ways and convince us to buy their products.

The knowledge of how our minds work ought to be used for positive purposes as well, and one area could be to inform the public in positive ways about how to protect our environment.

In many cases, the media has been used too much and has made many people feel complacent about the matter—"Oh look, another article on the environment and how much damage is being done." We can feel overwhelmed by the problem and feel that our small contributions are just drops in the ocean (no pun intended). But every little bit matters; our small contributions spread ripples across that ocean.

If we knew that industries and factories were on the same page as we were about polluting less, that would make our small, daily contributions much more worthwhile.

## 8. The Big Sinners

Why is it even allowed to make products that can take 300 or more years for nature to break down? Factories all over the world often use and emit harmful chemicals in the manufacturing process with no regard for the environment, and many of the products they make are not easily biodegradable.

We know the harm that certain substances, chemicals, and hormones can do to us and nature, but we still allow it. These harmful substances wreck the balance of nature and interfere with our future and that of our children. Pollution affects the air we breathe and the water we drink; it affects all marine life including those we consume, and it affects the soil in which we grow our crops.

It should be a birthright for all children to live in a comfortable and healthy place. We should make sure they too can breathe clean air, swim in the sea, walk in the forest, climb mountains, and eat safely what the earth and the oceans provide.

We should make sure that all areas of the planet are suitable and available for living. If we destroy this planet, is there another place we can go? Why should we destroy this beautiful, blue planet, our home and the home of so much life for millions of years?

Who are we to end that?

# Chapter 13

. . . . . . . . . . . . . . . . . . . . . . . . . . . . . . . . . . . . . . . . . . . . . . . . . . . . . . . . . . . . . . . . . . . .

# Cycles in Nature and
# in Our Lives

. . . . . . . . . . . . . . . . . . . . . . . . . . . . . . . . . . . . . . . . . . . . . . . . . . . . . . . . . . . . . . . . . . . .

Looking at how things work in nature might help illustrate our connection with nature.

Life, as nature, is always changing. Nothing stays the same forever. Our planet is alive; it goes through cycles and changes constantly. It is moving, evolving, rearranging, and healing just as we are. We go through daily, monthly, and yearly cycles in our lives, and nature goes through seasons.

Plants, flowers, and trees spread their seeds throughout their lifetimes. When the mother plants wither and die, they decompose or turn to soil and thus feed the baby plants.

Trees hibernate each year until of course they are very old and wither, but at some stage each year, trees and many plants turn their attention inward during autumn or winter to save energy and life force so they can bloom in the spring and grow bigger and stronger.

During our lives, we go through similar times when we need to pay attention to our life force—our energy—and our health. During these times, we get a chance to digest recent events and our experiences, thoughts, and feelings. We get a chance to turn our attention inward as well. We do this maybe often subconsciously to learn, grow, and become stronger and wiser.

However, some people do not take advantage of this internal attention time and feel stuck in the same situations. They may even eventually feel unstable or unbalanced in many ways. They do not grow as much as they could.

Maybe you feel you have plenty of time for yourself, but suddenly one day, you feel swamped; you have a million things to do, but everybody needs your attention. Life seems hectic. After that, you get some time to yourself again before the next hectic wave rolls in.

Sometimes, you may be able to focus on what you want, but at other times, you cannot seem to get anywhere because you feel you have lost the ability to focus.

Maybe that is when you are unable to move forward as fast or as far as you consciously want. You need to take time to turn your attention inward and digest the recent days or weeks. When you do that, you can recharge and accumulate the energy you need for your next growth spurt just the way nature does it.

## 1. Taking Time to Enjoy Nature

I like to take the long way home if I am driving. I put on one of my favorite tunes and drive slowly through the landscape. Music lifts my mood and adds to the pleasure. I notice the trees, bushes, hills, birds, and flowers I drive past. If I find a spot I like, I pull over, turn off the music, get out of my car, and take it all in.

When we take moments like this, we feel a oneness with everything. Our creativity and sense of joy get a boost. We feel grounded and connected. We get a feeling of grandness and humility at the same time. Nature is capable of doing that to us!

*Let children walk with Nature, let them see the beautiful blendings and communions of death and life, their joyous separable unity, as taught in woods and meadows, plains and mountains and streams of our blessed star, and they will learn that death is stingless indeed, and as beautiful as life.*
—John Muir (1838–1914), conservationist, writer

*The more we are separated from Nature, the unhappier we get.*
—Unknown

# Part 3

........................................................................

# Body

........................................................................

*With our bodies, we bring to life the essence of
our thoughts and spiritual virtues.*
-Marianne Johansen

# Chapter 1

........................................................................

# Creating Balance

........................................................................

We are multifaceted beings. We consist of bodies, minds, and souls or spirits that hold all higher knowledge. Our bodies, minds, and spirits need to be in balance and taken care of before the whole of us can feel good.

This part of the book looks at how we can increase our sense of general well-being by using our bodies in a way that lets in all things positive and healing.

The following chapters provide information about a selection of natural healing therapies, how to have a healthy relationship with food, and various "dis-eases" and how they manifest in our bodies.

## 1. Our Bodies

Our bodies are our physical links with nature. In this busy, bustling world, that can be easy to forget. We can take care of our bodies. We should be able to choose how we want to heal our bodies in case of imbalances.

We may sometimes forget we are responsible for our bodies. Have our bodies become allergic to natural remedies? No. The health of our spiritual and mental selves affects the health of our physical selves because they are all connected.

We are responsible for our bodies and accountable for our health. More than 90 percent of all physical imbalances are psychosomatic (*psyche* means mind, and *soma* means body). Many people even believe that all diseases and imbalances are due to mental or emotional and effectively spiritual imbalances.

Psychosomatic dis-ease manifests through an imbalance in the mind. It does not mean that whoever is ill is really just a hypochondriac; it means we can all manifest mental imbalances and negative thoughts into a physical imbalance often without our realizing it.

We may be so used to harboring negative thoughts or complaints that we do not notice it until somebody asks us to stop whining or points out that we always seem so gloomy. We may not consciously notice a mental or emotional imbalance until we get ill.

The fact that our thoughts can manifest into a physical dis-ease should not make us feel guilty or scared; it should only help us realize our potential to influence the state of our bodies and remind us that our thoughts as well as our actions affect the whole of us including our bodies.

Our physical bodies are the lowest of our vibrations, the outer, etheric bodies being of higher vibration. So in a way, our bodies are the last place for an imbalance to settle.

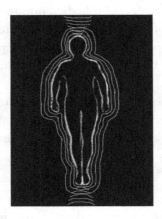

You can become more aware of the connection between your mind, soul, and body in a number of ways.

- Explore natural/pagan medicines and treatment methods. We all need treatments of some sort at some time. Choose one that appeals to you and feels right.
- Observe what activities (physical or mental) leave you feeling invigorated, recharged, and balanced, and then do those activities. Learn to listen to your ideas and follow through with them.
- Keep your feet happy—give them a good rub with a good lotion.
- Have a body massage regularly by a professional masseuse or masseur.
- Do some type of exercise daily that makes you happy.

- Notice what foods and drinks leave you feeling energetic and healthy and go with them. Avoid foods and drinks that leave you feeling tired and bloated.
- A well-groomed body can lift your mood.
- Give your body the rest it needs; listen to its signals before they turn into warning bells.

You can heal your physical, mental, and emotional layers because they are deeply connected. Your mental activities affect your emotional and physical states and vice versa. You comprise your body, thoughts, emotions, and feelings.

Your mental body is probably the one that often works overtime, so rest your mind. Let your thoughts wander. Enjoy a meditation, a massage, cozy time with your partner, music, or other things that will help your thoughts flow by. Start healing yourself step by step. Unravel yourself and heal what needs healing.

# Chapter 2

·····································

# Natural Healing Therapies

·····································

Millions of people are returning to natural healing therapies. They find that these methods work beautifully and that they can heal and harmonize body, soul, and mind simultaneously.

We take in air, colors, touch, sounds, feelings, thoughts, and energy from everything and everybody around us. We are sure to find a healing method that suits our bodies, moods, thoughts, colors, and energies. The following pages describe just a selection of gentle but powerful natural healing methods available, and I have tried many of them and like them.

Important note: the following is not to be construed as medical advice in any way. Be your own judge of who you want to let into your personal space to heal you. Always seek a qualified, trustworthy, and experienced practitioner to perform or guide the healing. Beware of possible contraindications.

## 1. Reiki

Reiki (pronounced *ray-key*) means "universal life force." Being a Usui Reiki master and a Jikiden Reiki practitioner, I have dedicated quite a few pages here to explain the wonderful powers of Reiki because they have changed my life since I received a brief treatment in 1995 in Munich.

A friend of mine once called Reiki a "massage of the soul," which I think is appropriate; Reiki helps the soul release toxins and negative energies in much the same way physical massage helps rid the body of toxins. You are also helping the whole you become recharged and harmonized.

You could also describe a Reiki session as a cleansing of yourself through your higher self or an energy healing session. You are letting go of negative energy and replacing it with pure healing light. Reiki cleanses your feelings, mind, physical body, and your spiritual body—all that is you.

Once you have received healing via Reiki or when you have actually passed on healing with positive intentions with your bare hands, you will realize how powerful we all are. You will believe in the power of intention and the powers beyond our physical reality.

As with all healing therapies, the client has to allow the healing to take place. Through experience, I have learned that it is also crucial to tune in to a client, to use and trust your intuition, and to know how to follow it.

Furthermore, over time, you will develop treatment routines, as I have, and may start using divine, celestial, and universal helpers, beings, symbols, mantras, and crystals.

## 2. Sensing Energies

Speaking of energies, reef sharks and hammerhead sharks seem to register electrical impulses from other fish around them. These sharks have so-called electromagnetic field receptors in their heads and can detect electric fields produced by certain prey. It is also thought that sharks navigate using electric fields generated by the magnetic fields of the earth (Wikipedia: "electroreception").

While we may not have electromagnetic field receptors, I think we do have a way of registering if not electric fields, let us call them energy fields, auras, or vibes from other people or our surroundings. If we do not pick them up with our physical five senses, what are we using to pick up these energies?

I mention the ability of the sharks to pick up electric fields to illustrate how we could also use senses other than our five physical ones.

## 3. Chakras

When you work with energy healing modalities, you work with the chakras or energy wheels of the body.

Chakras were first described thousands of years ago in Hindu sacred texts, and the knowledge of chakras plays a big part in Ayurvedic teachings originating in India. (*Ayurveda* is the science of life, conscious living, holistic prevention.)

It is believed that we each have seven main chakras (eight if you count the higher heart chakra) though we have other chakras beyond our physical bodies as well anchored in our etheric layers of our being.

The first of our physical chakras is our root chakra, which is at the base of the spine, and the seventh one is our crown chakra, which is on top of the head. In between are five main chakras and a number of minor chakras for example at our fingertips, toes, and temples.

## 3.1. Balanced and Imbalanced Chakras

The main chakras spin at various speeds. When they all spin at their healthiest speed, we are in total balance physically, mentally, and spiritually. Our energy levels are high, we feel charged up and healthy at all times, and we are completely in tune with our bodies, minds, and spirits. This is however rarely the case if ever for us on the earthly plane.

Most of us go through life with one or more chakras out of balance at any one time. A chakra can be overactive, in balance, or underactive. As energy sensitives, we can feel these imbalances. There can be various reasons for these imbalances.

- We are constantly picking up energies from around us positive as well as negative from other people or certain places or events, and we are constantly digesting all these energies. Some of them may stick to us and influence the balance of our chakras depending on how we cope with the input.
- We also produce negative energies through our thoughts and actions often without knowing it. If we have negative energy in us and our ethereal bodies, we may develop an imbalance that if not harmonized and healed will manifest and affect us physically.
- We may also feel our energies are depleted or drained. This can happen if we have been in contact with someone with ill intentions or someone who subconsciously drains energy from other living beings—an energy vampire if you will.

Someone may have left you feeling drained and empty. Someone consciously or indeed subconsciously taking positive energy from you or showering you with his or her negative energy causes this.

We may not feel anything or know about the effect of the negative energies we have picked up or developed. A qualified and tuned-in healer can tell if a specific chakra is in or out of balance. Reiki can balance the chakras. Often but not always, clients need several treatments to bring the imbalance to the surface of the conscious mind so they can be aware of what needs healing.

## 3.2. How We Feel When Our Chakras Are Imbalanced

Sometimes under various influences and according to how and what kind of energy we absorb, our chakras may start spinning faster or slower than their ideal speeds. Though we may not be aware of this, we will immediately feel the effects.

We may feel hyperactive, stressed, or restless, or we may start growing extra cells like psoriasis or eczema for protection depending on which chakra—which area of our lives—needs healing; we may become depressed, sluggish, and careless, and we may feel drained or with no zest for life. These are just some of the experiences we may feel when our chakras are not in balance.

As our physical and subtle bodies are all energy in different forms, we feel the effects of energy intake and output in our bodies.

If something is allowed to fester for too long without our knowing or our willingness to look at it, it can manifest physically. I lean toward believing that the physical reaction is the last resort for something to let us know it needs healing. For some time, we may have knowingly or unknowingly ignored several emotional, mental, or even minimal physical warnings. I have to do further research on this topic, but for now, I assume that certain things take longer to manifest physically rather than ethereally—in our spiritual bodies or auras—because our physical energy bodies vibrate at a slower rate.

## 3.3 Chakras in Relation to Color, Sound, and Body Parts

Chakras are energy wheels; they respond to other forms of energy such as sound, including music, and color. Each chakra has a corresponding sound, tone, and color as is also shown in various ancient records of chakra knowledge.

As our physical bodies are a form of energy, every chakra has corresponding organs in our bodies. Our chakras take in energy to nurture our physical bodies including our organs.

The brief guideline below of the chakras is based on my research and experience as an energy healer and reader.

Crown Chakra:

On top of our head; our connection with the universe, our higher selves, the cosmos, and higher realms beyond our physical senses.

Third-Eye Chakra:

Between our eyebrows and slightly up. It includes all our senses including our sixth sense. Understanding of the higher principles and visions.

Throat Chakra:

Throat. Communication, sound, expression of creativity, voice, writing.

Upper-Heart Chakra:

Thymus. Mid sternum. Understanding of higher love.

Heart Chakra:

Heart. Love. Compassion. Seat of the soul. Understanding. Self-love. Love of other beings.

Solar Plexus Chakra:

Below rib cage, mid. Personality. Feeling and being integrated. Expression of personality.

Navel Chakra:

Below navel. Creativity, emotions, sexual energy.

Root Chakra:

Near coccyx. Sense of belonging to the physical world. Security. Survival. Safety.

I mentioned Maslow's hierarchy of needs. It is tempting to mention how similar the needs of Maslow's pyramid are to our chakras even though the pyramid contains only five levels as opposed to the seven chakras. Interestingly enough, however, we see that the lower levels of the hierarchy of needs are concerned with physiological needs; as we move up the pyramid, the needs become more psychological and even spiritual.

Similarly, in the chakra system, the lower chakras have to do with our physical aspects while the higher chakras open up to the more spiritual and ethereal aspects of life.

## 3.4 Ruled by the Three Lower Chakras

When we are spiritually aware or learning to become more spiritually balanced, we acknowledge and use at least the main seven chakras.

When I was learning about pranic healing, Dr. Raj, my teacher, explained that many people are ruled by the three lower chakras; their lifestyles are based primarily on fulfilling their basic needs such as physical survival, procreation, fulfillment of physical needs including sexual, mental satisfaction, and ego fulfillment. "The remaining four chakras—i.e., from the heart to the crown—are very weak in these people," he told me.

Apparently, people who operate mainly through their lower chakras are not very spiritually inclined. They are emotionally cold; they do not make it a priority to think with their hearts or consider and respect others' feelings and lives. They have simply not woken up to the sound or vibration of their higher chakras. They consciously choose not to listen to their higher chakras because they are so attracted to the physical dimension with all its material and physical attractions, or they do not know how to open up to their higher chakras.

This was part of his explanation of some of the aspects and influences of our energy wheels.

## 4. Other Types of Energy Healing

Reiki and pranic healing are based on the same principles, namely that *ki* or prana is the universal life force that runs through everything. When the flow of the life force is blocked because of our experiences, thoughts, or feelings, imbalances occur.

There is a life-force energy. We are energy. I believe all physical ailments and diseases can be healed with energy healing—healing our chakras, thoughts, and emotions and healing our spiritual bodies.

When channeled through the hands of a competent, intuitive, giving, and committed person, Reiki can heal anything on anybody as long as it is in line with their overall plan. I can almost hear skeptics thinking, *Ah! Here's the escape route.* But the more you become involved in certain types of spirituality, the notion of each of us having an overall plan seems very natural.

## 4.1 Vedic Reiki

A wonderful friend of mine who is a Reiki master, teacher, author, and poet to mention a few of her many talents introduced me to Vedic Reiki.

She taught me how to make use of certain mantras during healing sessions when deemed appropriate and helpful. There are different mantras for different ailments, and the healer uses whichever feels right at the time. Vedic Reiki is very powerful and adds to the healing experience when performed with respect and humility.

## 4.2 Pranic Healing, Mahi-Kari, Mauri, and Lomi-Lomi Massage

I believe there are other concepts that fit the description of healing with energy. As mentioned above, pranic healing is another method of tapping into a greater power or energy. A session is similar to a Reiki session, and you also work with the aura, which is an energy coat, and the chakras, which are energy vortices.

Mahi-Kari is another form of healing that draws toxins out of your aura or energy field. It is also a very profound experience and powerful as well. As with Reiki, it leaves you feeling refreshed and able to reach deeper levels in yourself.

Mauri and Lomi-Lomi massages are other methods of healing I have also had the good fortune to try. They involve a physical massage, but the theories behind them are similar to energy-based types of healing.

Marui and Lomi-Lomi massages are also done with loving intentions.

The practitioner is in a giving and positive state of mind, and this is released to the receiver thus helping him or her heal.

This is another example of how we can use our minds to channel the energies around us. We just have to remember to protect our clients and ourselves so we are sure to channel only positive energies.

## 4.3 Body Massage

Nothing stimulates and soothes your body like a well-performed body massage. The benefits are multiplied if you receive a massage in beautiful, positive surroundings. The effects of a massage are many on the physical, mental, and emotional planes. Below are some of the conditions a massage can improve or even cure.

- back pain
- neck and shoulder tension
- arthritis and rheumatism
- mental and physical fatigue
- stress and anxiety
- removal of toxins that accumulate in muscles after sports or in general over time
- calf cramps and other muscle spasms
- improvement of muscle tone
- rehabilitation of stroke patients
- reduction in healing time of fractures, breaks, and dislocations
- sprains and strains
- improvement of circulation affecting greater mobility
- improvement of the function of internal organs
- digestion
- lymphatic system
- all types of headaches
- premenstrual tension and menopausal problems
- wrinkles and rejuvenation
- reduction of body fluids

Important note: some conditions may require a doctor's permission prior to a massage.

There are many types of massages; Swedish, Thai, Mauri, Lomi-Lomi, hot stone, and shiatsu to mention a few.

## 4.4 Reflexology

This involves applying pressure to and massaging the feet; it is also an ancient form of massage that offers amazing results.

Reflexology is known to have cured many ailments, aligned imbalances in the body, given relief to labor pain, and much more.

As with any massage, it is of highest importance that the healer is trained and has extensive knowledge of the physiology of the human body as well as a wide range of ailments and disorders.

It is equally important to know when not to perform a massage and be aware of possible contraindications. Please refer to other sources of further information on this subject.

## 4.5 Color Therapy

Color therapy is believed to promote general healing from within. It can boost your immune system, and it is particularly useful when it comes to alleviating psychological imbalances such as anxiety, depression, insomnia, behavioral disorders, SAD (seasonal affected disorder) syndrome, and learning difficulties to mention some. It can also boost creativity.

Color therapy can be given in colored rooms lit by colored lightbulbs via crystals or fabrics or even in modern spas where you can enjoy sitting in a Jacuzzi lit up alternately in different colors.

If you are allowing a healing to take place, you will feel how colors affect your mood and emotional state.

You can also use meditation to bring color into your life. During a meditation, see yourself bathed in a rainbow; see yourself sitting at the end of a rainbow and absorbing all the colors. The colors of the rainbow also correspond to the colors of the chakras!

Notice the colors in your house and clothes. What is your favorite color? Find the meanings of the different colors in books or magazines or on the internet. There is plenty of information on this topic as well as on colors in relation to our chakras.

## 4.6 Yoga

Yoga, which means "union," is a wonderfully calming and balancing type of exercise. When you do yoga, you unite your mind, body, and soul. After a session of yoga, you should feel elevated and more balanced physically, mentally, and emotionally. It is a real boost if done correctly.

Yoga should never be painful. You should never stretch or reach farther into a position if it causes too much pain. Go as far as you can, hold it there, and remove any discomfort gradually every time you exhale. If you do yoga regularly, you will soon be able to reach farther into the various positions.

Yoga originated in India supposedly around the third millennium BC; it is considered the oldest system of personal development in the world. However, another source states the following about the origins of yoga.

> Born in India, almost 26,000 years ago, Yoga is believed to have evolved during the period of the "Sat Yuga," also called the Golden age. This period became known as a time of everlasting peace and abundant blessings, filled with seekers of the Eternal Truth. That is why, probably, even today we associate yoga with sages and hermits. (www.medindia.net/yoga-lifestyle/yoga-origin.htm)

When you perform yoga, allow time while you are in the various positions or *asanas* as well as in between them so you can feel your body and muscles and any tension melting away. Regular yoga sessions will help you concentrate on and be aware of your body.

Equally important is taking the time to enjoy the relaxing last part (the *savasana* or corpse position) of a yoga session when you mentally go through every muscle to feel your whole body relaxing. Yoga is very much about awareness of self.

As I mentioned earlier, a yoga experiment was conducted in a prison, and all the inmates were enrolled in yoga classes. After a number of sessions, they were asked to describe their experiences, and they all said they had been positive. Prison staff noticed that many inmates' moods had improved radically.

Making a few lifestyle changes can have a big impact on our lives. I am sure most of us are aware of that; the challenge is again becoming consciously aware of it and then making changes.

## 4.7 Meditation

When you meditate, you will connect with and sense the real you. You will connect with an inner form of yourself and with something bigger than you, something around and in you. You will reach levels in your subconscious that can assist you in your search.

When you reach that state, you will see your life and life around you in a different light. You will have epiphanies—experiences in which you suddenly see, feel, know, or hear the answers to your questions or thoughts in your mind or system. The answers may come as visions, smells, colors, flashes, feelings, or physical signs.

You may become aware of something you did not know was in you because it was only in your subconscious mind until then. You may receive a revelation or a message you will want to investigate. It all depends on what you are ready for, what you are looking for, and how open-minded you are.

When conducted correctly and safely, meditation will leave you with a clear mind, a calm body, new energy, and a relaxed state that will enable you to face any of your challenges and stress.

You can do meditation on your own or in a group guided by a qualified healer. If you meditate on your own, simply put on some relaxing music, light a candle, close your eyes, and let your mind wander at first. Then tell your mind (your ego) to take a rest so you can reach that space where your mind is no longer in control and where your higher self will emerge.

You can use visualizations such as rainbow light surrounding you and keeping you safe, or you can ask angels or God to protect and heal you or whatever feels right to you. You can also ask your inner or higher self for guidance and answers. As long as you relax and take the time, something will come to you when you are meditating.

But remember to come back to reality! Notice your breathing for a few breaths, feel the ground you are sitting or lying on, notice again the noises around you, move your fingers and toes, stretch your body until you open your eyes, and realize you are back here in the present.

Give thanks to whomever you asked for protection and guidance. Give thanks to Mother Earth and anything or anybody who comes to mind—your higher self, deceased loved ones, and so on. Express your gratitude. Sit for a few minutes to soak it all in, and write down anything that comes to mind.

Meditating in a group is also recommended as you are always sure to find the wonderful feeling that you and those with whom you have meditated with are all somehow connected. It is also very comforting, exciting, and useful to share your experiences with your group.

You can also buy meditation tapes or CDs with guided meditations or download them from the internet. There are many wonderful meditations for different purposes. Whatever you choose, it should feel right and positive before you embark on your meditation journey.

## 4.8 NLP

Neuro-linguistic programming (NLP) describes the fundamental dynamics between mind (neuro) and language (linguistic) and how their interaction affects your body and behavior (programming).

NLP is a way of improving your life experience through awareness of your five senses, how you function, and how you adapt to and handle different situations. The theory behind NLP is that we do not know what reality is; we can know only what we perceive as reality.

All our observations, behaviors, actions, and feelings about things are based on how we process everything around us. Once we begin to understand the processes behind our minds and how our minds affect our behaviors, we can change our behaviors. Many psychotherapists use NLP techniques to promote a better understanding of self.

NLP ties in with many other forms of therapy as it includes the mind and body. What it does not seem to include is the spiritual aspect of our beings. However, it is an effective and tangible way to learn how we function.

For further reading, I recommend books, magazines, or the internet.

> The people who are most effective are the ones who have a map of the world that allows them to perceive the greatest number of available choices and perspectives. NLP is a way of enriching the choices that you have and perceive as available in the world around you. Excellence comes from having many choices. Wisdom comes from having multiple perspectives. (www.nlpu.com—Robert B. Dilts)

## 4.9 Crystal Therapy

Crystals are minerals in their most stable form that have crystallized over millions of years. They vibrate at different frequencies and have different healing abilities depending on their types and colors.

When crystals are used in a healing session, specific vibrations in our cells resonate with certain crystals' vibrations and thus return us to a healthy and stable equilibrium—balance.

Some people who have undergone experienced crystal therapy including my clients and me report getting tingling, blissful, or powerful feelings. Sometimes, crystals make you feel happy or bring out sadness. I have felt all of the above and more. It's amazing to have a crystal put on your body and feel its energy.

I also use crystals in my Reiki and other energy healing sessions with clients as I am intuitively guided to do so.

During and after crystal healing, clients may feel purified, light, and energized. As with Reiki, massage, and other alternative therapies, some people may need only a few sessions of crystal healing to clear away imbalances; others may need several sessions.

Besides being used for healing and balancing, crystals are also often used in meditation to enhance a specific feeling or emotion or to heal the vibrations of people who meditate.

You may suddenly find yourself wanting to buy crystals as I suddenly started to do twenty years ago, or you may feel attracted to a certain crystal and feel that you need it. My advice is to go with your intuition. Acquire the crystal and read about it in one of many wonderful books available. Letting crystals into your life can be life changing.

## 4.10 Aromatherapy

Aroma oils, essential oils, are used in massage and Ayurvedic treatments. Many people use essential oils in aroma lamps to fragrance their home, to create a special mood, or to clear an air of negativity. Our sense of smell is very important to us and is connected with our root chakras, which also link us with the physical world and with survival.

In aromatherapy—massage—different natural oils are mixed with a base oil so they can be used for massage. Natural oils have different healing qualities and are suitable for different ailments. The molecules of the oil are absorbed through the skin when applied and can treat the client.

Just smelling certain natural oils can have a healing effect emotionally and mentally; when we connect a certain smell with something pleasant, we feel good.

Many of us believe that frankincense can minimize feelings of anxiety and depression. People around the globe have used and still burn incense, dried sage, and essential oils in aroma lamps when praying, meditating, or practicing yoga or other forms of natural healing or religious ceremonies. The tradition of burning incense goes back to ancient times.

Today, many people need scientific proof before they will trust using natural remedies, but millions swear by the old, positive traditions and incorporate them into their lives.

Important note: aromatherapy must always be conducted by a professional; some oils are very strong; they may be contraindicated for certain conditions and may cause side effects.

## 4.11 Homeopathy

Homeopathy works around the symptoms of an ailment or disease. Different people may experience different symptoms of the same disease and may thus require different homeopathic remedies. When you experience certain symptoms, the substance to take is one that produces the same symptoms in a healthy body.

Homeopathic remedies are usually based on natural ingredients. They are very dilute, they are not addictive, and they can be taken on their own or with other medications without producing any unwanted side effects.

However, it may be difficult for the untrained to find the right remedy.

To do so, you need to be aware of a range of characteristics of yourself and your complaint. You can find help with that on websites or in books.

Homeopathic remedies can cure the underlying problem as well as its symptoms of any ailment. Homeopathic remedies can cure long-term, chronic conditions as well as short-term ailments. For best and safest results, consult a professional homeopath. As you build up your own knowledge and understanding of homeopathic remedies, you may become more able to prescribe a remedy or more remedies for your treatment.

Please remember this: consult with your doctor before you stop taking any prescribed medications; otherwise, you may endanger your health. If you symptoms get worse or do not go away, seek professional medical attention. Minor symptoms may be signs of more-serious conditions, so a timely diagnosis by your doctor could save your life.

## 4.12 Acupressure and Acupuncture

Acupressure and acupuncture use the same points on the body's energy pathways, called meridians, to stimulate the flow of *chi*, or life energy. It is the same as the *ki* in Reiki, and it restores balance and harmony in your body. It is thought that when chi becomes stagnant and its flow is disrupted, illness and disease result. There are more than 350 acupoints on the meridians.

Acupressure is the older of the two types of healing. It and acupuncture originated in China. Acupressure is applied with the fingers and can be done by you as long as you follow proper instructions and are aware of any contraindications.

Acupuncture is done by inserting needles into the meridian points. Acupuncture should be performed only by a trained professional acupuncturist who follows correct hygiene procedures.

Both forms of healing are believed to be around 4,000 to 5,000 years old and were introduced in Europe only around 200 years ago. Since then, they have become more widespread and popular in the Western world as well as an all-around art of healing.

## 4.13 Music

Music is very much connected to our feelings and moods. Most of us have listened to music that changed our outlook too. Music can for example

- make us want to dance, laugh, sing, and love,
- help us relive specific situations,
- bring back feelings from previous situations with the same music,
- bring relief to stressful situations,
- put us in a state of trance, relaxation and bliss, and
- help expand our imagination, our perspective, and our ability to solve problems or challenges.

Music can also have a negative effect on us.

- It can make a situation scary.
- It can make us feel irritated and aggressive.
- It can make us feel tired and drained.
- It can make us hyper or even stressed.

Since time immemorial, people seem to have preferred basic instruments such as drums and some types of wind instruments including flutes. If you have ever heard native or tribal drumming of any kind, you will know this way of creating rhythm speaks to us all in basically the same way.

Drumming can make us feel connected to our inner selves and others and with nature and the universe. Listening to and performing drumming is very grounding and can help release negativity in us. It creates a feel-good factor in most people.

Today, many bands and individuals produce the same feel-good factor in their music. Even if we all feel good about music in its many forms, we all have preferences based on our needs. What some people find energetic music may be perceived by others as draining or boring. What some find releasing or exciting may be downright noisy or negative to others.

This falls in line with my theory mentioned earlier that people are divided into different artificial groups depending on race, religion, material wealth, and so on, whereas a more natural grouping would be based on feelings, actions, values, and emotions. We instinctively create these groupings by choosing whom we let into our circles of friends and others.

Music can heal in its own right, and it is often a key component in other forms of alternative healing. It can be soothing and uplifting to listen to soft, relaxing music while having a massage for example, and it can aid in bringing forth calm emotions. Our choice of music tells us a lot about our inner state.[6*]

## 4.14 Affirmations

We are often our own biggest hindrances to achieving what we want because the biggest blockages lie in the way we think. When we use affirmations, we aim at turning our negative ways of thinking into positive ways of thinking. When we think positively and believe in the positive, we invite positives into our lives.

Affirmations are mantras in a sense. Using affirmations makes you conscious of what you are thinking and how you work. When you say things to yourself repeatedly, you change the negatives in your subconscious that make you act in certain ways.

When you use affirmations, you always use the present tense as if your new program or way describes your current life as if your wish has already come true. You can say the affirmations as often as you like whenever a situation arises.

Here are examples of affirmations.

- I have abundance in all life areas.
- I am surrounded by caring friends.
- Money comes easily to me, and I put it to good use.
- I can heal myself and others.
- I am running a successful business.

The list goes on and on. It is up to you to decide what you want to reprogram or install in yourself in a positive way. You can write your affirmations down and keep them in your pocket or purse so you will be reminded of them several times a day. You can stick them on your fridge, bike, dashboard—anyplace you are bound to see them several times a day to remind you.

When you have become more consciously aware of how you think in certain situations, you will notice what may have seemed like forced thinking in the beginning has become natural. When that happens, you will know your affirmations are working!

---

[6] * See more on this topic in my chapter dedicated to music.

It is important to be persistent. And it is important to believe in what you are telling yourself. It is equally important to start feeling as if your life has already taken a positive turn. Start feeling successful, balanced, wealthy, and so on. Move forward step by step whether they are little or big. And remember that thought is creation.

## 4.15 Visualizations

You might also call these visual affirmations. Using visualizations to promote balance, harmony, a positive direction, or general well-being for yourself can help you consciously focus on whatever kind of positivity you need to build up. Visualizations may also come to you more or less automatically during a healing session; you might see images in front of your closed eyes.

To use visualizations consciously as a healing tool, create an image of your choice with your inner eye with your eyes closed. You can add to the image or take things away until you are happy and at peace with what you are seeing and feeling.

The images may become distorted or negative from time to time when your ego and thoughts try to take control, but just acknowledge that, let that happen, ask the thoughts to go away, relax, breathe, and then consciously go back to the positive image you want to work with.

When your visualization is strong and you can hold it, get into the feeling of it. Does it give you the feeling you desire? Maybe you need to add more or take some things away. Is your mind trying to erase your lovely image? If so, steer your thoughts and feelings back to the desired image again.

As is the case with affirmations, it is important to visualize your desires as often as possible and feel that they are already a reality. Even if this seems manipulative at first, you will soon start feeling your new reality for real.

## 4.16 Hypnotherapy

Hypnotherapy—hypnosis—is a way of reaching your inner mind, your subconscious mind, to provide positive suggestions and harness your inner powers so you can make the changes you desire—e.g., gaining more self-confidence, stopping the pollution you put your body through by smoking, clearing a phobia, and so on.

It is also very similar to affirmations, but instead of you programming yourself, you are using the help of a professionally trained therapist.

It is important that you see a qualified and professional therapist with whom you feel comfortable and you trust.

Your hypnotherapist will guide you through hypnosis. Contrary to popular belief, you will not be asleep or in a trance. You will be awake and aware of what is going on, and you will feel very relaxed. After the session, you will be able to remember what was said as if you had had a normal conversation with someone.

You might feel very empowered after a session, or you may feel nothing. Yet when you encounter a situation similar to the one you have been treated for—e.g., a situation that normally made you feel insecure—you may find that you are able to deal with it in a more self-confident way.

Hypnotherapy helps to reprogram your inner mind much as affirmations and visualizations do toward more-positive actions and thoughts that replace your old negative patterns and behaviors.

# Chapter 3

## The Senses of Our Bodies

Think of your body as your companion while you are on earth. You take your body with you wherever you go. It is a shell that protects you and enables you to live. Your body is your connection with the physical plane, with nature, and with natural things. Through your body, your mind is your connection to a higher consciousness as well.

No matter what your body looks like, it allows you to experience and enjoy so many sensations emotionally and externally. Think about some of the pleasures your body can bring you.

- a sensation of fullness after a meal
- a feeling of relaxation
- sexual excitement
- a sense of happiness or excitement
- a sense of rejuvenation after a good sleep
- a sense of belonging and relaxation when lovingly touched
- a sense of energy being replenished when standing in a forest
- breathing in fresh air
- water tickling your skin
- good memories associated with a certain smell
- a feeling of happiness when seeing something beautiful
- a sense of peace and light and purpose during meditation

These are just some of our "It feels good to be alive" sensations, and our ability to experience these feelings and appreciate them plays a big part in how we actually feel about life. Our ability to feel plays a big part in how we live.

# Chapter 4

## Looks, Looks, Looks

Some people have been blessed with natural good looks while others have to work hard at looking good. But on what grounds do we find someone good looking or not?

According to research, there is apparently a formula for universal beauty that involves ratios between different facial features that most of us find appealing.

We all like to look at beautiful or handsome people. We like to admire the features of those we consider attractive or sexy. We can admire their body types, eyes, hair, and hands or the way they move. We might even admire people of both sexes albeit not necessarily in a sexual sense.

### 1. Good-Looking = Kindhearted?

Nevertheless, we have all met people who were not particularly handsome or beautiful on the outside, but when we got to know them better, we discovered they had hearts of gold.

Alternatively, we may have met a gorgeous hunk or a beautiful honey who made our hearts beat fast but who turned out to be an unfeeling womanizer or someone who simply played with our feelings just to gain something.

To confuse us completely, we may have met people who were not physically attractive and who were not kind as well. We may have met people who were very attractive on the outside as well as on the inside. Maybe they were not always beautiful on the inside, but they may have learned some lessons along the way. So maybe there are no definite rules about the connection between our appearance and our virtues or character traits.

I think our physical features give off some information about who we are on the inside, but I also think we have not all yet learned how to gather that information consciously.

We still need to look inside others to find out what they hold in there. Maybe this is so to teach us to see others with our hearts and intuition.

Imagine that no matter what we look like on the outside, our inner core is filled with light, understanding, compassion, and love. Around our core, we may have gathered layers of low self-esteem, fear, pride, greed, vanity, and selfishness. Shedding and healing those layers however we choose helps us get closer to our inner core. Beautiful image, isn't it?

Sometimes, vanity is our biggest weakness, and looks may seduce us. We may feel great if we are seen with very good-looking partners; we may feel proud that we caught gorgeous people, Sometimes, we are so happy with the way somebody looks that we forget to look inside as well.

No matter how somebody looks, there will always be one or more who admire him or her. We may be instinctively attracted to someone who is universally beautiful, but we are also individually attracted to certain types. We can be attracted to someone based on a physical, mental, or spiritual attraction or on a combination of these. The point is that everybody has different features and everybody has admirers.

Many gorgeous people have insecurities and obstacles; they are not necessarily comfortable in their own skin. No matter what you look like, embrace your features and find your ideals so you can be comfortable in your own skin.

That's often easier said than done, which is why we can seek help from others. We are here to help each other!

# Chapter 5

## Stages of Well-Being

The better you feel mentally, spiritually, and physically, the more you want to do for yourself and your surroundings. It is almost like Maslow's pyramid of well-being. His concept is an appropriate way to describe and symbolize many things in life.

Start with a solid foundation of essentials and build your way up to a more refined and harmonious way of living. You end up naturally wanting more balance and harmony in yourself and your physical surroundings including your house, clothes, what you eat and drink, and so on.

Take for instance a simple gesture such as lighting an aroma oil lamp or an incense stick, which I do when I am in a certain state of balance and well-being mentally, physically, and emotionally. It is the icing on the cake when I do that. When I add a soothing aroma to my surroundings, it means that I have a generally good and balanced feeling.

It can be the other way around; sometimes, lighting an aroma oil lamp can help elevate me to a state of calmness and balance that helps me see which areas in the lower stages I need to work on and inspires me to come up with new ideas or concepts for that work.

Lighting an incense stick is just one gesture that could symbolize a heightened sense of internal balance. For others of course, lighting an incense stick is just part of their daily routine.

When certain people are in a heightened state of balance or harmony, they may listen to certain music, perform a certain dance, paint, dress differently, get a fantastic new idea, write something profound, share their experience with others, host a party—on and on—but I think common to all these activities is that they fall into the more creative or sensory area of life.

Just as I think our stages of overall well-being fit into a pyramid shape, I think they correspond well with our seven major chakras. First, we need to tend to our lower chakras, which broadly speaking are the more physical and survival-oriented chakras.

Once we feel connected, grounded, and physically present, we can turn our attention to the middle chakras, which have to do with our sexuality, creativity, emotions, feelings, personality, and ability to give and receive love.

Last, we work on expanding our higher chakras, our communication skills and our imagination, our links with the spiritual, and our awareness of our oneness. With our higher chakras, we link with a higher intelligence, our higher selves, the universe, our core—whatever you like to call it.

When we are balanced inside, our balanced energy pours out into our physical world. We even like things to just look balanced. An imbalance in our outer, physical world can show us there is an imbalance inside caused by stress, blocked emotions, negative thoughts, and other factors.

Think of the days when you get a rush of energy to tidy up, clear out, declutter, organize shelves or papers, and other such tasks. Then think of days when you have no energy for those chores. Notice the difference in what you might have been doing a day or two before you got that positive rush. What gave you the motivation? How can you keep getting motivated like that?

## 1. Psychosomatic Dis-eases

The challenges and problems you face in your physical world reflects the conflicts in your inner world.

Illnesses tell us what types of imbalances are going on inside us—not only those that have manifested on the physical level but also on our mental, emotional, and spiritual levels.

We get the complete picture of what we are here to learn through the internal and external conflicts and imbalances we face. I believe we can heal their causes through one or more of the natural healing therapies we have today if the disease or imbalance is meant to be healed as per our bigger purpose here.

I am not sure where the boundaries are, where energy healing must give way to medical treatment to reach healing. I do not think enough research has been done in that field yet. People have tried alternative therapies before switching to mainstream medical treatments, which can treat the symptoms rather than their causes. The level of medical knowledge and expertise doctors and researchers have today is remarkable, and of course, that saves many lives each day. However, I think many alternative therapists wish there could be greater cooperation between medical doctors and alternative therapists.

## 2. Your Body Manifests Your Thoughts

Below is a brief overview[7]* of the possible link between physical symptoms and their emotional or spiritual counterparts. For those interested, read *You Can Heal Your Life* by Louise Hay and *Reiki—Universal Life Force* by Bodo Baginski and Shalila Sharamon. I have practiced and studied Reiki as well as psychological well-being and metaphysics for many years; the research in these books resonates very well with my experiences and findings.

## 2.1 High Blood Pressure

Blood is the manifested life force flowing in us. It is the giver and distributor of life force in our bodies. High blood pressure can come when we feel pressure internally or externally and have not been able to distribute or ease the conflicts and reach long-lasting calmness of thoughts or feelings. The pressure builds up.

## 2.2 Varicose Veins

Again, this has to do with the flow of the life force manifested as blood in you. You may feel weak, resistant, or inflexible about what you do, and it could be linked to your work.

## 2.3 Overindulging in Fatty Foods and Sweets or Not Eating Enough

You are missing the sweetness of life; you are looking for something to fill you up emotionally and feel the need to fatten up some part of you perhaps for emotional reasons. Think about this when you sink your teeth into a piece

---

[7] * This brief overview is in no way to be construed as a substitute for medical advice; it is merely meant as an inspiration to help you think about the link between your emotional, mental, and spiritual states and your body.

of cake or fried food. What are you missing? How can you fill the gap in a way that gives you what you are really looking for?

And when you do not eat enough, you might be afraid of living to your full extent in whatever package you are in. You could be reluctant to accept your sexuality, sensitivity, self, the way you do things, and your insecurities about how to live and open your treasure chest of talents and skills.

## 2.4 Diabetes

You are yearning for unconditional love and may feel you are not able to open up to receive love.

You may feel bitter with life. You may feel a victim, but what you are really looking for is the sweetness of life. Focus on giving unconditional love; that will help you learn how to receive it.

## 2.5 Hoarseness, Laryngitis

Your throat is your communication gateway. When communication is compromised, that is a sign that you should look for ways to express your dissatisfaction or anger more in tune with your heart, that is, more-loving ways or more-assertive ways, and not be afraid to express your feelings and thoughts.

## 2.6 Substance Abuse, Alcoholism, etc.

You feel a need to cloud and soften reality to deal with the circumstances in your life. You are looking for ways to live a problem-free life as an expression of yourself so you can satisfy your desires and experience things you do not know how to reach otherwise. What are you looking for? Have you yet found love and confidence within?

## 2.7 Digestive Problems

Our stomachs and digestive systems have to do with what we take in and how we process it. This is not only food. Digestive issues also involve the impressions and information we take in through our senses.

We may be too open and take in too much to digest, or we may take in something not right for us. It can have something to do with for example self-confidence or expressing emotions in relation to our intake. Look at what you take in and see the reasons or purpose behind what you allow in. Accept your feelings, and let them flow through you.

## 2.8 Infections (Generally)

A conflict or something else that has been bugging you for a while has not received attention or noticed with the view to resolve the matter.

The above excerpts from my guidelines can maybe inspire you to look at imbalances in a different way and do further research. Physical imbalances hold information for you to heal yourself from within.

## 3. Food, Weight, and Exercise

When we talk about our bodies and healing therapies, we must also turn to topics such as food, weight, and exercise to maintain our bodies.

With increasing numbers of obese people at least in the Westernized world, it is no wonder that so many diets and tips on how to lose weight are available. However, sometimes, the only thing we might actually lose is our general overview and the use of common sense about what to eat and what not to eat.

Whether you are trying to lose or gain weight (which for some can be equally tough challenges), use available guidelines that can show you the average and healthy weight for your height and bone structure. Try not to get obsessive; you still have to feel good in your own skin. As with exercise, it should make you feel good and make you smile. Exercise can nurture body, mind, and soul at the same time.

We are responsible and accountable for our results. It is up to us to do all the work, and it is up to us to listen to the signals from our bodies and stop if we feel discomfort or pain.

Besides our food and drink intake, many components such as our metabolic rate, stress level, blood pressure, genes, mental state, exercise regime, and so on play major roles in how we look and feel about ourselves.

Sometimes, medical conditions can make people put on or lose weight to such an extent that their weight management needs to be controlled by professionals.

## 4. Learn the Basics

Most of us know how to eat sensibly. Many have been taught about the basic concepts of how food affects our weight and health.

- Too much sugar and fat may increase our weight.
- Natural foods such as vegetables and fish are generally good for our overall health.
- Fruits and vegetables are filled with vitamins and often minerals as well.
- The cells of our bodies need minerals, protein, healthy fats, etc. as basic building blocks to maintain our bodies at a healthy level.
- Too much or too little of something can alter the balance.
- Our bodies thrive on alkaline foods and drinks.

When we eat too much of one thing, we may actually start to contaminate or malnourish our bodies instead of nourishing them. For example, eating only salad and drinking water (although both are healthy) do not give us all the other building blocks our bodies need.

To keep your body in a healthy and balanced state, learn some of the basic ideas of how your body works. If you are not receiving or have not received this information through your education or at home, then do some research.

Here are some keys to maintaining a healthy body.

- Take responsibility for what you put in your body.
- Use common sense.
- Eat and drink what you know is good; avoid what you know is potentially bad for you.
- Know when to stop.
- Do not be afraid to look yourself in a mirror.
- Forgive yourself.
- Accept your present now, and vow to improve your health.
- Do not stop eating or eat excessively because you are hurting inside. Balance your mind, body, and spirit to find out where the imbalance lies so you can get to the root of the problem. Ask for help if needed.

Your look is the one you have when you are and feel healthy, glowing, and comfortable with yourself. Nobody else can decide how you should look.

Treat your body like a buddy with love, respect, and care. Help your children to become healthy individuals. Teaching your children about the effect that food has on our bodies is an important task. Why would we not teach our children about the very basis of their existence, i.e., how to make good food for themselves?

Most of us know food and drinks made from scratch are healthier than processed and prepacked foods. However, millions of parents do not always have enough time to prepare home-cooked meals every day.

Decades ago, in many households in many Western countries, the father was away at work every day while the mother was at home cooking, cleaning, washing, and taking care of the children.

Nowadays, many dads and moms are at work most of the day, and many household chores have been compromised, put off until the weekend or delegated to a housekeeper.

If you are working and do not have help at home, finding the time to cook everything from scratch among all the other household chores that need doing every day can be a big challenge.

Many parents feel guilty because they feel they cannot give their children enough time to show them that they love them. Some parents try to compensate by letting their kids eat junk food. Unfortunately, they are not doing their children any favors, at least not if that is a regular occurrence.

*Eat Foods That Are as Close to the Source as Possible*
(from Magenta Pixie, Youtube.com)

You give your children a much healthier option if you cook your meals from scratch with natural ingredients and if you start buying basic natural ingredients that can be jazzed up into very tasty dishes. The trick is knowing how to do just that and eventually passing that knowledge on to your children.

## 4.1 Introducing Your Children to Healthy Foods

When your children are young, introduce them to healthy foods. They may want to try next week what they do not want to try today. If you keep a positive approach and attitude about eating healthy foods, your children will take note and might eventually become curious enough to try.

They may not immediately like something new, but if you give it to them again after a while, they may end up actually liking it. Even if they do not, at least you have tried and can offer something different for them to try.

From my own experience, however, this can be difficult if you have a child who has grown accustomed to asking for and getting sweets or junk food. I have found that a strong conviction and a no-other-option policy on my part over and over has been a necessary step.

Giving our children sweets just because they make a scene otherwise and we want a moment's peace gives us only that—a moment's peace. We will have more moments of peace in the long run if we teach our children right from the beginning. Investing that time in them pays off.

## 5. Organic Foods

In the past before the introduction of additives, pesticides, and other chemicals, all our foods, crops, produce, and livestock were organic. What . we call organic food today was called simply food then.

With the space age in the 1960s came powdered foods and long-lasting canned foods. People got so used to this type of food, fast food, and processed foods that this suddenly seemed like normal or natural food. However, the longevity of such food is the result of chemicals and additives.

In the face of a global disaster of such a magnitude that we were unable to grow crops or breed livestock for food, canned foods could of course been our lifeline. The only other arguments for canned, jarred, and frozen food could be these factors.

- **Time** as it saves us time spent in front of the stove.
- **Choice** as in our ability to buy products other than local ones.
- **Money** as in export possibilities (ties in with choice).
- **Land** as in the growing population/urbanization makes it difficult if not impossible for everybody in a city or town to have a garden to grow crops.

Our view of traditional, natural foods has undergone a transformation or rather a conditioning. Those who showed an interest in organic food were often ridiculed and called hippies in a derogatory way. The term *organic* came along some twenty years ago to define produce and livestock grown or raised without chemicals.

Many in the Western world at least may think that organic is old-fashioned, but when you look at the reasons for using chemicals in our food, you may wonder why that is a better idea.

Nowadays, many people buy only organic products though these products are more expensive.

## 6. You Are What You Eat

You have heard the phrase "You are what you eat." I never gave it much thought until one day some years ago when I started connecting that phrase to the spiritual way of interpreting how our bodies and lifestyles are manifestations of our inner selves.

How we live, how we take things in, and what we take in—food and drink—reflects what is going on inside us and the state of our inner selves. We could turn the saying around: "You eat what you are." As mentioned earlier, we put things into ourselves to fulfill our needs, urges, or cravings. We can change what we take in by becoming aware of our thoughts, feelings, and actions.

If you want to change your diet, you can seek and find many skilled and caring professionals be they dieticians, life coaches, or sports professionals. Maybe a visit to a trained and qualified naturopath could help.

The optimal diet will be nourishing and free of toxins and help us maintain healthy and strong bodies. It is probably not possible to keep all this up at all times, but if we notice the signals our bodies give us, we will have a good chance of maintaining balance.

## 7. Natural Foods

As we grow older, it may seem natural to some of us to revert to old, natural, and basic recipes for food or for natural remedies. When we are young, we tend to go more for the practical and the quick. Young people want everything fast.

However, food can still be made from scratch quickly with all natural ingredients and be healthy.

Natural foods, those we find in nature, are part of the living ecosystem we are part of. These foods help us sustain ourselves. If nature is left to its own devices and if people use the abundance that nature supplies, there would be no food shortages.

I have seen orange and lemon trees in the Mediterranean area bursting with fruits that eventually fall and rot because nobody was allowed to pick the fruit. That leaves me puzzled; there is no common sense behind that.

## 8. Think Simple

Know which foods and how much of them are good for you. Know which foods and how much of them are bad for you. Notice how your body feels after a meal. Eat in moderation. Exercise or do stretches regularly. Feel at peace with your body and what you put in it. A balanced mind leads to a balanced body.

# Chapter 6

........................................................

# Learn to Use Nature's Resources

........................................................

## Disclaimer

Any interaction between natural remedies and medicines prescribed by your doctor or health caretaker could have serious consequences. If you are taking any medications or have any doubts about your health, check with your doctor and/or health caretaker before using nature's medicines.

Besides becoming aware of the spiritual or psychological side to diseases, we can also aid healing of ourselves by trying to heal our physical sides.

The list below is not exhaustive of all properties of each food; it is meant only to help awaken an interest in using natural remedies.

# 1. Some of Nature's Healers

- **Peppercorn** tea w/honey can help loosen phlegm.
- **Pomegranate** seeds can alleviate muscle cramps.
- **Oranges** can boost immunity.
- **Ginger** can cure nausea and morning sickness.
- **Bananas** can help against diarrhea.
- **Broccoli** can prevent cancer.
- **Peppermint** can alleviate nausea and sore throats, soothe mucous membranes, and increase the flow of calcium in muscle cells so sore muscles can relax.
- **Thyme** can inhibit growth of bacteria and loosen phlegm.
- **Hyperikum** tea can help against mild depressions (discuss possible side effects with your doctor prior to drinking hyperikum tea).
- **Licorice root** tea is filled with antioxidants and can be a laxative.
- **Anis** tea can help with flatulence.
- **Chili/Ginger/Horseradish** can increase metabolism.
- **Garlic** can lower blood pressure and relieve the formation of gas in the digestive system.
- **Indian Gooseberry** can control high blood pressure.
- **Lemon** can control high blood pressure and help maintain capillary fragility.
- **Grapefruit** can prevent high blood pressure.
- **Watermelon** can safeguard against high blood pressure.
- **Rice** is low-fat, low-cholesterol, and low-salt. Brown rice can soothe the nervous system.
- **Boiled potatoes** can lower high blood pressure.
- **Parsley** raw or as tea can be very useful against high blood pressure and help maintain blood vessels.
- **Carrot juice** (raw) can be beneficial in treating high blood pressure.
- **Spinach juice** (raw) can be beneficial in treating high blood pressure.

Cutting down on salt, high-cholesterol foods, fats, tea, coffee, and alcohol can help you keep tabs on high blood pressure.

## 2. How to Attain Your Body's Building Blocks

Our bodies need protein, minerals, vitamins, carbohydrates, fats, and other compounds to grow and stay strong and healthy. Below are some foods that will provide you with some of the building blocks you need.

- **Vitamins**: apples, bananas, carrots, green beans, mango, mint, pears, peas, potatoes, spinach, sweet potatoes
- **Minerals**: broccoli, brown rice, bananas, green beans, red lentils, pears, peas, potatoes, quinoa ("mother grain"), spinach, sweet potatoes, black beans
- **Protein**: red lentils, meat, chicken, fish, quinoa ("mother grain")
- **Carbohydrates**: potatoes, bread, brown rice
- **Fiber**: apples, bananas, black beans, broccoli, brown rice, carrots, pears, peas, sweet potatoes
- **Antioxidants**: black beans, butternut squash, pears, lemon, broccoli, carrots, green beans, mango, mint, peas, potatoes, spinach, sweet potatoes, butternut squash
- **Fats:** Broccoli, chicken, fish

The above are examples of where to find what we need to keep our bodies healthy. There is plenty of information available on how to use natural ingredients in the alleviation of many of our physical symptoms.

Be healthy, be curious, and stay balanced.

## 3. Something about Chemicals

Scientists around the world believe that increasing rates of cancer, diabetes and infertility could be reduced by removing certain hormone disrupting chemicals from products that we use in our daily lives. But to date although EU politicians have expressed concern, political action has been half-hearted. (http://assets.panda.org/downloads/edc_chemical_cocktail_leaflet.pdf)

The above leaflet from the World Wildlife Fund contains tips on how to reduce our exposure to chemicals. It also looks at what governments can do to better protect human and wildlife health.

Still, safety regulations vary greatly from country to country. To be best informed and to protect your loved ones and yourself, find more information on the various sources on the internet and magazines that are concerned with the health of all living beings on the planet and the environment.

## 3.1 Chemicals in Food and Staying Informed

Also worth mentioning is the occurrence of additives in consumable goods, the so-called E and A numbers, flavor enhancers, sweeteners, and coloring. You can find abundant information from the ministries of several countries on the possible effects of some of these chemicals in leaflets or on the internet.

Research on nutrition is ongoing. Sometimes, what was thought to be good for us turns out to be not so healthy and vice versa, so keeping informed is always advisable.

## 4. Extracting Information from the Past

To live naturally and sustainably on all fronts, we should seek sound advice from the past. What did our grandparents eat? What did they use to clean and maintain their houses, furnish their houses, and groom themselves?

Of course, times were different then; many people lived in the country and had land to grow crops. Towns were not as crowded, and bartering for food and other goods was very much part of getting what was needed.

However, we can still look at how they got through everyday tasks and what they ate for inspiration. Our grandparents might have used vinegar, baking soda, and lemon as household cleaners and egg yolks or beer as hair conditioners. They may have made their furniture, grown crops in their gardens, or made compost for their garden needs.

Some of these things may be difficult for many of us to do because of our living conditions and circumstances, but we can start to live more naturally and sustainably in a number of ways. We can research the ways of our ancestors and use some of their ideas today.

*Food is Medicine—let your Medicine be Your Food.*
—Hippocrates, ca. 400 BC

# Part 4

## Quick Tips

Below I have compiled some highlights of the ideas on the various topics that have been presented throughout this book:

## 1. Key Points on How to Help Yourself

- Be basic. Think of what we all basically want, need, and like so we can become and stay positive. If it is something you want, you can be sure that everybody else wants it too. You can start a ripple effect. I am talking about e.g. love, compassion, care, understanding, humor, support, etc.

Even if you are afraid of rejection, show care or interest in other people Know that positive attention flatters everyone.

- Influence and comparison can mean pressure. You may feel an enormous pressure trying to live up to certain standards, role models, expectations, and so on around you. Think about the different kinds of people or circumstances that influence you, and think about if it actually feels more like pressure and stress than a healthy, positive influence. Then choose not to be pressured anymore or care what others expect or want from you. Think about what you want, what you care about, and what you would like to give to others.
- Accept that you are not a completely balanced human being. None of us is fully balanced; we all still have lots of issues within us that we need to work on. Do not feel discouraged if you fail; look at the situation as one you can learn from and move away from knowing more than you did before.
- See yourself as part of nature and simple things. One of my favorite mantras is "The more we are separated from nature, the unhappier we get." It reminds me of what is important here. The separation from nature is happening to a great number of people on this earth today. Too many of us are getting so far away from nature and the simple things due to stress, confusion, and greed, and we are running around in circles trying to keep up with payments for housing, food,

clothing, transportation, education, luxury items, on and on. We often forget to take the time to enjoy nature's bounty and harmony.

- When do you take the time to stop and ask yourself some basic questions such as *Am I happy?* or *Do I really want or need this?* or *When did I last have a good laugh with my wife, husband, or children?* When do you ever just sit and watch a sunrise or sunset with someone? When did you last go for a walk along the beach or in the forest or listen to a fantastic piece of music and really take it in and let it ring through every cell of your body?

- Further, think about if you feel that you are going down the wrong path. Are you losing touch with nature, natural things, simple and basic things that cost nothing and that are there for you to enjoy at any time?

- You may suddenly realize that your priorities are all lopsided, upside down, and inside out. When I feel I am getting sidetracked a bit, I paint a world picture—I imagine a situation such as a big regional or global catastrophe or another type of upheaval in some way. Next, I think about what would be of importance to me. As mentioned earlier in this book, this exercise often gives you a different perspective on your current situation.

- Ground yourself! If you feel that you are beginning to lose touch with yourself and you feel that you are beginning to stop caring about yourself or those around you including loved ones, that could be because you are trying to escape some kind of pressure.

Get yourself grounded again. There are some very easy ways to help you feel grounded and part of everything again.

*Sounds.* Pay attention to nature's sounds or natural sounds in your surroundings— birds chirping, running water, wind in trees, truck or cars passing by, rain drumming on a roof, construction sounds, meditative music, other types of music—whatever sounds give you a sensation of being connected to the planet.

*Visualizations.* Sit in a quiet place and imagine roots growing from your feet into the ground; this works even if you are in a tall building or on an airplane. Even if you are moving around, your roots are still connected to the ground. At the same time, imagine that you are connected to the universe, you have upward roots, a channel, from the top of your head that connects you to something positive as you yourself define that and your whole body is in a bubble of white shimmering, protective light. This is a very powerful visualization, and you can use it for some minutes or until you feel energized and grounded!

- Take the time to think about how you could go about solving something in your personal life that has been bothering you. Stay focused on the result you want. This could be for example, "I want to live in peace, harmony, and positivity," or "I want a warm, compassionate relationship with my partner," or "I want to be a good friend and role model to my children." Keep your goal in mind whenever you think of ways to solve a specific challenge and whenever you go through that specific challenge!

- Remember that no matter how much you try to be in balance physically, mentally, and spiritually, you will still get some blows and experience challenges whether they are new ones or the same old challenges you seem to encounter over and over; they are inevitable.

We are all moving, life is ever changing, nothing stays unchanged forever, so let yourself flow with the changes. Look for ways to get through the changes, and find ways to lift yourself further up.

## 2. Quick Tips for "Today's World—and Some Challenges"

- Be critical of what you spend your time on.
- Be aware of the focus of your attention, thoughts, and feelings. *The Law of Attraction: The Basics of the Teachings of Abraham* explains, "Without exception, that which you give thought to is that which you begin to invite into your experience."
- Be curious. See that being here on earth is an opportunity to investigate how everything works, functions, and interacts.
- Be critical of what types of entertainment you fill your mind, body, and spirit with.
- Be aware of your surroundings and natural environment.
- Care about our planet.
- Compare our world today to how it was during for instance the Stone Age. Imagine the Stone Age briefly: what was life like? What was important? How did people fill their lives? Then think about today's

world: How much in today's world is actually superfluous? How much in today's world clouds our view?

- Do not be discouraged by but do not ignore the seemingly enormous amount of news of sad, unfair, and violent episodes coming from every corner of the world. There are plenty of positive stories and events too, and there are many people in the world trying to make a positive change. Collect stories like that for your own treasure chest of positivity.
- Declutter your intake and stock of information. Keep only that which really means something to you.
- Try not to watch the news for a month. Read only headlines in papers. Notice any change in your outlook.
- Be grateful for what you have, be grateful for life itself, be grateful for opportunities, and acknowledge and go through all emotions you have both negative and positive, but think positively and keep a positive focus!

## 3. Quick Tips for "Our Children"

- Do not be pressured into any decision regarding your children. Talk to your children about how they feel about a certain situation that needs a decision. How can your children come out of the situation in a positive way and for the long term? How can you guide them? Do not always think short term only when it comes to making decisions.
- Observe your children and figure out how you can help them feel more happy and untroubled. Notice what you do that makes them feel good. Keep trying to add more feel-good experiences.
- If children misbehave, it is often because you or others have not conveyed instructions to them in a way they understand. Explain kindly to them again what it is you expect from them so they understand that. Their behavior is partly a reflection of what you teach them, so you should accept this responsibility.
- Be critical in a helpful way about the kind of information you allow them to take in.
- Take an interest in what they learn and what they are exposed to from outside sources such as toys, media, school, peers, other adults, and so on.

- Take the feelings of your children seriously.
- Take the ideas of your children seriously.
- Children are more in tune with their intuition, so listen to what they have to say.
- Teach children how to become and remain humane human beings.
- Even the toughest, meanest child really just wants love, compassion, a hug, or a caring conversation.
- Appreciate the gift of foresight, that is, being able to see or imagine what is best in the long term for your children, for you, for the planet, and so on.
- Watch what you give your children to eat. The more natural the better. Avoid colorings and other additives that may make children hyper or allergic or may interfere with the development of their hormones.
- Remember that children look to you for inspiration and guidance on how to handle everyday situations. Let that inspire you to become a positive influence with long-term, positive effects on your child. Do not use it as an opportunity to soothe your own (bruised) ego.
- Spend time with your children. Be open to learning from them as well.
- Stand by your positive values when it comes to your children. Do not be afraid to intervene if you deep down feel that the short-term or long-term effects of an action could be negative on them.

## 4. Quick Tips for "Your Thoughts and Feelings"

- Take your own thoughts and feelings seriously.
- When alone, observe your general feelings about yourself and your life.
- If you want to influence your thoughts and feelings, start by noticing your current thoughts and feelings. Notice how different things make you feel and what thoughts they trigger in you. Reset your focus onto something positive. Seek information on how to heal whatever is troubling you.
- Notice and observe any negative feelings or thoughts you may have. Ask for instance the universe, the positive energies, an angel, or God to heal your negative thoughts and feelings.
- Instead of nurturing feelings of regret, forgive yourself or patch things up with someone whom you might have hurt. Promise yourself to make things better from now on.

- Give your mind and soul a rest through yoga, meditation, Reiki, walking, horseback riding, vacuuming, listening to a favorite piece of music, watching a sunset, sitting on a hill, laugh, gazing into candlelight, dancing—whatever it is that gives you peace.
- Imagine living in natural surroundings and according to your own methods, beliefs, choices, and observations much as the pagans did and how many indigenous cultures did and still to an extent do. Then fast forward to today. What are your beliefs, values, and rituals now? How true are they to nature?
- Replace jealousy, hatred, and irritability with friendliness, understanding, and acceptance.
- Do not be afraid to feel grateful. You will not run out of things to be grateful for. The quota is infinite, and abundance is yours too.
- If you feel you cannot find compassion in your heart for other people, find a method of healing that appeals to you. When you pass from this world, would it not be nice to leave knowing that during your lifetime, you showered others with warmth and compassion?
- Notice the thoughts you spend time on. If they are negative and leave you feeling not so good, find the cause of that. Could you treat people around you in a nicer way so you would not have to think *I shouldn't have said or done that* or *I hope she or he didn't misunderstand that.*

Be nice to people around you; then, you will not have to worry that you might have hurt somebody. When you have hurt somebody, it will make you worry, it will occupy your mind and thoughts, and it will give you an uneasy feeling. Make sure you spend time on positive thoughts.

- Never think that you are invincible because you are not. Someday, you will need the help and kindness of others, maybe even from somebody you have treated badly, and you may feel ashamed and guilty. Think ahead and avoid situations that could create negative vibrations.
- Follow through with your thoughts and ideas of how you want to live your life. Practice what you preach. I think many of us are guilty of not doing that all the time. It can sometimes be very easy to think how we want things, but we need to put action and feeling behind those thoughts as well. We need to heal much in ourselves first. But when we do actually practice what we preach, that will create a very good feeling.

- Be proud of who and what you are, and hold those feelings inside you.
- Take the time to do the things that make you feel you are living life fully.
- Start somewhere! Promise yourself to make a new start toward a positive way of life. You might not know where to start, but just start somewhere and take it a little step at a time. Start by doing even small and positive things for yourself and for others.

## 5. Quick Tips for "Choice, Responsibility, and Accountability"

- When you make decisions that are based in your higher self, you creative positive energies within you and you feel good to your very core. When you base your decisions on your ego's desires or your mind alone, you create negative energies within you, and you may end up feeling guilty, fearful, or doubtful.
- Every choice you make has repercussions. This is the case even if you choose not to choose anything.
- Remember that you will always have choices at any given time in your life.
- You might be in a certain or perhaps even desperate situation but suddenly find yourself having at least two choices to get out of it. Go with what your heart and your mind can agree on because that choice will be the right choice for you.
- Remember that you are always responsible for your choices.
- If something makes you feel uncomfortable, choose to move away from it.
- Start moving in the direction you want your life to go.
- To change any negative behavior or patterns in yourself, you first need to become conscious and aware of your negative behavior and negative patterns. Then you can choose to heal them and move away from them.
- Even with the concept of "What will happen will happen" in mind, we are still blessed with our free will as part of the equation of life. Our free will is there for us to use. Certain things will happen, but how we handle those life events and how we make our choices is up to us.

# 6. Quick Tips for "Your Relationship with Others"

- Respect and care about other people's concerns and feelings.
- People who act tough and cold are not evil deep inside; spiritually speaking, they have not yet opened up to their hearts. They have not yet learned how to be humane human beings. (See more in Part 2: Being Spiritual)
- Sometimes, putting common sense before tradition or societal expectations is the better choice for someone in a dire situation. Wanting to help and take care of others in need is a basic instinct in us humans.
- In a conflict, do not take advantage of someone who you sense is in any way weaker than you; give him or her the advantage instead.
- A bit of humility will get you a long way.
- Stop and ask yourself, *Am I hurting somebody with my actions or words?* If you are, then think about making the choice to heal yourself so you do not continue to hurt other people knowingly or unknowingly. Heal your own pain—you can do it. You are entitled to your own happiness, and you are entitled to be in harmonious relationships with others. Heal yourself so you can have positive, healthy, and giving relationships with other people.

Bring yourself into balance via for instance yoga, meditation, care from other people, psychotherapy, music, or through whatever method or methods appeal to you.

- Try not to take control of somebody you would like to help. If you see friends or relatives who are in a destructive cycle and whom you want to help, encourage and support them in what they do. Give them a little caring push if they need it.

Keep in mind, however, that they will take in only the advice they are ready for. See their lives and yours as separate, but be ready with support and encouragement once again if they approach you for help.

Helping others should not drain you; helping others should generate a positive exchange of gratitude or other positive results. You can ask or imagine that only positivity flows between you and your friends or relatives in need of something. If they are not able to accept your help, they may be in need of other types of healing or help.

- Learn to be truly happy for others. Know that jealousy can stem from for example feeling left out, from doubts that there is enough for all, from low self-esteem, and other sources. These feelings, however, can be healed, and when you heal them, you will not need to feel jealous of other people anymore. Jealousy is based in the ego and in your mind, and it breeds negative feelings and actions in you.
- Think ahead and think about what is best in the long run.

## 7. Quick Tips for "History"

- Use the past to learn from it and understand the present.
- Find inspiration for the future in the past.

## 8. Quick Tips for "Spirit"

- Spirituality and healing are ongoing processes for everyone. Everybody evolves and learns from experience. We all have different starting points, and we move at different paces.

Spiritual growth occurs when something higher or deeper if you like replaces something negative in you that you have acknowledged, recognized, and dealt with. A lesson has been learned; you have moved away from that particular negative aspect.

- We may not always be able to agree with other people's ways of spiritual living, but we can always try to respect their ways if they are not harming anyone.
- Create space for growth and inspiration by healing and releasing the negative in you.
- Research the backgrounds and lives of your role models whether they are alive or in the past.
- Keep in mind that everybody's spiritual path is different.
- Think of your troubled and negative feelings, emotions, and thoughts as a coat you are wearing. Then decide that you want to take that coat off. Find out what is in that coat—define your feelings or thoughts, and tell yourself that you do not want to wear that coat anymore.

Say to yourself that you want to release and heal all that is negative. Imagine that all negativity is dissolving into light. Tell yourself that you want to wear a coat filled with positivity, and then imagine putting it on. Define your new feelings and thoughts. And remind yourself every day that this is what you are wearing from now on. This visualization could maybe be of help to you.

- See every challenge and disease as a way to improve yourself and move forward and upward toward a positive goal.
- Meditate regularly. You will be amazed at the benefits you will experience on all levels. It will open up a new world to you!
- Go with your own intuition, and trust signs that make themselves known to you. Go with them as long as they are positive and not harmful to you or others and as long as they feel right for you in your body, in your thoughts, and in your soul.

## 9. Quick Tips for "Music"

- The type of music we like at different stages and times of our lives is a good indication of the state of our bodies, minds, and souls.
- Use music to improve or express your mood.
- Use music to express yourself.
- Give some attention to some of the great music masters from all cultures and times. Think about the incredible flow of inspiration they have received or possessed. Let that thought inspire you if not in a musical manner, then perhaps in another way.
- Listen to all kinds of music; be open to new experiences and inspirations. Some types of music may grow on you after some time.
- The tones resonate with our chakras.
- Music creates moods, feelings, emotions, and images and can be used as a healer.

## 10. Quick Tips for "Nature"

- Observe the natural world. Notice how nature works and changes to survive and adapt.
- Nature's cycles and your life cycles are all connected.

- What happens in nature happens in you and in the universe around you.
- Spend more time in nature, and study it—notice every little small and big thing. Take it in through your soul.

# A Look at Our Future

We are over two thirds of the way through this twelve year period of intensity which from an astrological perspective represents the crunch point for humanity and its futures.

The decisions we take over the coming few years, both globally and personally, will resonate for many generations into the future. The concentration of planetary energy, originating in the early 60's, maturing in the 80's, escalating since the mid 90's and accelerating wildly since 1999 is at peak now. From our time reference, now means August 1999 - August 2010.

This is not a drill. This is the final lead in to the prime time, the omega point that our lives and the lives of our ancestors have built toward. It's the time we have all been anticipating and fearing, knowing that we as individuals are being called to account for our honesty, conscience and integrity, and then being asked to move into a better future for every being on earth. Within our lifetimes, there will be an evolutionary leap the like of which we have not seen since Cro-Magnon man superceded Neanderthalis. The acceleration of population matches the acceleration of technology and spirituality, and now we're approaching prime vertical.

Do we collapse in on ourselves, as perhaps we did 12,500 years ago? Or do we move on beyond existing boundaries into a multi-dimensional future where the only limits are those of the imagination? The time lines are drawing in; the options are running out, the fences are coming down. Do we acquiesce to the dominators and become even more insane, contributing to the ruination of the earth, the domination of nature, the suppression of the feminine and other spiritually bankrupt policies? Or do we eliminate fear, guilt and the sanctions that the media, churches and governments/corporations have imposed on us, and move ahead into a cleaner world of our making? A world unpolluted by power, secure in our sense of individuality, yet aware of our function, our space, our role in a society based on love, community, consciousness expansion, empathy and a sensuality and sensitivity to the environment.

Because - and this is the big one - if these things are not a part of our future, what kind of future will it be? (From Astrologer Steve Judd's 2007 forecast of the future)

How have we done in the past decade??

# References:

hierarchy of needs—Maslow, Wikipedia.

archetypes—Carl Jung, Wikipedia.

multiple intelligences—Howard Gardner, Wikipedia.

Guardian.co.uk/uk/2007/mar/19/schools.children.

Wapedia.mobi/en/Grief.

Helpguide.org/mental/grief_loss.htm.

Hugh Everett, Wikipedia.org/wiki/many-worlds interpretation.

Safeyouth.org/scripts/faq/mediaviolstats.asp (now safeyouth.gov).

Chinesefacereading.blogspot.com.

Pete Jennings, *Pagan Paths.*

Central Art, Aboriginal Art Store, Alice Springs, Australia, www. aboriginalartstore.com.au.

hippie, Wikipedia.

electroreception, Wikipedia.

Medindia.net/yoga-lifestyle/yoga-origin.htm.

Robert B. Dilts, Nlpu.com.

WWF (World Wildlife Fund),

assets.panda.org/downloads/edc_chemical_cocktail_leaflet.pdf.

Iroquois, "Basic Call to Consciousness," edited by Akwesasne; notes, Book Publishing Company, Tennessee, 1977.

Sutton, 1988.

Christine Comaford-Lynch, *Rules for Renegades—How to Make More Money, Rock Your Career, and Revel in Your Individuality.* Published by McGraw-Hill, New York, 2007.

Bodo Baginski and Shalila Sharamon, *Reiki—Universal Life Force.*

Steve Judd, astrologer, forecast from 2007.

R.C.L., "Meaning of the Universe," fractalwisdom.com, www. abchomeopathy.com.

# Inspirational Reading

*Embraced by the Light* by Betty J. Eadie
*Journey of souls* by Michael Newton, PhD
Testimony of Light by Helen Greaves
*Water Bugs & Dragonflies*
*Explaining Death to Young Children* by Doris Stickney
*Ageless Body, Timeless Mind* by Deepak Chopra
*Siddhartha—An Indian Tale* by Herman Hesse (1922)
*Reiki Intentions* by Anubhaa Sharma
Books by Louise Hay, Doreen Virtue
Historical books about the Sumerians, Phoenicians, the Mayas, and other ancient civilizations, cultures, traditions, religions, etc.

## Suggested Topics: music, nature, the environment and its protection, chakra, foods for optimum health

www.fromthestars.com: alternative and spiritual theories about our origin, our present, and the future
www.crystalinks.com: extensive website by Ellie Crystal about the metaphysical, ancient history, science, our origins, our future, spiritual development, multidimensional realities, etc.
www.spiritualresearchfoundation.org: about the spiritual level of the entire human race
www.karmastrology.com/rek_usui.shtm: about Reiki and Dr. Usui
www.reallifespirituality.com: amazing website by Akemi Gaines on ascension, star children, akashic records, a new era, etc.
www.starchildglobal.com: by Celia Fenn. Her book *The Indigo-Crystal Adventure* explains more about the metaphysical aspects of the indigo-crystal experience, for example, about golden auras, human angels, and multidimensional consciousness.
www.cainer.com: (Jonathan)/Oscar Cainer, astrologer, author
www.stevejudd.com: Steve Judd, astrology and astrocartography

www.shiftfrequency.com: various inspiring and thought-provoking articles compiled by Gillian on the ongoing shift and ascension of humanity, the earth, and the universe.

www.edgarcayce.org

www.fractalwisdom.com: "Meaning of the Universe" by R.C.L. You can also find many other intriguing articles here of scientific and spiritual natures.

www.ddewey.net/mandelbrot: more about the Mandelbrot fractal and fractal theory

www.digitalcenter.org/webreport94/credits.htm: "Television violence monitoring project," UCLA Center for Communication Policy

www.cdc.gov/ViolencePrevention/youthviolence/electronicaggression/index. html: information on electronic aggression.

www.surgeongeneral.gov/library/youthviolence: "Youth Violence: A Report of the Surgeon General"

www.surgeongeneral.gov/library/youthviolence/chapter4/appendix4bsec2. html: specific violent TV and video game information

www.youtube.com: search word: "Magenta Pixie"; many inspiring and enlightening videos about spirituality, ascension, earth changes, light beings, etc.

www.rense.com/ufo5/undergiza.htm: another look at our world

http://native_viewpoints.tripod.com/Native_Perspective/my_thoughts.htm: thoughts on the Lakota people

www.ratical.org/koya.html: inspirational website with articles that make you think; link to Hopi statement and thoughts

www.lifedesignstrategies.com: about designs according to who we are

www.coloryourspirit.com/morecolortherapy.html: gives a good overview of the meaning of the different colors in relation to your physical, mental, and spiritual bodies and has information on how to balance your chakras

www.spiritlibrary.com/doreen-virtue: for some inspirational reading on number signs from your guides and angels

http://sacredscribesangelnumbers.blogspot.dk/p/index-numbers.html numbers and their meaning, seen as messages from angels and guides

Printed in the United States
By Bookmasters